This book belongs to : Madison J. Mitchell

Intelligent Virtue

Intelligent Virtue

Julia Annas

OXFORD
UNIVERSITY PRESS

OXFORD

UNIVERSITY PRESS

Great Clarendon Street, Oxford OX2 6DP

Oxford University Press is a department of the University of Oxford.
It furthers the University's objective of excellence in research, scholarship,
and education by publishing worldwide in

Oxford   New York

Auckland   Cape Town   Dar es Salaam   Hong Kong   Karachi
Kuala Lumpur   Madrid   Melbourne   Mexico City   Nairobi
New Delhi   Shanghai   Taipei   Toronto
With offices in
Argentina   Austria   Brazil   Chile   Czech Republic   France   Greece
Guatemala   Hungary   Italy   Japan   South Korea   Poland   Portugal
Singapore   Switzerland   Thailand   Turkey   Ukraine   Vietnam

Oxford is a registered trade mark of Oxford University Press
in the UK and in certain other countries

Published in the United States
by Oxford University Press Inc., New York

© Julia Annas 2011

ISBN 978-0-19-922877-5

Printed in the United Kingdom by
the MPG Books Group Ltd

Preface

This is my second attempt to write on this subject. I first wrote most of a book on virtue ethics, only to find that publishers' deadlines did nothing to get me to finish it, until it became clear from my reluctance that I was writing the wrong book. I no longer wanted to write about virtue ethics; I wanted to start further back and get clear about virtue. Accordingly, I ditched the first version completely and started again; and this time I did finish.

I have been working on virtue for so long that I have acquired embarrassingly many intellectual debts. I am especially grateful to Rosalind Hursthouse for a long-standing warm friendship and intellectual companionship, Dan Russell for discussions over the years, Frans Svensson for valuable insights and objections in our enjoyable discussions, my colleague Rachana Kamtekar for many enjoyable and fruitful philosophical interchanges. I am also particularly grateful to Paul Bloomfield, Christopher Gill, and Mark LeBar for written comments that have given me much to think about. My thanks go to Lilli Alanen, John Armstrong, Robert Audi, Neera Badhwar, Hugh Benson, David Brink, Andrew Cohen, David Copp, Michael DePaul, Julia Driver, Stephen Gardiner, Alasdair MacIntyre, Christian Miller, Allan Silverman, Rebecca Stangl, Fred Stoutland, Christine Swanton, David Solomon, Sean Patrick Walsh, and Linda Zagzebski. I am grateful to colleagues at Arizona who have read and commented on my work: Tom Christiano, Terry Horgan, Rachana Kamtekar, Uriah Kriegel, Chris Maloney, Dave Schmidtz, Houston Smit, and Mark Timmons. Clerk Shaw and Rachel Singpurwalla, when visitors, also gave invaluable help. I am grateful to all the graduate students who participated in my seminars on virtue, especially Michael Bukoski, Ginger Clausen, Jacob Daly, Chris Freiman, Michelle Jenkins, Emil Salim, Daniel Sanderman, and Robert Wagoner and I am particularly grateful to Rachana Kamtekar for continued discussion of ancient and modern virtue and eudaimonism.

My interest began over a decade ago, and was greatly furthered by a memorable virtue ethics conference in Christchurch, New Zealand, organized by Stephen Gardiner in 2002, and by my being given the honour of delivering the Hägerström Lectures at the University of Uppsala in 2003. I am grateful to all the audiences who have sat through lectures on related material at the Universities of Canterbury, Otago, and Auckland in New Zealand, the Australian National University, the Universities of Arizona and Nebraska at Lincoln, James Madison University, the University of California at Berkeley, the Merson Center at Ohio State University, the Universities of Colorado, Minnesota, Notre Dame, and Princeton. I am grateful to Dartmouth College for inviting me to give the 2004 Gramlich Lecture, to the University of Connecticut for inviting me to give the 2004 Parcells Lecture, to the University of Oklahoma for inviting me to give the David Ross Boyd Lectures for 2004, to the Pacific Division of the APA for my invitation to give the Presidential Address in 2004, to the Collegium for Advanced Studies at the University of Helsinki for inviting me to give the Collegium Lecture for 2005, to Haverford College for inviting me to give the Altherr Symposium for 2006 and to St Olaf College for inviting me to give the Belgum Lectures in 2007. I was one of the contributors to John Doris's Author Meets Critics session at the 2003 Pacific Division APA meeting; the proceedings have been published in *Philosophy and Phenomenological Research* for 2005. My participation in a workshop on moral phenomenology organized in 2005 by my colleagues Terence Horgan, Uriah Kriegel, and Mark Timmons enabled me to develop some ideas about virtue in unexpected directions. So did an invitation from the UK project on Nietzsche and Moral Philosophy to write on Nietzsche and virtue ethics for a workshop in Southampton in 2008.

For help of all kinds in my work on the second version I have particular thanks. This work is a contribution to an interdisciplinary project on The Pursuit of Happiness: scientific, theological, and interdisciplinary perspectives on the love of God, neighbour, and self, established by the Center for the Study of Law and Religion at Emory University, and supported by a grant from the John Templeton Foundation. I am grateful to all the participants in this project, whose discussions have been very helpful, especially discussion of the material which ended up as Chapter 8. I am particularly grateful to Corey Keyes for our joint work on eudaimonism in psychology and its relation to Aristotle, and to Philip Reynolds and Timothy Jackson for discussions of happiness and agapism. I hope to work more specifically on the topic of eudaimonism and agapism at some future date. I also owe thanks to the project on Happiness in Antiquity at the

University of Oslo for their hospitality at a period when I worked on this material (as well as on another project on virtue in ancient thought), especially to Eyolfur Kjalar Emilsson, Hallvard Fossheim, Øyvind Rabbås, and Svavar Hrafn Svavarsson. I owe special thanks to Paul Bloomfield, Dan Russell, and Frans Svensson for comments on this latest version, as well as thanks for helpful comments to two referees for Oxford University Press. To all these people who have helped me, many, many thanks. It has been difficult to work through to what may now seem like the simplicity of the ideas I put forward here. Whatever their reception, I am very grateful to those who have assisted me on my way. My greatest thanks, as always, are to David and Laura, for sustaining me always with love and support.

Contents

1

Introduction

This book aims to produce an account of virtue. Do we need one? In the last two decades there has been a deep and widespread revival of interest in virtue and systems of ethics centred on virtue, and we have had theories featuring versions of virtue presented in the tradition of Aristotle, the Stoics, Hume, Adam Smith, Kant, Nietzsche, and even consequentialism. It is reasonable to wonder whether we need yet another account of virtue. I have two reasons for thinking that the answer is yes. One is that these debates have made it clear that different theories do not share an agreed conception of what virtue is. It seems worthwhile, then, to begin with virtue, rather than with a type of ethical theory, and to see what kind of account can be produced. Even though disagreement will certainly remain, we may be able, if we can focus clearly on an account of virtue, to see more plainly ways in which disputes between kinds of ethical theory centring on virtue depend on their claims about what virtue is, and so we may be able to get a better view of the alternatives within this ethical tradition.

Second, I think that the present distinctive account of virtue results from attending to two ideas. One is that exercising a virtue involves practical reasoning of a kind that can illuminatingly be compared to the kind of reasoning we find in someone exercising a practical skill. Rather than asking at the start how virtues relate to rules, principles, maximizing, or a final end, we will gain by looking at the way in which the acquisition and exercise of virtue can be seen to be in many ways like the acquisition and exercise of more mundane activities, such as farming, building, or playing the piano. The other idea is that virtue is part of the agent's happiness or flourishing, and that it is plausible to see virtue as actually constituting (wholly or in part) that happiness. I shall develop these ideas in turn, but by the end of this book it should be clear that they are interrelated.

These two ideas turn up as familiar themes in the ancient ethical theories that I have studied for many years, and I have come to think them applicable to contemporary debates about virtue. Contemporary theories, of course, need support from, and relevance to, contemporary concerns, and the features of the skill analogy that I shall be focusing on overlap only partially with those that interest the ancients—unsurprisingly, since in a very different culture the skills we emphasize are different and we are interested in different aspects of them. What results is a distinctive approach to virtue ethics, one that runs contrary not just to many contemporary assumptions in ethics but to the assumptions of some contemporary virtue ethical theorists. This approach can be judged, I hope, by its attractions and its promise as a contemporary ethical theory.

The idea that the practical reasoning of the virtuous person shares important features with that of the expert in a practical skill is often referred to simply as the skill analogy. Some readers may come to think that 'analogy' is not the best term for a relation so close that some have come to think of virtue as itself being a kind of skill; but what is most important is to bring out the shared features and their importance. The idea that virtue constitutes (wholly or in part) the happiness or flourishing of the virtuous person will be discussed when I get to the part of the book on happiness in the tradition of thought which has been called eudaimonist. In the discussion of eudaimonism in Ch. 8 I face the question of whether we should think in terms of the agent's happiness, or whether modern influences on our use of that term are a barrier to that, and make it better to use the term 'flourishing'. Until that chapter I shall use the term 'flourishing', since the discussion will be neutral on that issue up till then, and a more neutral term is preferable.

I will plunge into developing the theory without first defending the skill analogy and eudaimonism in the abstract. There are two reasons for this. First, these terms are not part of contemporary ethical debate (indeed they are often misunderstood). Trying to establish them by offering definitions, or necessary and sufficient conditions, would fail to engage with familiar terms of ethical debate; moreover, it would miss the important point that these ideas are far more intuitive and empirically rooted than often assumed. Working from the ground up helps to make this clear. Second, I aim to present virtue and flourishing as parts of a theory in which neither of them is, in modern terms, foundational (in this the theory is like some ancient ones). Virtue and flourishing are both central in it, but neither is a basis or foundation from which other parts of the theory can be derived, nor do they jointly form such a foundation. Rather, the theory is holistic in structure; the different parts are mutually supportive. This is, obviously, something that can be apparent only by the end of the book.

I shall develop an account of virtue in which I show how central to it is the idea that the practical reasoning of the virtuous person is analogous, in important ways (which I will bring out in turn) to the practical reasoning of someone who is exercising a practical skill. This will go on to illuminate various aspects of virtue, and will in turn enable us to meet in a satisfactory way various kinds of objection that have been raised to the project of making virtue central to an ethical theory. I will then show how a virtue ethical theory with this conception of virtue enables us to see how virtue is constitutive (wholly or in part) of the agent's flourishing. Many contemporary virtue ethical theories see virtue as having a further aim, but one other than the agent's flourishing. This work will fall short of exhaustive arguments against them, but will show at least how their failure to connect virtue to eudaimonistic flourishing leads to problems for them, and also connects to their failure to deal with aspects of virtue that the skill analogy illuminates. The project is not intended to be an exhaustive discussion of all the disputable issues involved in a theory of virtue, but it will shed light on some: the unity of virtue, the relation between virtue as an ideal and virtue in everyday life, the relation between being virtuous and doing the right thing, and some others.

Two points about method will now be flagged. First, the following account focuses on the virtue of individual people, and although I stress, heavily, the importance of social context for the development and exercise of the virtues, this is a contribution to ethical rather than to social and political thinking; thus I discuss justice as the personal virtue of fairness rather than as a virtue of institutions.

Second, I talk throughout ot what 'we' think and say. Who are 'we'? I take this to be an inclusive, invitational, use of 'we' rather than an exclusive one privileging the views of the writer and those like her.[1] 'We' are the readers of this book, as well as the writer. If you, an individual reader, find yourself disagreeing about a claim, this is relevant to your receptivity to the account as a whole. The account, however, is not

---

[1] Bernard Williams (1985) has perceptive remarks on the use of 'we' in this connection.

presented as a theory which can be refuted by a single counterexample, nor as a theory with foundations such that if these are weakened the superstructure collapses. In both respects the account is holistic: virtue and happiness are central in it, but not foundational, and the account answers to our experience as a whole. Disgreement with some aspects of the account thus does not cut off the possibility of agreement over others. Further, I use the term 'account' rather than 'theory' to avoid the idea that I am doing something common in philosophy, namely setting up a 'theory' on the basis of 'intuitions'. To accept this as a description of what I am doing would be to accept assumptions I am concerned to avoid, mainly the idea that the notion of 'intuition' can be introduced without a philosophical account of what intuitions are, something I do not have. In what follows I talk simply about what we think and believe about virtue, and also about skill and expertise.[2] I will return to the issue of methodology in the final chapter.

In what follows I bring out a number of different points about virtue, which, I hope, develop into a cumulative whole.

In Ch. 2 I make the preliminary point that virtue is dispositional; a virtue is a disposition of character to act reliably, not a passing mood or an attitude. Nor is it just a trait or a mere disposition to perform acts that have been independently labelled as virtuous. Further, a disposition has to be acquired by habituation, but a virtue is not a matter of being habituated to routine. It expresses the kind of habituation that a skill does, one in which the agent becomes more intelligent in performance rather than routinized.

In Ch. 3 the skill analogy helps to show us how a virtue can be learnt and taught. Like learning a skill, learning a virtue requires us initially to trust the teacher and the context of learning, but also to go on to act from our own independent understanding. The important point emerges that this account of virtue is essentially developmental; we must always distinguish between the expert and the learner. The analogy with practical skill further helps us to see how thinking in terms of virtue can guide action; here I raise the issue of the relation of virtuous action to right action. We can then appreciate how the kind of learning involved in acquiring a virtue

---

[2] This is another reason for avoiding talk of 'intuitions', since intuitions about virtue are often taken to be 'moral intuitions', and, whatever these are, we surely do not have them about building or plumbing.

always takes place within an already given social and cultural context, but also always involves the aspiration to do better.

A problem remains for this picture, discussed in Ch. 4. If virtue is always learnt in given social and cultural contexts, and the learning of virtue requires that we progress by first trusting the teacher and teaching context, will the result not be essentially conservative? Virtue involves aspiration, but will the aspiration be strong enough to criticize the contexts and institutions within which virtue has been learnt? The answer is yes: this charge underestimates the resources of virtue, at least on this conception of it.

In Ch. 5 I turn to the point that any account of virtue should be able to say something about the difference between the virtuous person and the person who does do the virtuous thing, but reluctantly and against his inclinations. Virtue requires not just acting on reasons, but having the right feelings and attitudes, doing virtuous actions in an easy and unconflicted way that is characteristically enjoyed. This is generally taken to mark a sharp distinction between virtue and skill, since skill can be exercised without the right feelings, and is not usually associated with enjoyment. However, I argue that here too the skill analogy can help us to get on the right track for understanding the way in which virtue requires agreement of reason and feeling. I appeal to some contemporary psychology of pleasure (of a kind that fits Aristotle's approach to pleasure, though not that of most contemporary philosophers). There remain, of course, important differences between virtue and skill, but these support, rather than undermine, the analogy.

In Ch. 6 I turn to some important implications of the account so far, particularly the role in virtue of practical reasoning. We are led, I argue, to see the development of the virtues as aspects of an overall and unified development of character, and thus to see that there is much to be said for a version of the idea that the virtues form a unity. This discussion also brings out the ways in which virtue functions as an ideal in this theory, and how the ideal is related to virtue in everyday contexts.

The account of virtue is cumulative; each chapter has examined an aspect of virtue, so that we have built up an account of virtue from critical reflection on the analogy of skill. Chapter 7 takes up two important points about virtue that are independent of the skill analogy. Virtues are unlike other dispositions, such as wittiness, tidiness, or punctuality, in two ways: first, a virtue is admirable for itself; if we find a disposition valued as excellent is so valued merely instrumentally, it is not a virtue. Virtues are dispositions worthy of a distinct kind of admiration, which inspire us to aspire to them as ideals. I discuss how this distinguishes between virtues and other dispositions.

Second, a virtue requires a commitment to value. For a disposition to be a virtue, possessing it involves the person's orientation to something the person takes to be valuable. Some 'pluralist' theories stop at the stage of finding different values as the aims of different virtues; others unify these values as different aspects of the good. At this point there are many options, corresponding to different conceptions of what the good is that virtue is committed to.

Chapter 8 turns to the task of showing how virtue is related to our flourishing, and whether we can reasonably take eudaimonistic flourishing to be happiness. First, we have to distinguish between various different understandings of happiness. It is not episodes of feeling, or just getting what you want, but something achieved over a life as a whole. I introduce the notion of happiness in the eudaimonist tradition, and show how it avoids dilemmas that confront some modern accounts of happiness, and, unlike the latter, gives us a satisfying framework for ethical thought.

Chapter 9 takes up the challenge of showing that the virtues can plausibly be taken to constitute (wholly or in part) the agent's happiness or flourishing. The main obstacles to this come from the aspects of virtue brought out in Ch. 7, but I shall show that these problems can be met, and that theories which hold that virtue's commitment to value conflicts with eudaimonism run into problems which make their theories unattractive. I shall then show that we do justice to the points we have seen developed about virtue in the earlier chapters only if we do take virtue to be constitutive (wholly or in part) of the agent's happiness or flourishing.

Given the argument so far, we can see how the claims that virtue is either necessary, or necessary and sufficient, for the agent's flourishing are not far-fetched and implausible, but have much appeal to many of our everyday thoughts. We can also see why, with due caution, it is not unreasonable to think of flourishing as happiness.

In Ch. 10 I return to the issue of methodology, reiterating the point that I have stood aside from the philosophical project of producing a 'theory' as opposed to 'intuitions'. Rather I have sketched a holistic account whose claim to acceptance comes partly from the way it hangs together and partly from its answering to the way we regard virtue and happiness in our experience. I suggest briefly that further backing for the claims I make could well come from philosophically informed research in psychology. Critics of the so-called 'situationist' challenge to virtue have established that we need more sophisticated research than hitherto on the nature of virtue, and I think it is clear that we will be helped by empirical study of practical skills and the ways in which virtue is similar to them.

This way of proceeding inevitably brings the disadvantage that a straightforward account of the kind I propose will probably seem mundane at first, and it may take a while for the material in the early chapters to appear as a coherent whole with the resources to produce arguments against alternatives. I hope that the patient reader will be rewarded for forgoing, at the start, sophisticated arguments against contemporary alternatives in favour of working up from what is, as Aristotle says, familiar to us.

2

Virtue, Character, and Disposition

In ordinary life, although we may not often use the term 'virtue', we think and talk all the time in terms of virtues. We think (and frequently say) of others and ourselves that we are generous or stingy, kind or mean, helpful or selfish. What are we talking about? People, obviously, but are we focusing on their actions, their feelings, or something else?

What is it for Jane to be generous? It is not merely that she does a generous action, or has a generous feeling. Either or both could be true without Jane's being generous. She may have done a generous action, suppressing her normal stinginess, in order to impress a friend who really is generous and will respond favourably to her action. She may have had a generous feeling triggered by a sentimental song she has just heard. In neither case is *she* generous, because the action and feeling neither come from nor lead to anything lasting. For Jane to be generous, generosity has to be a feature of *her*—that is, a feature of Jane as a whole, and not just any old feature, but one that is persisting, reliable, and characteristic.

A virtue is a lasting feature of a person, a tendency for the person to be a certain way. It is not merely a lasting feature, however, one that just sits there undisturbed. It is *active*: to have it is to be disposed to act in certain ways. And it *develops* through selective response to circumstances. Given these points, I shall use the term *persisting* rather than merely lasting. Jane's generosity, supposing her to be generous, persists through challenges and difficulties, and is strengthened or weakened by her generous or ungenerous responses respectively. Thus, although it is natural for us to think of a virtue as a disposition, we should be careful not to confuse this with the scientific notion of disposition, which just is a static lasting tendency. A classic example is that glass has a disposition to break under certain circumstances. This is not the notion we need, since glass does not have a disposition by way of *doing* anything, nor can it learn to develop selectively as a result of encounters with different circumstances. A virtue is not a static condition like this; it is a disposition as a result of which Jane acts and thinks in a certain way, and which is at any time strengthened by her generous responses and weakened by failures to have them. If she is generous, her generous actions and feelings both come from a virtue and fortify it.   *repetitive ; active ; developmental*

A virtue is also a <u>reliable</u> disposition. If Jane is generous, it is no accident that she does the generous action and has generous feelings. We would have been surprised, and shocked, if she had failed to act generously, and looked for some kind of explanation. Our friends' virtues and vices enable us to rely on their responses and behaviour—to a certain extent, of course, since none of us is virtuous enough to be completely reliable in virtuous response and action. This is an aspect of virtue which we are more aware of in others than ourselves; we have some idea of who can be counted on to be generous or stingy when collecting for disaster relief or a wedding present, even when we surprise ourselves sometimes by our readiness, or reluctance, to give.

Doing things w/ pleasure + right motivation

Further, a virtue is a disposition which is *characteristic*—that is, the virtuous (or vicious) person is acting in and from character when acting in a kindly, brave or restrained way. This is another way of putting the point that a virtue is a *deep* feature of the person. A virtue is a disposition which is central to the person, to whom he or she is, a way we standardly think of character. I might discover that I have an unsuspected talent for Sudoku, but this, although it enlarges my talents, does not alter my character. But someone who discovers in himself an unsuspected capacity <u>to feel and act on</u> <u>compassion,</u> and who develops this capacity, does come to change as a person, not just in some isolated feature; he comes to have a changed character.[1]

One point is implicit right from the start in a virtue's being a disposition of the person to be a certain way, a disposition which expresses itself in acting, reasoning, and feeling in certain ways. This is that we do not, as in some kinds of theory, start with an account of what it is to make virtuous judgements and then, separately, go on to an account of how the person

---

[1] There are other dispositions, neither virtues nor vices, such as a disposition to be tidy, punctual, or hardworking, for example, which could in some circumstances come to be central to a person. We won't be in a position until Ch. 7 to see why these are not virtues.

can be motivated to act according to these. Our motivations to be fair, brave, and so on are not extra ingredients that have to be sought for after the account of virtuous judgement has been developed. We *already* start with motivations, and our dispositions are ways in which those motivations have been educated and developed. To ask how someone who thinks he should act bravely can *then* be motivated to be brave is a mistake. It is to forget that a brave person is not someone who has learned about bravery, decided that he should be brave, and then somehow found a motivation to follow up on this. He is someone whose existing character tendencies have been formed in such a way that he acts, reasons, and reacts bravely, rather than in some other way. This is why virtue is a disposition which is from the start an active and developing one. It is not a passive product of a string of impacts from outside; it is the way I (or you), an active creature, develops a character through formation and education.

As we shall see several times in this book, it is crucial to bear in mind that by the time we reflect about virtues, we already have some (and vices, and a lot of traits which are neither). We have developed to have the characters that we have by having been brought up and educated, and then living and reflecting, in ways that developed and built character in certain ways. This did not involve injecting new motivations into us, but in forming the unformed motivations that we start with. Aristotle discusses what he calls 'natural virtue', the character tendencies that we have before learning about virtue and vice. Some of these tendencies already suggest virtue, but, as we can see readily from studying small children, many do not. As parents and teachers know well, we teach children to be fair and honest not by teaching them what they should do and then trying to interest them in having a new motivation to do this. Rather, we try to educate and form motivations that are present already.

Both the reliability of a virtue and its being expressive of character have been challenged in recent years. Some philosophers have relied on results in social psychology to make two claims. One is that our actions are brought about much more than we think by the impact of the situation we are in and much less by the influence of our character traits.[2] If this

---

[2] The terms I use in this account of virtue are meant to be ordinary and accessible, and do not conform to those familiar in the 'situationist' debates about virtue. I treat virtue as a disposition in a broader sense than the one it has in this literature, where 'disposition' is standardly *opposed* to a trait sensitive to situations. (See Russell (2009: pt. III).) Similarly, I have

were true, it would cast doubt on the reasonableness of taking virtue as a central concept in ethics. It would, for a start, cast doubt on the account I have just given of how the virtues are educated developments of our unformed motivations. The other claim is that the practical reasoning on which we act is, in ways that we are unaware of, faulty; we act on the basis of mistaken reasoning, and sometimes in ways that bypass reason altogether. We will return to these issues later (in Ch. 10), when we have a fuller account of virtue, since we clearly do not have enough material in hand at this point for there to be a fruitful discussion.

We can, however, ask at this point why we make the disposition of the generous person central to an account of generosity. Actions and feelings are just as correctly called generous as are people. Perhaps a generous person is just a person disposed to do generous actions and to have generous feelings?[3] If so, we will be taking the actions and feelings to be more basic than the disposition, since we will need to be able to identify generous actions and feelings independently in order to understand that Jane is a generous person, disposed to do generous actions and to have generous feelings. For it would obviously be circular to say that Jane is generous because she does generous actions, if we could say no more about these actions than that they are the actions of a generous person.

We will see in the next chapter why this is not the right way to think of the relation between virtuous disposition and virtuous actions. At that point we will see that the fact that we can, as a matter of fact, identify generous actions and feelings before having a good grasp of generous dispositions is no objection to making virtuous dispositions central to an ethics of virtue.

There is, however, another point we can make at this stage. If generosity is just the disposition to do generous actions and to have generous feelings, the question arises why we would value having a *disposition* to do and feel these things. Why ever do we value having persisting, reliable, and characteristic dispositions to do and to feel these things? One response might be that we value the disposition to do generous actions because we

---

used 'persistent' to suggest the active aspect of virtue and 'reliable' to suggest those aspects of it wider than mere frequent performance of stereotypical actions. Both persistence and reliability cover consistency of response in the same type of situation and also 'cross-situational consistency' over different types of situation.

[3] Thomson (1997), Hurka (2006).

value the performance of generous actions, and if a person has a generous disposition then she will probably produce more of them than someone without such a disposition.[4] On this view thoughts about the value of dispositions will always be dependent upon thoughts about the value of actions and feelings. This conflicts sharply, though, with our everyday thinking about virtues; when we praise someone as loyal we are praising *them*, and it is absurd to suggest that this is really based on (subconscious?) calculations about how many loyal actions they will perform and loyal feelings they will have.

Since virtue is a disposition of the above kind, becoming virtuous will naturally take time. Scrooge may have been converted suddenly to compassion and kindliness on Christmas Eve, but the story is careful to tell us that he continued over time the process of becoming a compassionate person. Coming to see that being loyal or brave is a worthwhile way to live is just the first step. Becoming virtuous requires habituation and experience. We encounter habituation first through our education, both in school and in the family. We are not just told what to do but given role models and encouraged to act in ways that promote and show appreciation of loyalty or bravery. Either in real life or in books or movies we experience (really or vicariously) situations where people behave loyally or disloyally, and we are encouraged to find what makes them praiseworthy or blameable. We need experience to understand what it is to be loyal or brave, and our experience is guided through habituation by parents, educators, and the ways our culture impinges on us.[5] We are trained and formed through being habituated to act in loyal and brave ways and to respond positively to presentations of loyalty and bravery. Small children, for example, are discouraged from cruelty to animals, and read and see stories where cruel children are presented negatively. They are encouraged to share their possessions, and told stories where generosity is rewarded and selfishness is presented as repellent.

It is natural to worry at this point whether habituation is just habit, and whether a virtuous disposition is just one built up by force of habit. Our

---

[4] If we think it obvious that more is always better, of course. Generosity is a case casting some doubt on this, since an efficient way to produce more generous actions will often be to prolong, rather than to remove, the need met by generosity; but this can hardly be the product of *generosity*.

[5] We may reasonably worry whether this starting-point can be adequate to produce developed ethical thought: this issue will be discussed in Ch. 4.

experience leads us, in a number of areas of our lives, to develop habits which save time and effort. If developing a virtue is like this, why should we think it amounts to anything more than habit and even mere routine?

Here is an example of habit becoming routine. I drive to my university job every day, following the same route to the parking garage. At first I have to think consciously about the best way to do this, avoiding traffic without going too far from the most direct way, modifying the route at different times of day and so on. Gradually I become used to driving on this route, and it becomes habit with me. I no longer have to think about which way to turn at every corner, where to slow down and the like. My driving has become routine. This does not make it mindless: I am still at some level aware of where I am going, since I stop at red lights, drive at the right speed, and behave cautiously around dangerous drivers. But driving has become detached from my conscious thinking, and my conscious and deliberate thoughts may fail to be properly integrated with it. I may find myself at the garage when I started out intending to go somewhere else en route, or find myself at the usual entrance even when I know it is closed for construction. A decision to act differently from usual has not penetrated the patterns of routine, which carry on unaffected. A change to routine has to be conscious, explicit, and sometimes repeated if it is to have appropriate impact.

Virtue is unlike routine in a host of ways. But rather than simply claiming this, we shall first look at cases where habituation does not lead to routine—practical skills. Suppose I am learning to play the piano. As with driving, I need first to work out consciously what is the right thing to do and then get used to doing it over and over again. This goes on from learning notes to learning scales and arpeggios and then learning how to play sonatas. As I become a skilled piano player (here the 'I' becomes fictional) I can play sonatas and other pieces in a way that, as with driving, proceeds without conscious thinking. My fingers pick out the right notes in the right relation to one another at the right speed, without anything like a decision or conscious thought before each action of striking the keys.

When we see the speed with which a skilled pianist produces the notes we might be tempted to think that constant repetition and habit have transformed the original experience, which required conscious thought, into mere routine. But this is completely wrong. The expert pianist plays in a way not dependent on conscious input, but the result is not mindless routine but rather playing infused with and expressing the pianist's thoughts about the piece. Further, the pianist continues to improve her playing. The way she plays exhibits not only increased technical mastery but increased intelligence—better ways of dealing with transitions between loud and soft, more subtle interpretations of the music, and so on. Rather than the rest of the mind being shut off from patterns of routine and proceeding independently, the ability, though a habituated one, is constantly informed by the way the person is thinking. If the pianist resolves to play the first movement in a different way, her playing will all reflect this in subtle ways; she won't 'wake up' and find herself at the end having played it the previous way, as I find myself at the parking garage despite having intended to go elsewhere. The practical mastery is at the service of conscious thought, not at odds with it.

This is, of course, an idealized picture; no doubt pianists do sometimes 'wake up' to find they have played the piece the standard way. But if so, this is a failure in the skill: if practical skills become routine they ossify and decay. Actual pianists also become worse as well as better at their skill, as any pianist will tell you. This emphasizes the point that a habituated activity does not reach a plateau of routine which, once established, is unchanging and can be left alone; it needs constant monitoring for improvement or worsening. Skilled dispositions are not static conditions; they are always developing, being sustained or weakened.

One of the major suggestions of this book is that virtue is like practical skill in this respect (as well as some others). Because a virtue is a disposition it requires time, experience, and habituation to develop it, but the result is not routine but the kind of actively and intelligently engaged practical mastery that we find in practical experts such as pianists and athletes.

The intelligence displayed in an expert tennis player's strategy, for example, has come from practice and habituation, but it is not mindlessly repetitive. Similarly, a brave person (not someone who has just decided to be brave, or read a book about it, but someone who has become brave as a result of habituation) is now disposed to be brave in a way which is persistent, reliable, and characteristic. But when faced by an occasion when he should face risk or danger for something worthwhile, his response is not a mechanical, habit-based one. Like the expert tennis player, he responds directly to the situation in an intelligent way, one which takes account of all the relevant factors; habituation has sharpened rather than blunted his response. Bravery may be shown by rushing to the rescue; it may also be shown by first carefully assessing the situation. Loyalty may be shown by unflagging support; it may also be shown by seriously questioning the person who demands unflagging support.

A central feature of routine is that the reaction to the relevant situation is always the same, which is why routine can be depended on and predicted. But practical skill and virtue require more than predictably similar reaction; they require a response which is appropriate to the situation instead of merely being the same as that produced in response to other situations. This appropriateness comes from the habituated disposition that a virtue is. As Aristotle says: 'It . . . seems to be characteristic of the more courageous person to be unafraid and unruffled in sudden alarms rather than to be so in those that are foreseen; it comes more from his state of character [*hexis*, often translated 'disposition'], because less from preparation. Foreseen actions can be rationally chosen on the basis of calculation and reason, but unforeseen ones only in virtue of one's state of character.'[6] Virtues, which are states of character, are states that enable us to respond in creative and imaginative ways to new challenges. No routine could enable us to do this.

The analogy with practical skill, then, enables us to see how virtue can be a disposition requiring habituation without becoming mere routine.[7] I have introduced the skill analogy in a way which I hope indicates how important it is for understanding virtue. Much more remains now to be said about it, what it reveals about virtue, and what its limitations are.

[in margin: ✳ persistance "Living Deliberately"]

---

[6] Aristotle (2000), *Nicomachean Ethics*, trans. Crisp, 1117^a17–22.

[7] Many of Kant's problems with virtue spring from suspicion that habituation will produce mere routine, virtuous actions being performed mechanically and thus without the proper participation of the agent's will.

3

Skilled and Virtuous Action

Skill and Virtue: The Need to Learn and the Drive to Aspire

Virtue is different from mere routine in a way we can also discern in practical skills such as piano playing and tennis. What is the basis of this similarity?

It is one which is not to be found in every example of everything that we are prepared to call a skill. Some practical skills do seem to involve mere routine—this is true of daily activities such as getting to work which we are sometimes prepared to call skills, though at other times we call them routines or rituals.[1] Nor is it true of skills where there is a large contribution from natural talent; where this is the case, the similarity we are interested in does not apply to the contribution made by talent. (In the contemporary world athletic skills are usually developed in a context of competition, and a particular skill may only be developed where there is enough natural talent to win competitions; nonetheless we can appreciate the exercise of skill apart from this.) We find the important similarity of virtue to skill in skills where two things are united: the *need to learn* and the *drive to aspire.* positive model

Aristotle famously notes an important similarity between virtue and skill: both are practical, and so can be learned only by practice, by actually doing what needs to be done. Moreover, both involve *learning.* '[W]hat we need to learn to do, we learn by doing; for example, we become

---

[1] This account thus has little in common either with those which emphasize virtue as 'know-how', or with those which take the virtuous person to rely on immediate sensitivities to navigate the world. Neither of these kinds of account puts emphasis on aspiration. See Clark and Churchland (2000), Dreyfus and Dreyfus (1990). 'Know-how' is often used in a way which obliterates the distinction between learner and expert, which is so important in this account.

builders by building, and lyre-players by playing the lyre. So too we become just by doing just actions, temperate by doing temperate actions and courageous by courageous actions.'[2]

Building is not what we think of as a particularly intellectual skill, but there is still no such thing as learning to be a builder mindlessly, by rote copying. Even simple building skills are not easy or effortless to learn; they involve more than copying a role model and then learning by repetition how to do it routinely. We need experience and practice, and we have to learn from someone who can teach us. But from the start something is conveyed in the teaching which is not grasped by the person who merely tries to do exactly what the teacher does. The learner needs to trust the teacher to be doing the right thing to follow and copy, and to be conveying the right information and ways of doing things. And further, from the start the learner of a skill needs also what I have called the drive to aspire, manifesting itself first in the need the learner has to understand what she is doing if she is to learn properly.

The learner needs to *understand* what in the role model to follow, what the point is of doing something this way rather than that, what is crucial to the teacher's way of doing things a particular way and what is not. A learner who fails to do this will simply copy the teacher's mannerisms and style along with the teacher's exact way of doing things. But this is clearly a failure to learn the skill, not a success. Imagine a pianist whose goal is to play like Alfred Brendel, but mistakenly thinks that she will achieve this by copying all his mannerisms and niceties of style, playing only the pieces he plays and playing them just as he plays them. The result would be an impersonation of Brendel, not the achievement of his skill. The person who really learns to play in a way that could be called 'playing like Brendel' might do so in playing quite different pieces, in different ways from Brendel, but in ways that show that she has learnt about playing from Brendel and grasped what is central to his style.

What the learner needs to do is not only to learn from the teacher or role model how to understand what she has to do and the way to do it, but to become able to acquire *for herself* the skill that the teacher has, rather than acquiring it as a matter of routine, something which results in becoming a clone-like impersonator. To acquire the skill you have to be

Handwritten margin notes: "Have to want to be a virtuous person"; "Hallmark of virtue approaches"; ""Focus on the self""

---

[2] Aristotle (2000), *Nicomachean Ethics*, trans. Crisp, 1103^{a}32–^{b}2.

able to do it yourself, rather than stopping at a plateau of routine, where you can turn off thinking about further improvement. This is a point familiar in a whole range of skills: the moment comes when you have to stop just following the teacher and play, skate, dance, speak in Italian, for yourself. It is also clear that this is the point of the instruction: if you can't do it yourself in a way that is not merely parroting the teacher then you have not yet learned the skill. This point about self-direction links naturally to the first point: you have to make the effort to understand what you have been taught, and to grasp it for yourself, because this is the point at which you can exercise the skill in a self-directed way.

Finally, aspiration leads the learner to strive to *improve*, to do what he is doing better rather than taking it over by rote from the teacher. This is what a lot of practice is about—not perfecting a routinized movement but learning to do what is being done, but better: how to steer a car, skate a double axel, translate Homer, clear a hurdle. That there is this aspiration to improve might be doubted, since it often seems to disappointed teachers that some learners lack it, and have to be unwillingly prodded to go through the motions. These are, however, people who are not learning. The disappointed teachers will notice on their tests that they simply parrot what they have been taught, and have not learnt it; with physical skills they never advance to the next level. Where the aspiration to improve fails, we lapse into simple repetition and routine. This is a very demanding feature of a skill.[3]

「I feel always present / developing

Does the need to improve eventually recede, or is it always present? If it is, this seems to imply that nobody can master a skill completely. The need to improve never in fact entirely disappears, but the implication is simply that mastery of a skill is incompatible with its being mere routine; experts in a skill need to maintain it as a skill and not mere routine. Expert pianists, golfers, and climbers face this issue: if they don't use the skill they lose it, though they may retain mastery of technical matters required to exercise the skill. Experts thus face the same issues as learners, though in a modified form, since they have more resources of self-directed activity to draw on.

active is important

What is involved in coming to have a skill in this way, learning partly consisting in the drive to aspire? Something has been conveyed from the

---

[3] It is the point at which some may feel that the notion of a skill here has been made too demanding, since we do not demand aspiration to improve in tying our shoelaces and a range of such activities. This point, however, really tells against calling such routine activities skills.

expert to the learner which cannot be reduced to showing the learner something to repeat. So far I have talked of the point of the activity. This may be a simple aim, easily understood, or it may be something more complex, involving grasp of a principle or a set of principles. Learning how to fix a computer involves more complexity than learning to ride a bicycle. The more complexity, the more there is to learning to exercise the skill for yourself.

With skills of any complexity, what is conveyed from the expert to the learner will require the giving of reasons. The learner electrician and plumber need to know not just *that* you do the wiring or pipe-laying such and such a way, but *why*. An electrician needs to know more than she can learn by rote, since she will be dealing with a variety of different situations and will need to adapt what she has learnt to these; lessons learned by rote could lead to disastrous mistakes. Reasons enter in here as a medium of *explanation*: the teacher can, by giving reasons for what she does, explain to the learner why she must wire or lay pipe in such and such a way, as opposed to just showing her that you do it this way. The explanation enables the learner to go ahead in different situations and contexts, rather than simply repeat the exact same thing that was done. The ability both to teach and to learn a skill thus depends on the ability to convey an explanation by giving and receiving reasons. It thus requires some degree of articulacy.

This idea, that conveying and acquiring a skill requires articulacy, often meets resistance. This may take the form of pointing to skills where articulacy does not appear to be necessary; sometimes gardening is given as an example. In some cases, such as physical skills, the person outstanding in the skill may not be the best at conveying it (as with athletes and coaches). Many of these will be cases where what is at stake is really mastery of technical matters needed for the exercise of the skill, or where what is important is natural talent. In any case, it does not matter for this account if there are such cases, since the claim is simply that virtue has a structure which can be found in cases of skill which do exhibit the features of need for learning and drive to aspire. That we sometimes use the notion of skill more broadly than this does not affect the account.

This is a point on which our understanding overlaps with that of the ancients, but also differs. In ancient ethical theory, the analogy with skill is readily brought in and uncontroversially used. This is in large part because the ancients find unproblematic just the feature which apparently seems difficult to many contemporaries, namely the requirement of articulacy in explanation, the ability to convey why what is done is done. Indeed, just this serves to mark off skill (*technē*) from an inarticulate 'knack' (*empeiria*); the skilled person can 'give an account' of what he does, which involves being able to explain why he is doing what he is doing. Such a person understands what he is doing, unlike the person who can pick up a knack in a purely unintellectual way, without understanding what it is he is doing and why.[4] In the contemporary world we use 'skill' so broadly that this distinction seems less obvious. What matters, however, is that we can recognize at least some skills as having these two important features of the need to learn and the drive to aspire: to aspire, that is, to understanding, to self-direction, and to improvement. The need for reasons and articulacy emerges from the aspiration, and so is not to be found in cases which do not display it, whether or not we are nowadays prepared to call them skills.

Virtue can most illuminatingly be seen as like this kind of skill; it shares the intellectual structure of a skill where we find not only the need to learn but the drive to aspire, and hence the need to 'give an account', the need for articulate conveying of reasons why what is done is done. The learner in virtue, like the learner in a practical skill, needs to understand what she is doing, to achieve the ability to do it for herself, and to do it in a way that improves as she meets challenges, rather than coming out with predictable repetition. This comes about when the virtue is conveyed by the giving and receiving of reasons, in contrast with the non-rational picking up of a knack.[5]

That virtue has these features, and that they are centrally important to what virtue is, is one of the main claims of the book, as is a further claim, namely that this gives us an account of virtue which is both intuitive and readily accessible, and also theoretically well defended against many contemporary criticisms. Ancient ethical theorists did not doubt that practical skill was a good analogy for virtue, but the case has to be made for contemporaries with a contemporary understanding of skill and a stress on some features which the ancients passed over.

---

[4] This point about skill (*technē*) is put forward famously by Plato in the *Gorgias* (463a–466a, 500a–501c), and built on by Aristotle at the opening of his *Metaphysics*.

[5] For contrasting views on the relation of reasoning to picking up a habit see Pollard (2003) and Snow (2006).

It is important here to start in the right place, which is not by examining a mature adult to find virtues of this kind. The crucial point about skill under discussion is a point about how it is taught and learnt, and so the context to examine is the analogous one for virtue, namely contexts of teaching and learning. This also does justice to an important point about virtue ethics, as opposed to other kinds of ethical theories. Understanding the process of ethical education is a part of virtue ethics. Ethical education is not something 'merely practical' and so extraneous to theory. We cannot understand what virtue is without coming to understand how we acquire it. Virtue ethical theories are thus not theories which recommend themselves on other grounds—economy of basic terms, simple structure, and the like—and leave us to find out for ourselves whether such a theory can be put into practice.[6]

By the time we think about virtues, we all have some (and some vices, but I will not mention vice every time I mention virtue). For we have all been brought up, and that is where we have learned to be virtuous (or not, or not very). Our parents and teachers, and the people in our culture generally, teach us many things: mathematics, manners, how to read and write, how to interact with animals. They also teach us to be honest, loyal, and generous—not in separate lessons, but in the ways they teach us these other things, and in the way they act themselves, giving us examples and role models to follow (and to avoid). In what follows I will often speak of the context of parents and children, as this is the clearest case of ethical education, but other contexts are important also.

We always learn to be virtuous in a given context; there is no such thing as just learning to be generous or loyal in the abstract. One child will learn to be generous in the context of buying friends presents, another in the context of spending time building a house for the homeless. This point can be summed up by saying that learning to be virtuous always takes place in an *embedded* context. We learn in a multitude of embedded contexts, which can stand in various relations, from overlapping to conflicting: family, school, church, employment, siblings, friends, neighbourhoods, the internet. When we learn to be virtuous, then, the need to learn is less

---

[6] See Hursthouse (1999a), and Baier (1997). Some contemporary ethical theories still talk only about mature adults, assuming that they do not need to provide an account of how children can be brought up to be those adults (even where the theory is very revisionary about what sort of people mature adults will be).

obvious than it is with skills, since our surroundings are overflowing with teachers, and often it is not obvious at the time that we are learning to be generous or brave in learning how do things; most people discern this only much later. Moreover, it is also not till much later that we are in a position to ask about our teachers' credentials as teachers of virtue, or to feel ourselves in a position to correct them.

Many accounts of virtue give insufficient weight to the drive to aspire. They assume that we learn from our family, school, and friends to be brave, loyal, and generous, and that this process is something like mindless absorption: we allegedly just come to take on the dispositions which our family and society call virtuous, without having the distance to criticize them. If this were so, however, each generation would simply replicate the past one in the dispositions they encourage or despise, whereas what we find is that each generation alters its predecessor's conception of some virtues, while others fall out of favour altogether. As Aristotle puts it, everyone seeks the good, not what their parents did.[7] It is sometimes retorted that this is true only of modern liberal societies, not of pre-modern or very traditional societies. However, even in an ultra-traditional society with official uniformity about the virtues there are different groups with different perspectives, some of which may be officially ignored or even suppressed; we should not take at their word the people who claim to present the views of such a society.[8]

We learn to be brave and loyal, then, in embedded contexts. What happens when we do? As with skill, we learn from a teacher or role model who shows us how to do something which we then try to copy for ourselves. We don't learn to be virtuous from books, even books about virtue, though these help our understanding. Aristotle is right here: virtue is like building in that learning to be brave is learning to do something, to act in certain ways, and that where we have to learn to do something, we learn it by doing it (not just by reading books about it). A boy will learn to be brave, initially, by seeing a parent chase off a dog, say, and registering that this is brave. But right from the start he will see that his coming to be brave does not consist in his chasing off dogs. This has at first to be got across by the parents: some dogs are not a threat, some dogs which are are

✳ learnedus an example

---

[7] *Politics* II. 8.

[8] It is clear nowadays, for example, that the perspectives of women in traditional societies often differ greatly from those of the men who claim to speak for the whole society.

so big that they will hurt the child if he stands up to them, and so on. The child comes to see that bravery is not rushing to confront any danger, but requires thoughts about what is dangerous, and what is appropriate as a response to things that are.

From the start, then, the child will learn by copying the role model (or, more sophisticatedly, trying to act like heroes in books or movies). But this will not lead to bravery, as opposed to foolish repetition, unless *at the same time* the child is led to aspire in the three ways already indicated. He needs to come to understand why, not just that, the parent chased off the dog, and the factors involved, such as the dog's being a threat. He needs to come to be able to act bravely himself in similar situations, and we can see how much understanding this will require: he has to learn the difference between bravery and recklessness, the importance of realizing one's abilities, and also one's limits, the importance of realizing what merits a defensive response and what does not. And he needs to come to appreciate that his own attempts may be blunders, and that he has far to go before getting it right in the way adults do. All three aspects of the drive to aspire that we saw in practical skill turn out to be crucial for the acquiring of virtue.

Learning as complex as this requires the conveying of explanation from the parent, and upshot on the part of the child. Many people have stressed that a lot of this is not, especially with small children, explicitly articulate. We certainly don't have to imagine the parent always spelling out every time the point that acting in such and such a way is brave, generous, or whatever; a lot of learning takes place by the child's efforts simply being rewarded or discouraged. Nonetheless, parents are engaged, in a lot of what they do, in explaining to their children what it is that is brave in chasing off a dog or generous in spending your time for other people, in getting them to see the point of acting in certain ways, and the importance of achieving that by acting differently in a different context, rather than mechanically repeating the original action. An important aspect of this in getting children to see that they are learning to be brave or generous is, as with mathematics or writing, conveying that they still have a way to go. Doing what your role model does is not repeating that action, but coming to understand what they were doing, in performing that action, and being able to do *that* yourself, perhaps in a quite different way.

Although I have started with the example of parents and small children, examples of learning to be virtuous can be found throughout our entire lives. While very small children have to be taught not merely to copy examples slavishly, but to think about what in them to follow when they act, they acquire at a very young age what I have called the *drive* to aspire. The child starts thinking for himself what in examples to copy and what to do to be brave or generous in new situations. This point is one that psychologists have done a great deal of work on, but unfortunately hitherto always asking about children's thoughts about rules. Kohlberg claimed that his researches showed that children adopted rules from their surroundings and failed to distinguish ethical from merely conventional reasons for obeying them until going through various developmental stages. More recently the work of Turiel and Smetana has shown that this picture needs correction: children as young as 4 are able to distinguish a merely conventional rule from an ethical rule, and recognize that if an ethical rule holds here, it holds elsewhere, whereas a merely conventional rule would not hold in the absence of the relevant convention.[9] It is a pity that this research has restricted itself uncritically to rules as the relevant instruments of ethics, and has not extended research to the virtues. At any rate we can be confident of the general point that from a very early age children have the ability to distinguish doing what is merely copying what is done by authoritative figures from thinking for themselves about what the point of this is. Children can from early on, that is, come to learn not only passively to copy and develop routine, but actively to aspire to understanding, self-direction, and improvement.

This picture may strike some as too optimistic. Some people seem ethically lazy, with little or no drive to aspire. This does not threaten the account, however. The ethically lazy person merely takes on the patterns of action of her parents or other role models, without trying to understand what their basis is, or thinking about it for herself. Such a person will tend to develop rigid dispositions which will be ill-suited to coping with the world (since even in traditional societies one generation's circumstances will be different in many ways from that of the previous generation). The ethically lazy person may come to learn that her reactions are inadequate the painful way, in encounters with the world which may end up driving

---

[9] See Turiel (1983), who in ch. 7 effectively criticizes the developmental accounts of Piaget and Kohlberg, who assert that children retain an unthinking deference to rules until a much later stage of development.

her to aspire, if only to avoid the ethical disasters which come from routine mimicking of role models.

We can see the importance of the two aspects of the skill analogy which I have underlined: the need to learn and the drive to aspire. The need to learn does justice to the fact that virtues are always learned in particular embedded contexts, and that by the time we are mature and rational enough to reflect about virtue we have already been through a process of character education in which we were learners. We do not start ethical reflection as blank sheets.[10] The drive to aspire stresses the equally important aspect of coming to understand what we are learning, the move to self-direction, and the point that we are always improving (or at least sustaining) virtue. Virtue is not a state you achieve and then sit back, with nothing further to do. It is the drive to aspire which enables the learner to come to be able to assess and criticize what he has been taught, and to be able to correct the teacher and the context and culture in which he has been taught.[11] Hence we can already see why virtue is a dynamic, rather than a static, disposition.[12]

The role of reason-giving in a practical skill illuminates the role of reason-giving in virtue. A lot of what is involved in the learning and teaching of virtue is not articulate: at all ages we are guided not just by what the teacher or role model says but simply by what he does and the specific way he does it. Still, virtue is like practical skill in being more than a subrational knack, and accounts of virtue make a bad mistake if they downplay the role of reason-giving, and demands for reasons, as we are educated to have the virtues. One of the major problems with the subrational, 'knack' picture of virtue was pointed out already by Aristotle in the distinction he draws between virtue proper and mere natural virtue,

[margin annotation: persistance ("self-flourishing")]

---

[10] This is a feature of ancient theories, which is stressed in Annas (1993) and (2002). Some contemporary ethical theorists think that we begin ethical thinking by reflecting on principles, or good, in the abstract; these are then taken to commit us to changing our lives radically. The problems we have doing this are often merely chalked up to ethical laziness. It is far more realistic to face the point that we come to ethical reflection with a character already formed.

[11] The extent and force of this ability to criticize will be the subject of the next chapter.

[12] It is this dynamic character which is brought out by the idea of the 'drive to aspire' rather than simple aspiration. The stress in this work on aspiration should not lead to confusion with 'perfectionism', which in some of its varieties treats virtue as aiming to achieve ideal targets already set up by some distinct part of the theory (a distinct account of human nature, for example). (For a thorough discussion of this issue, see Lebar and Russell, forthcoming.) Aspiration on the present account comes from a drive internal to virtue.

[margin annotation: Not perfect but better; adaptable personality views]

a natural predisposition to be bold or sympathetic or the like. The latter may seem to do the work of a virtue, but because the person lacks the ability to demand, and give, reasons for what he does he is not equipped to deal with new and unforeseen circumstances. Never having learnt not to take people at face value, for example, the 'naturally brave' person may get into a serious fight over a slight intended as a joke, while the 'naturally sympathetic' person may find herself the victim of scams. As Aristotle says, they are like powerful but blind people who stumble and fall over.[13]

Another serious problem with the subrational picture is that it disables us from giving any plausible account of ethical advice or disagreement. A loyal person, say, is asked what someone should do who wants to be loyal to their friend, but has realized that the friend is taking drugs. We expect the person asked for advice to be able to offer reasons for and against breaking off relations with the friend. It would obviously be absurd if they replied that there was no way they could explain; the questioner should just watch some loyal people and pick up what they do. We also realize that in a case like this there might well be disagreement as to what the questioner should do. Two people, both indisputably loyal, might pick on different features of the case and give diverging advice. When this happens, we think that they are giving the questioner diverging reasons, and that each recognizes that the other has reasons which can be met in argument and debate. If the subrational view of virtue were true, there would seem to be nothing they could do other than accuse each other of being badly brought up.[14]

Finally, there is a range of issues about virtues which arise in everyday life, which we discuss in terms of reasons rather than abandoning them to the area of subrational knacks. One of these is the issue (to which we shall return) of how to individuate the virtues. Two people become parents, and naturally wish to bring the child up well. Do they need a specific virtue of parenting, needed only by parents and having a specific shape and demands? Or do they simply need to apply virtues they already have (to some degree) such as sympathy and patience, and learn to apply these in a new context? Which of these ways of looking at the matter they take may make a large difference to the way they go about learning to be good

(margin notes: "A Deceiving", "Is many?")

---

[13] Aristotle (2000), NE 1144^{b}4–14.

[14] We resort to this, normally, only when what is at stake is not central enough to be a virtue or vice, as in cases of rudeness.

parents. How we decide between these two positions about virtue is something that we discuss and give reasons for; that is, even on the way to getting clear on this issue, and thus well before having a clear idea of the answer, we reject the idea that the virtues, whatever they are, are nothing more than subrational knacks that can just be picked up independently of reason-giving.

Another issue is that of natural virtue, in the Aristotelian sense of traits that we are born with, and develop without being taught. Parents recognize that natural assertiveness, for example, is not a trait to be uncritically encouraged; this could lead to bullying and not listening to others' views. The child's natural tendency needs to be educated so that he becomes aware of reasons to act and not to act assertively, and he does so by being given reasons by parents and role models. *not to be confused* This is not fundamentally different from the way a child with a natural aptitude for a practical skill is educated to develop it in ways which are flexibly responsive to a range of different challenges and situations.[15]

The skill analogy, then, turns out to answer to a number of our ways of thinking about virtue. As already stressed, this conclusion is not undermined by our finding that we are sometimes prepared to count as a skill something like tying our shoelaces, which does not answer to the above account of skill; I feel fairly confident that few have thought that being loyal or beneficent is much like tying shoelaces.

Not all accounts of virtue put forward by philosophers, however, are receptive to the above idea, namely that virtue is to be understood in part by the way it is acquired, and that its acquisition involves both the need to learn and the drive to aspire, as sketched above. Virtue on the above conception is a disposition not just to act reliably in certain ways but to act reliably for certain reasons. The latter comes in because a virtue is not just a habit of copying what others do but a disposition to act which involves understanding what you do, self-directedness, and a drive to improve. The virtuous person will act, dispositionally, on reasons which reflect the extent to which she has achieved the condition just described. The reasons will reflect what she has learned in what has been conveyed by her

---

[15] This is different from the case of a child with a natural talent for an intellectual skill, such as chess or mathematics. These skills develop in ways unlike practical skills and virtues, and as a result may be far advanced in a way that is unintegrated with the rest of the child's character. (If this lack of integration persists to adulthood, the result is *idiots savants*.)

teachers; yet they are also the point at which she is able to depart from
what her teachers do and act for herself on the basis of her own understanding of why acting this way, rather than that, is honest, or loyal, or
brave. So, even before we further develop our account of virtue, we can
see at this point that virtue cannot be adequately understood just as a
disposition to perform actions; the virtuous person is someone whose
actions are performed for certain reasons.   *— motivation; want; dr.*

Is such a conception of virtue too intellectualist? I have already mentioned the point that the development of practical reasoning has not been
supposed to be developing in a motivational void. We come with motivational tendencies which, by the time we learn anything, have already
developed in various ways; the ways we learn develop them further.
It is a mistake to ask how practical reasoning can subsequently acquire
motivation to act; practical reasoning has been developing as part of the
development of a disposition to act. The present account is thus not
intellectualist in the sense of developing an account of reasoning uncon-
nected with action.

There are other ways, though, in which the account might seem over-
intellectual. First, it might be thought that the account so far makes the
virtuous person sound, unrealistically, as though they were always busily
thinking about reasons. An attraction of the subrational model is that it
seems to answer to one aspect of the behaviour of the virtuous, namely
that they respond *directly* and *immediately* to situations in a way that often
contrasts with the more inhibitedly thoughtful response of the less virtuous. In a case of need, the generous person will at once respond to the
need; the person who stands around wondering what to do and has to
figure out how to respond is not (yet) a generous person. When we ask
brave people why they responded as they did, the answer will typically
be in terms of the situation they responded to—'They were about to be
swept away', 'He was going near the wasps' nest', and so on—and this does
not look as though they had to think much, or at all, about the reasons
why they had to respond.

This is not the last we shall see of this objection, which we will deal with
in greater detail in Ch. 5 and will return in Ch. 9. At this point I shall just
show that it ignores something about virtue which we can learn from the
analogy with skill, and which goes some way towards enabling us better to
understand the point made in Ch. 2: the virtuous person's response is
immediate, but it is an *intelligent* response, not a rote one. We can now see

why it is intelligent; it is an *educated* response. Think of the person learning to play the piano. At first she will have to acquire the skill by consciously thinking what to do, and will be running through thoughts about reasons the teacher has given her for playing the arpeggio one way rather than the other, adjusting the left hand speed and so on. As we saw, where skill differs from acquiring a rote habit it requires thought about acting. Understanding what you are doing is acquired as you think before acting in ways which incorporate what has been learned. As the pianist improves, she will need to think less and less as she plays about how she should play the next chord, attempt the next scale, and the like. The result is a speed and directness of response comparable to that of mere habit, but unlike it in that the lessons learned have informed it and rendered it flexible and innovative. The conscious thoughts seem to have disappeared; they are not taking up psychological room, or we would never see learners speed up as they become experts. The thoughts have, in a useful philosophical term, effaced themselves. The pianist is not aware of them at the time, and it would interfere with her performance if she were (as thinking about how to skate and ride a bicycle interferes with actual skating and riding). But they have not disappeared entirely. If asked how she produced a certain effect, the pianist would have something to say about how it was done; just as she was taught, she can go on to teach others.[16]

Similarly with the virtuous person. Someone who is loyal will have learnt, from parents, teachers, and other role models, the value of loyalty, and reasons for being loyal and for ceasing to be loyal. In a crisis, she may stick by a fellow worker suspected of misconduct. This is an immediate response—'He needed support'. But when asked she will be able to give reasons—reasons, for example, for sticking by fellow workers whose character you know, rather than believing the worst of them because of someone else's suspicions. If she can think of no such reasons but just insists on solidarity without any reason, we move to thinking that this is not loyalty but unreasoning attachment. For one important lesson we learn from the analogy with skill is that reasons for acting can efface themselves without evaporating entirely. Moreover, it is the fact that these reasons

---

[16] With some physical skills, the practitioner may find himself unable to do this. This may be because a large part of the accomplishment is due to natural talent (perhaps the trainer or coach, with less natural talent, may be better able to convey the skill). This effect will vary between different skills.

cease to take up psychological room at the time of action which enables the virtuous person to become someone who is disposed to act generously or sympathetically without hesitation or the need to work out the options. The reasons have left their effect in the person's disposition, so that the virtuous response is an intelligent one while also being immediate and not one which the person needs to consciously figure out. There are people who apparently act virtuously but prove completely unable to explain why they did so; as with skill, this makes us think that we are dealing with a natural gift which has not yet been educated to become virtue proper.

There is another issue about the alleged intellectualism of this kind of account of virtue, which is that it is elitist. This has been memorably stated by Julia Driver. On a view like the present, she holds, virtue requires the kind of wisdom that comes from reasoning and thinking, acquiring ethical understanding in an intellectual way. This implies that to become virtuous you must become practically wise. This is certainly what Aristotle himself demands; the virtuous person is *phronimos* and has *phronesis*—practical wisdom. But this means that virtue will be limited to a few, and for most of us will be merely an ideal we cannot achieve. 'Virtue must be accessible—to those who are not wise but kind; to those who had the misfortune to grow up in repressive environments that warped their understanding, yet who are capable of showing the appropriate compassionate responses to human suffering.'[17]

We are not all wise, certainly, but it can be doubted whether we are all kind, either. If virtue is linked to sympathetic response rather than to ethical understanding, it will still not be universal, since many lack sympathy or have it only in very limited or even distorted forms. Moreover, there is little or nothing the person lacking in sympathy can do about it, whereas the drive to aspire in what we learn is more plausibly something accessible to all.[18] We can see as much from the skill analogy itself. We can all learn to acquire skills; if some of us have a better natural endowment for them then the others will find it harder, but they are not excluded.

---

[17] Driver (2001: 54).

[18] We can, of course, make efforts to extend our sympathies, by making efforts to find out about deprivations and miseries normally hidden from us. But unless this is done intelligently there is no reason to think it will lead to virtuous compassion, rather than sentimentality. Feelings of compassion and sympathy on their own can be led in many directions.

This response, however, brings up another point in the quoted passage. Some of us grow up in bad environments which warp our ability to come to understand the virtues.[19] Are we not excluding these people from the community of the virtuous for something they can do nothing about? There are very many people in the world today who live in terrible conditions of poverty and violence (for example, in the slums of large cities) which make it unreasonable to expect them to reflect on and criticize the lessons they are taught by the role models they have, people who frequently (and understandably) emphasize the importance not of the virtues but of looking out for yourself, not getting held back by caring about others, becoming used to violence and cruelty, and worse. It is important, though, not to confuse the fact that we do not expect virtue here, which is reasonable, with the different thought that these people are incapable of virtue, which is mistaken. Most of these people fail to become virtuous because of the difficulties of their situation, not because they are not capable of it. Analogously, we do not expect someone from such a slum to make much headway on making a grant application or playing the piano. This is obviously not because they lack native capacities, but because their situation is such that these ideas, and opportunities, are shut off from them; they don't own pianos, have never heard of grants, and may well not have learnt even to read and write. We do not expect people raised on garbage dumps outside a Third World megalopolis to be kind and generous in their everyday behaviour, but this is, I suggest, for the same kind of reason that we also do not expect them to play the piano or to do crosswords. Their environment has obviously lacked the opportunities to learn and do these things, and because this is so obvious we do not assume that they are naturally unable to do them. The same holds for failure to develop the virtues.[20]

The present account is not, then, committed to elitism about virtue. We are all capable of developing the kind of understanding that virtue requires. For some their circumstances make it hard for them to develop this, but

[19] Driver's own example is Huck Finn, but I concur with Hursthouse (1999a: 150–3) that this is not a good example of virtue.

[20] Some skills can be developed in the absence of much by way of external opportunities; some famous soccer players developed their skills early in street playing, for example. Similarly, we do sometimes find outstanding examples of kindness and other virtues among people whose external circumstances gave them very limited opportunities for their development.

we have no reason to think that any are naturally incapable of it.[21] It remains the case that, given the world as it is, not everybody does actually develop the virtues; but this is a problem for every account, not for this one in particular.

Action Guidance

How does thinking in terms of virtue actually help you to act, when you need to do something? Looking only at the account of virtue so far may make this question appear misguided. How can being generous guide you to act generously? This looks like the question, How can having learned to speak Italian guide you to communicate with Italians? The answer seems painfully obvious. (In this case, we can also contrast the practical skill of having learned to speak Italian with the skill of having learned Italian as an object of theoretical philological study, which is not itself practical and thus does allow the question to be sensibly raised.) What we learn, as we learn to be virtuous, is practical understanding, which is understanding how to act; if we are left puzzled by the question, how this guides us to act, we have been learning the wrong thing.

There is a problem here, however, which we can see clearly if we look at disputes that arise about ethical theories in which virtue is central. Although I am exploring the notion of virtue rather than that of virtue ethics, a serious issue is raised about the practicability of the kind of account of virtue presented here, one which needs to be faced especially by an account which, in stressing the skill analogy, emphasizes that this account foregrounds the practical nature of virtue. I shall accordingly not aim to cover the entire debate, but to consider only the way in which an account of virtue like the one presented here can meet three demands which are frequently made of an ethical theory.

The first demand is that an ethical theory *direct* us, that it issue *commands*, in short that it *tell us what to do*. Where it is assumed that these demands are

---

[21] Paul Bloomfield has emphasized to me that the development of virtue does require a minimum of intelligence not possessed by, for example, people with Down's syndrome. Such people can develop analogues to the virtues, but not the virtues themselves. I think that any ethical theory has to allow that in cases like this there is a qualification to the way in which such people can be full members of the ethical community in so far as this is thought of as a community of active reasoners. (Of course they are members of it as objects of concern.)

legitimate, it is often claimed it is not clear how being virtuous results in anything like this. If I am honest, I will do the honest thing; but how can my honesty issue commands, either to me or to others, to do particular actions? A theory in which virtue is central, then, appears, given these assumptions, to lack the resources to provide the kind of directive force which, given these assumptions, ethics should have.

We should, however, examine just what is involved in this notion of direction or telling us what to do. Being *told what to do* brings with it the idea of *doing what I am told*—that is, straightforwardly conforming to a directive. We normally take this to be appropriate to areas where directives can be given and where it is appropriate for the person on the receiving end of the directive to conform to them. One obvious such area is that of technical instruction, where to learn to do something I have to follow rules. To learn how to fix a computer or a car, for example, I have to follow the rules in the technical manual. This is how we learn many techniques. This does not amount to learning a skill, though many skills are made easier to learn if we already have certain techniques. Someone will become good at fixing a computer or learning Italian only if he has first learnt the technical matters in the computer manual or the grammar. But to fix a computer or speak Italian in a skilled way the person must have got beyond the point of doing what she is told. Being versed in the technical matters does not bring with it any move to understanding, self-direction, and improvement; that comes only with the development of skill.

It is sometimes (less often nowadays) thought that an ethical theory should provide action guidance in something like the manner of providing a technical manual which would tell us what to do. This is often called 'providing a decision procedure'. One advantage of this is that it is ethically egalitarian, for the demand is that ethical direction apply to all alike, regardless of the level of their virtue or intellectual achievement. And this initially sounds attractive; surely ethical direction should apply to everyone in just the same way? How could it be relevant what age you are, for example? The simple model of a decision prodecure, telling everyone alike what to do in the manner of a technical manual, answers to this.

It turns out to be less attractive on examination, however. It is implausible, for example, that ethical direction could be the kind of thing at which a clever adolescent could excel, though clever adolescents are

"If it were easy everybody would do it"

notoriously good at learning technical matters fast and accurately.[22] More-over, if ethical direction were something that all of us are in principle equally good at, this would render it not only possible, but actually required, to separate ethical direction from character. Whether someone's ethical advice was good would have nothing to do with their character. But we would find it at least odd to take ethical direction from somebody whose character we recognize as loathsome. This is sometimes denied, but I suspect that people denying it are thinking in terms of a romantic villain who nonetheless sees deep into the human heart. It is more realistic to ask if you would take advice from somebody who is stupidly brutal and cruel, or an insensitive airhead. We would take advice from such people on technical matters that they were expert on, but hardly ethical advice on what matters to us; and this illustrates what is faulty in the decision procedure model.

Apart from problems with the person giving the advice, we should in any case look closely at the very idea that ethical thinking requires us to do what we are told. Doing what we are told is appropriate at the learner stage in technical matters, and this seems to correspond only to the very early stages of ethical education, if there. Very small children perhaps have to do what they are told in order to orient them rightly, but good ethical education does not encourage the habit of doing what you are told. Imagine a grown adult who always unquestioningly does what his mother tells him to do. This is a sad case of arrested development. And what is problematic about him does not depend on the point that it's his mother he is depending on; it does not go away if we replace his mother by an ethical theory telling him what to do. Whatever we are looking for by way of action guidance has to be more complex, and more suited to adults, than the idea of telling us what to do.[23]

A second demand often made of an ethical theory is that it give us instructions which, even if they are not just telling us what to do, are specific and definite. We need not only to be told what to do, but to be told *exactly* what to do. This is more puzzling than the first demand, because even if you are persuaded that we need to be told what to do,

---

[22] This objection is due to Hursthouse (1999a).

[23] This demand is now less frequent, though the notion of an ethical decision procedure, which would mechanically tell us all what to do, has not entirely disappeared from contemporary ethical theory.

why should we need exact, specific instructions, with no leeway for our own judgement? This is not true even of technical instructions, beyond a very simple level, and even the most authoritarian mother presumably does not tell her son *exactly* how to put on his socks.

Ethical theories in which virtue is central are sometimes criticized on the grounds that they do not give us exact and specific directives as to what to do. We are directed to do the virtuous thing—the brave, generous, loyal, etc. thing; but is this not far too vague to be helpful? It is, however, completely unclear how we are to assess objections like this, given that there is no agreement as to how specific, if at all, ethical directions should be. We can agree that ethical direction will be useless if too general—'be a brave person', 'always be loyal', and the like—and also that it is unrealistic and unmotivated for a theory to be required to tell us exactly what to do, at a level leaving no room for our own judgement. But there is no agreement as to how specific ethical direction should be, and so no independent traction to an objection that theories in which virtue is central give us ethical direction in too general and unspecific a way. In what follows I will try to home in on the kind and level of direction that theories centred on virtue can provide.

[margin handwritten: ✓ not what to do, but what's right to do; virtuous actions]

The third objection is often posed as the thought that a theory centred on virtue cannot produce what is called a *theory of right action*. It is not immediately clear what this objection amounts to. This point is often missed in philosophical discussion, since frequently the notion 'theory of right action' is transferred from theories in which it does have a well-defined place, and it passes unnoticed that in discussions centred on virtue this is no longer true, and use of the notion requires discussion and defence.

I will start from a common formulation of the objection: we cannot get, from considerations about character and the kind of person to be, direction as to what we *ought* to do, what our *obligations* and *duties* are, what we *should* do—in short, what is the *right* thing to do. When we are wondering what to do we often think in terms of the right thing to do, or which action is right. The assumption is frequently made that an ethical theory must be able to deploy these notions in guiding our actions, and it is made an objection to theories in which virtue is central that it is not clear how they can do this, and that ways of getting to these notions from those of virtue and character are systematically inadequate. Either our theories just don't tell us how to get from virtue and character to right action, in which

[margin handwritten: ✗ Inadequate assumption]

case they are failing to give us *action guidance*, or they have to find some way of getting from virtue to right action, and all such attempts have been subject to criticism.

What resources has an honest person from honesty, in herself or her teachers, when she wants to do the right thing? The most helpful approach to being directed to do the right thing is to look first at being directed to do the honest, generous, etc. thing to do. So we shall first go deeper into this process.

Virtuous Action

How are we directed to do virtuous actions? When we learn from our parents and other teachers, they guide us by giving us rules to follow which are stated in terms of the virtues. 'Be honest', they say, 'don't be greedy', 'don't be unkind', and the like. These are what Hursthouse calls the virtue rules or 'v-rules'; she argues powerfully that they are in no way vaguer or direct us less specifically than such rules as 'don't lie', 'don't tell tales', and the like.[24] We have seen, however, that learning to be honest or kind involves a development, and so when we learn to be honest, or brave, there is a development in our understanding of what it is to be honest or brave, accompanied by a corresponding development in our understanding of what honesty and bravery are.

We start as learners, and our notion of what the honest or brave thing to do is what our parents and teachers tell us is honest or brave. A child, for example, is told to be honest in contexts of sharing treats and toys without cheating, not taking things in shops without paying for them, and similar circumstances. He is told to be brave in the doctor's office when a vaccination will hurt, and when other boys are mean to him and he wants to cry about it. His notion of what is honest and brave is the parents' or teachers', not yet his own; he can as yet apply it only to circumstances which are intuitively the same as the ones in which he has learned it. Many movies will underwrite the notion of bravery he has learned, and will also extend it, via scenes of fighting and battles, to the idea of doing what

---

[24] Hursthouse (1999a: 36–9, 58–9, 80–1). This leaves open the question of how specific ethical direction should be.

warriors do. Books praising sports- and war-heroes will likewise enlarge his view of what actions are brave. Experience will also bring in occasions which lead to conflict, or discomfort, with what he has been taught. He may find, for example, that his parents, scrupulous about honesty with money, are not honest with the truth about family history.

If the person we are concerned with develops in an ordinary way, his learning will be infused with the drive to aspire. At an early stage this may take no grander form than learning from mistakes and discoveries. When he learns that his parents are scrupulous about honesty with money, but lax about honesty with the truth, this will produce confusion about what honesty is, and a need to clarify it. He may refine his conception of honesty or conclude that honesty takes ultimately diverse forms. Further, he may find that a friend is behaving bravely in the hospital with cancer. This situation is very unlike any glamorous warrior situation, and may produce confusion as to what bravery is. He may, however, remember being told to be brave when faced with pain, and relate the friend's behaviour to earlier contexts that linked bravery with endurance rather than contexts of violence.

All this is familiar and commonplace, but important in the present connection. I have emphasized that the drive to aspiration involves coming to understand what you are doing, doing it in a self-directed way, and trying to improve. All these points can be found in the way we learn to acquire a virtue such as honesty or bravery. In the process of learning, we acquire the momentum to compare different contexts and notice how different they are, notice what seem like conflicting applications of the same virtue term by others, and work on our own confusion by thinking about the virtue in question.

Some of us may not think very deeply; we may conclude nothing more ambitious than that there are different kinds of bravery, shown in warriors and in people enduring pain, but not asking about what makes all these kinds of *bravery*. This is, for instance, the situation of the people Socrates prods into thinking about bravery in Plato's dialogue *Laches*. Similarly, we may conclude that there is honesty about money and honesty about truth, and that people may have one without the other. If so, the confusion produced by further difficulties may get us to think productively about honesty and bravery. Both honesty and bravery are complex and difficult concepts, and getting them right goes beyond what most of us can muster

your experiences can change your views/opinions/outlook

(margin note, handwritten) life changing (moment?)

unaided.[25] What we can achieve, however, is to think for ourselves about them and reflect on whether our own understanding of them is confused or conflicted. Most of us will need to be spurred into action by some experience—perhaps an occasion when our unclarity leads us to do something we then recognize as wrong, perhaps meeting someone like Socrates who examines the defects in our understanding of bravery and honesty and the like.

What has emerged from examining the acquiring of virtue is that virtue itself is an essentially developmental notion. We do not go suddenly or in a simple move from being pre-virtuous to being virtuous (pre-brave to being brave, for example), being then able to stop, as though we had acquired a static condition. Virtue is not a once for all achievement but a disposition of our character that is constantly developing as it meets new challenges and enlarges the understanding it involves (this leading to self-direction and improvement). ♡

As we develop in virtue, our understanding of the corresponding virtue also develops. In the case of bravery this happens in an obvious and unavoidable way, as we encounter the enlargement of the range of situations in which people are said to be brave. The same thing happens less obviously with other virtues, such as generosity. If someone is brought up to be generous in the context of giving money she may associate generosity with the writing of cheques, and it may take experience to get her to recognize generosity in contexts such as giving time to work on volunteer projects. Doing so will not only enlarge her view of the situations in which people are generous, it will alter her notion of what generosity is, since personal contact foregrounds the need for generosity not to be condescending or to insist on one's role as the giver, something not obvious when one just writes a cheque.

These developments inform our view of what the virtuous thing to do is. The person who has learned to be generous with time in contexts of working with others will now be more aware of the fact that a generous action needs to be performed in a way which also takes note of the

---

[25] Problems about bravery have been brought out since Plato's *Laches*. Some of the problems with honesty were brought out by an experiment done in the 1930s with school-children which appeared to show that honesty in some situations was relatively unlinked with honesty in others. Sreenivasan (2002) discusses the experiment and its methodology. (The experiment, unfortunately, impressed Kohlberg enough to make him abandon hope of a virtue-centred account of moral development.)

recipient's dignity, and is not only helpful but tactful. The person used to finding bravery in many radically different contexts will be less likely to rush to the assumption that a colleague is not brave if the latter does not immediately face down a challenge; he will be able to reflect that the colleague may be bravely defending something less obvious. The child worried by his parents' dishonesty over the truth when they are honest over money may not be able to resolve the problem himself, but he will be aware that honesty is not a simple concept, and that people honest with money cannot be relied upon not to be dishonest in other kinds of situation.

As our understanding of honesty, bravery, and generosity develops, we act, when we act with these virtues, in ways that embody increased understanding of them, and hence increased understanding of what we are doing. From passively taking on our parents' and teachers' understanding of these virtues we have progressed to acting virtuously in a way that reflects greater understanding, acquired from experience and reflection, greater ethical independence of our teachers, and a move towards doing better—not just being surprised by experience or treating it as mere extra information, but responding to it in a way that leaves us better prepared the next time. It is because we do this that each generation's understanding of honesty, bravery, and other virtues is not an exact reproduction of their teachers'; even in a society as traditional as Aristotle's he noticed that people seek to act and live well, not to produce a replica of their parents' lives. How revisionary the process can become is the topic of the next chapter.

It should be clear by now that there is no threat from an alleged dilemma often presented to those who hold that we learn to be virtuous by following the v-rules.[26] If we are guided to be generous, we are being guided to do what generous people do; but this, it is alleged, will be either circular or lead to arbitrariness. Doing what's generous will be doing what generous people do. But how do we go about doing this? We look for the generous people, and who are these? They are the people doing generous actions! We avoid circularity only by picking out generous people independently of their performance of generous actions. But this, it is alleged, will be arbitrary, or will reflect nothing deeper than the prejudices of our culture.

---

[26] See Harman (1999) and (2001), Doris (2002), Johnson (2003).

This ignores what has been stressed here, the developmental nature of virtue.[27] When we begin, we do indeed take over and act on what our parents and teachers say is generous or brave. Where else could we learn this from? This is no more threatening than the fact that when we learn to play the piano or ski we learn from teachers whom we accept as experts at a time when we are in no position to check their credentials. If becoming virtuous never got beyond this stage then indeed it would have a weak claim to be taken seriously as an ethical option. But as we have seen this is just the beginning; we develop to using virtue terms on the basis of our own understanding and in a self-directed way, improving either from the need to make sense of new experience or as a result of more conscious reflection. When the beginner acts generously, this is on the basis of a passive and partial understanding of generosity. When a truly generous person acts generously, this is on the basis of a far fuller and deeper understanding of generosity, and her actions will exhibit what the beginner's may lack: awareness of the way generosity requires tact, awareness of others' dignity and a host of other considerations. The beginner does the generous action, the generous person does the generous action as a generous person does it. The latter action is the characteristic action of a generous person, that is, the action of a generous person acting in character. The alleged dilemma gets going only by ignoring the crucial difference between the beginner and the truly virtuous person.

What I have called the truly virtuous person is obviously analogous to the expert in a practical skill, the person who actually has the expertise. There are unquestioned experts around in a variety of skills. Does the skill analogy then pressure the present account at this point to hold that there actually are truly (completely? perfectly?) virtuous people in the world? This is an issue which will be further explored in the next chapter. When I use the phrase 'truly virtuous person' I imply only someone who contrasts with the beginner, someone of whom we truly say that they are generous, brave, or honest.

[27] Perhaps this is because many modern theories don't see education, the process of acquiring the theory and learning to act on it, as part of the theory proper, and so insist on starting with the adult virtuous person and ignoring the importance of the process of becoming virtuous.

Right Action

What happens when we move outside the language of virtue and restate the demand that our account of virtue provide a theory of *right* action? The notions of *right, ought, should,* and more formally those of *duty* and *obligation,* are notions which clearly belong together, and are often classed as 'deontic'; their relation to virtue is not obvious. Until recently, the philosophical trend was to think that we can be helped in finding action guidance[28] by looking at the deontic notions and trying to extract rules and principles by following which we would be doing the right thing. I shall not comment on these attempts here, but will start from the influential analysis put forward by Rosalind Hursthouse to link rightness with virtue: an action is right if and only if it is what a virtuous person would characteristically (acting in character) do.[29] We have been examining the way in which a virtuous action is what a virtuous person would do, noting that this is not something fixed but will depend on whether the virtuous person is a learner or more like an expert. When we go from virtuous action to right action, what do we find out about rightness?

An honest, generous, or brave action is (barring exceptional circumstances) right—this much holds from our ordinary concepts of virtue and rightness. It might initially look, then, as though talking about right action is a generalized way of talking about virtuous action: a virtuous action will be a right action and vice versa. The difference will be that the virtue terms are richer in content and more informative about the action, whereas 'right' will just gather together all the actions picked out by the virtue terms.

If the present developmental account is correct, however, we will need to take account of the point that when an action is virtuous it may be done at any point on a range of development from the learner, who merely parrots what her teachers tell her, to the truly virtuous person, whose actions are based on understanding gained through experience and reflection, self-directed, and coming from a disposition which continually improves through active engagement with experience. If we insist that a right action must be done by a truly virtuous person for whom this is

[28] Usually construed as definite and specific action guidance, but I will not focus on that aspect here.

[29] Hursthouse (1999*a*: pt. 1).

characteristic, then we will get the result that only the truly virtuous person does the right thing. Learners who are dependent on their teachers' understanding, and people still struggling to be virtuous, will not be doing the right thing, though they may be on the path to becoming virtuous, and hence to doing the right thing. This position is unappealingly rigorist, and at odds with our ordinary ways of relating rightness and virtue.[30]

Another response is to say that 'right' has two senses here: when the learner does the right thing it has the sense of 'barely acceptable' while when the truly virtuous person does the right thing it has the sense of 'exemplary'. This has an advantage over the first suggestion in that we do recognize these two senses, or better uses, of 'right'. We say both, 'He acted tactlessly and blunderingly, but at least he did the right thing,' and 'He did the right thing in responding to the situation in an exemplary way.' Still, it is unrealistic to hold that the virtuous person must be doing one or the other, when virtue is a matter of continuous development.

The most satisfactory solution is to recognize 'right' in this context as a weak notion, which does not introduce independent ethical force itself, but gets its force from its connection with virtue, adjusted to the developmental account of virtue. 'Right' is a 'thin' ethical concept, lacking independent ethical content of its own, as opposed to 'thick' ethical concepts like the virtues.[31] Hence when we claim that the right thing to do is what the virtuous person would do, we recognize that the right thing to do can range from what the learner does to what the truly virtuous person does. These are different ways of being the right thing to do, since the learner acts in a way dependent on the teaching of others, and so does the right thing only in the sense of doing something acceptable, while the truly virtuous person acts on the basis of her own understanding, and so does the right thing in the sense of doing something exemplary; and there are many ways in between of doing the right thing, depending on the stage of development of virtue that the person has reached.

This answers satisfactorily to the point that when we hear merely that someone did the right thing, we have as yet no idea whether they barely

---

[30] The Stoics held the rigorist view that nobody is virtuous except the ideal 'sage' (of which we have not yet had any examples), but even they thought that people who are not virtuous could do the right thing.

[31] The contrast between 'thick' and 'thin' ethical concepts was introduced by Williams (1985).

managed to do the right thing, did the right thing from the right reasons and in the right way, or would be located somewhere in between. That is, an action's being the right thing to do merely locates it somewhere on a range from a barely acceptable action to a highly meritorious action, but with no indication where on that range it falls. This is not very informative about an action, especially since an action's being right is also no indication of what kind of action it is: brave, generous, loyal, kind, and so forth. When we move to the richer vocabulary of virtue, we find more about the kind of action it is. Further, the vocabulary of virtue, unlike that of rightness, directs us to the kind of reason relevant to the performance of the action, and the kind of consideration relevant to being someone who performs that kind of action as a matter of character (as opposed to accidentally, casually and so forth).

One consequence of this is that an action's being the right thing to do is almost totally uninformative; we cannot hope for anything from it alone like a systematic way of guiding people's actions. To do that, we have to refer them to virtue and to an account of what it is to be virtuous and do the virtuous thing. This is surely the correct result, however, given how weak a concept for guidance 'right' is, being thin and poor in content. Why would we expect much useful action guidance merely from recognizing that something is the right thing to do? The only thing useful for guidance that it does is to direct us towards the richer virtue concepts, whose content we do have some reasonably specific understanding of.

This is, to put it mildly, a very different account of 'right' than those available from ethical theories in which virtue is not central, and it may seem startling. It is worth pointing out, however, how intuitive this understanding is of the relation of rightness and virtue when we consider the matter independently of theory. It has been objected, for example, that we recognize cases of the right thing to do which are not what the virtuous person would do.[32] Suppose I have done something wrong; the right thing for me to do would be to apologize—but this is not what the virtuous person would do, since the virtuous person would not have done the wrong thing in the first place. It is easy to see how the developmental account deals with this.[33] It is reasonable for the learner to apologize for

---

[32] See n. 26 above.
[33] The same holds for other such examples. I have not dealt with the case where the truly virtuous person is in a situation where it seems impossible to do the virtuous thing and hence

wrongdoing; the learner can be expected to make mistakes and to need to apologize. The learner can still properly be called virtuous; apologizing for wrongdoing is doing the right thing only in the sense that it is acceptable, minimally OK, better than not apologizing, and this is precisely what is appropriate for the stage of the learner. It would be problematic to say that a truly virtuous person could be in this position, since the truly virtuous person has the understanding not to be in the situation in the first place. The truly virtuous person does the right thing in the sense in which this is doing something truly good and exemplary, and there is nothing very good about doing wrong things that you have to apologize for. Both, however, have done the right thing. Doing the right thing covers, as stressed above, the whole range from the barely acceptable performance of the beginner to the highly meritorious performance of the truly virtuous person. It is perfectly familiar that there are things that are right for the learner to do which would not be right for the truly virtuous person to do. Thus the complaint that there are cases of doing the right thing where this is not what the virtuous person would do relies on ignoring the difference between learner and expert that is fundamental to a developmental account of virtue.

The complaint also flouts the way we understand doing the right thing. We find it perfectly natural, after all, to think that someone can do the right thing for a variety of reasons. At one end of the spectrum we find agents who do the right thing because this is the unforced product of a virtuous disposition. Someone may do the right thing, when this is, for example, a generous action, and do it from a generous disposition—that is, in the appropriate circumstances and in appropriate ways, suiting the contribution to the need. As is by now familiar, we also find people who do the right thing, but from a disposition which aspires to be generous, but suffers from mixed motives, or immaturity, or lack of experience or of developed intelligence in dealing with the relevant kinds of situation. Going further down the spectrum, we find Eliot's Becket famously saying that the last temptation is to do the right thing for the wrong reason. We find ourselves doing this either because we are tempted in some way, like Becket, or because we lack the understanding to find and act on the right reason. Even further down, we find that bad

---

the right thing, through no fault of her own. Hursthouse (1999a: ch. 3) deals impressively with this issue.

people can do the right thing. A cruel person can do the right thing, where this is a compassionate action, because she is motivated by sentimentality, for example. We can even find cases, at the other end of the spectrum, where someone can do the right thing only because they *can't* exercise the relevant virtues in that situation; the right thing is the best they can do. An example of this is the couple in Muriel Spark's short story *The Black Madonna,* whose progressive views about race evaporate when their own child turns out to be dark-skinned, revealing African ancestry in the wife's family. Unable to accept or love the child, they put her up for adoption. They have done the right thing, since keeping a child you cannot love would not be the right thing; but this is the right thing for them to do only because they are incapable of exercising any of the virtues appropriate to the situation.[34]

It fits right into the way we think of doing the right thing, then, that people who are brave, not very brave, or outright cowardly can all do the right thing. We need to know more about the person to know how to interpret their doing the right thing. On its own the mere fact that they are doing the right thing tells us very little—indeed it can be misleading in the way it lumps together the actions of such different people with such diverse motivations.

The fact that there is no problem in someone not very virtuous doing the right thing also underlies the way we regard people in societies very different from ours, especially societies in the past. Take a slave-owning society such as ancient Rome. If we find an ancient Roman acting humanely to his slaves, we find it odd to deny that he did the right thing. He did not, after all, do the wrong thing, which would have been to treat them cruelly, something he could have done with impunity. Does it follow that we think the ancient Roman virtuous? He is certainly virtuous by the standards of his society, where there is nothing illegal about abusing slaves. But if we ask whether this is what a truly virtuous person would do, we at once find ourselves inhibited, since this person lives in a slave society, and thus his exercise of all the virtues is constrained

[34] Spark (1985). The story ends, "'We've done the right thing,' said Lou. Even the priest had to agree with that, considering how strongly we felt against keeping the child. "Oh, he said it was a good thing?" "No, not a *good* thing. In fact he said it would have been a good thing if we could have kept the baby. But failing that, we did the *right* thing. Apparently there's a difference."'

by the point that the conventions of his society, from which he learns the virtues, are systematically unjust.[35] A truly virtuous person, we think, could not stand to others in the unjust master–slave relation. If we hold, as is not unreasonable, that nobody can become truly virtuous in a systematically unjust society, then the Roman is not, however hard he has tried, truly virtuous. Nonetheless, he has clearly done the right thing, since he clearly qualifies as virtuous at the stage of the learner. It was, after all, open to him safely to do the wrong thing, and he did not do that; he saw what was wrong about it and chose to act differently, even though it was not open to him, in that society, to get to the point of rejecting the master–slave relation.

Often when we think about people in other societies we admire them, but realize that features of those societies present, or presented, systematic obstacles to the development of virtue. We recognize that it is foolish to judge these people anachronistically, by standards unavailable to them, yet we recognize that the standards of their society did present systematic problems for becoming virtuous. Yet we do not have the same hesitation about allowing that they did the right thing. The claim that someone did the right thing can be made in a much broader and less critical way than the claim that the person was generous or brave, or overall virtuous. And it is reasonable to hold that this is because the claim that the person did the right thing is in itself a thin claim which can amount to as little as that what the person did was acceptable, and as much as that what they did was exemplary. We find it natural, then, to allow that often people in systematically unjust societies did the right thing, and exhibited virtue—but only as much virtue as their society allowed of, which we recognize as falling short of the truly virtuous person.

It should be stressed that this is a thought which leads not to complacency but to caution about our own claims to ethical progress. When we reflect on many of the systematic injustices in our own society, after all, it is clear that future generations will think of us in many of the ways that we think of the ancient Romans. They will allow that we often did the right thing, but that our exercise of the virtues was severely constrained by systematic injustices in our societies.

---

[35] This issue is raised in Tessman (2005). The issue will be revisited later.

It is open to all of us to do the right thing, but for many of us this will not exhibit much virtue—we are just being honest, fair, or kind as our society understands that and to the extent that we have picked that up. Only the truly virtuous do the right thing as the virtuous person would do it, exhibiting independent understanding of what should be done in a way which that takes into account all relevant features of the situation. Doing the right thing, then, turns out not to be a very helpful notion in an ethics in which virtue is central. A virtue ethical theory will be interested in *virtuous* action, but will not get much out of the notion of *right* action.[36]

Finally, I say something about a very common assumption which would render the above account of rightness moot. It is very often taken for granted that if an action is a right action, or the right thing to do, then this must be in virtue of some *right-making features* (or *characteristics*). The issue then becomes, what these right-making features are.

It is not clear what is meant by this claim; a number of distinct issues can be raised by it. Sometimes this is regarded as an issue in meta-ethics, the metaphysics of ethics, taking the form: what kind of entities are these 'right-making features', and what is their metaphysical status? From here we go on to ask what our epistemological access to them is, and perhaps ask where they are located.[37] It seems to me that the bare claim about 'right-making features' is too indeterminate to give rise on its own to determinate issues of this kind, and actual discussions take place within assumptions (metaphysical or otherwise) provided by various theories. I will not consider these meta-ethical issues here, since I do not have scope in this work to go into detail about these other theories.

---

[36] Anscombe (1958) made this point in a memorable way. See also Murdoch (1970: 42), where she argues that we act on realizing 'This is A B C D (normative/descriptive words)' rather than 'This is right'. She continues: 'As the empty choice will not occur the empty word will not be needed.' Cf. Hursthouse (1999a: 69), where she says that virtue ethics can come up with an account of right action, 'But it does this under pressure, only in order to maintain a fruitful dialogue with the overwhelming majority of modern moral philosophers for whom "*right* action" is the natural phrase.'

[37] If we do ask this, a dilemma is sometimes put forward: if these 'features' are 'in the person' then virtue itself becomes the source of the value of right action, while if they are 'in the situation' then right action has value independent of virtue. See Das (2003). However, the unacceptability of both arms of the dilemma should make us wonder if a forced choice between only these options is appropriate to the issue.

What I will do is to consider a common and apparently quite reasonable interpretation of the 'right-making features' idea. This is the following: a claim that I or someone else did the right thing commits me to providing some kind of *justification* of what was done. What is it that *made* (rendered, etc.) the action right? It can't, surely, *just* be the right thing to do, with absolutely nothing further to be said on the subject. This point is obvious where we are thinking of justification of an action which I or someone else has performed; but it is equally clear when we think of the giving of advice about a future action. If I tell you that standing up to someone is the right thing to do, I surely have to provide some kind of justification; I can't, at least not reasonably, just keep repeating to you that that *is*, just *is,* the right thing to do. If I could think up no answer to the question of why it's the right thing to do, you would not pay much attention to my advice.

The point is reasonable; but is it damaging to a theory in which virtue is central? Surely, if I need to justify my claim that standing up to that person *is* the right thing to do, I have plenty to say. It is the brave thing to do, I may say, and then point out various features of the situation that call here and now for bravery, rather than patience, and so on. If I am talking about a past action, then I have justified what I did in a familiar and adequate way. If someone wants to challenge me, they can retort that it was not brave at all, but foolhardy; or, that it was brave but also tactless, and so on; in each case they will point out the salience of features of the action and situation which they claim that I have missed, or over- or understated. If I am talking about a possible future action, giving someone advice, the advisee has been adequately oriented to the aspects of the situation relevant to their action. They might of course challenge my orientation in the same way as the person challenging the account of the past action. Whether my account will motivate the person will obviously depend on how brave or cowardly they are.

It is commonly objected to this kind of response that it misses the point: what is required, by way of justification of a claim that some action is the right thing to do, is to show in some way what justifies it as the *right* thing to do, where this does not just mean the brave, generous, etc. thing to do. 'Right-making features' will on this objection be features that all right actions have in common, and so can't be identified with what makes this right action a brave one, that right action a loyal one, and so on. The request for justification is focused on the *rightness* of right actions, so that explications of these actions in terms of virtue leaves the main point untouched.

There are many ethical theories available for which this demand is legitimate, and in which various types of answer are already developed. What makes all right actions *right* is: their conformity to the Categorical Imperative, their being demanded by God, their maximizing some form of utility, their being demanded by Reason, and so on. Given this, we can then ask, in the terms of these theories, whether a theory in which virtue is central can deliver a comparable answer; to which the answer is clearly, no. This is not an independent objection to the theories, however; it merely shows that a theory in which virtue is central does not ask the same questions about right actions (what makes them all *right*? What justifies my saying that this action is *right* (*as opposed to* virtuous)?) as do these theories.

Does the question, what makes all right actions *right* (as opposed to virtuous)? have any independent traction? If it does, it will be reasonable to ask *all* ethical theories to provide an answer to it, and theories making virtue central will be no exception. If we free our minds from theories in which this question is already part of the structure, and look for truly independent traction for the question, the skill analogy may be helpful again. Suppose I tell someone that in speaking Italian they have said the correct thing. This is because they used the indicative correctly (correct number, tense, etc.) and also used the subjunctive correctly (correct type of clause, etc.). For each correct utterance, there is a justification for what makes it correct—namely, in terms of grammar and syntax. Now suppose someone claims that this misses the point: what is needed is a justification for what makes all correct utterances *correct*, independently of explanations of what makes this indicative correct, this subjunctive correct, and so forth. We need an account of the 'correct-making features' of all correct utterances independent of the kind of explanation we give of what actually makes each of them correct. This demand would rightly puzzle us. What could such 'correct-making features' be? What would be the point of an account of them? They seem to do no work; we cannot appeal to them to show why any particular indicative or subjunctive is correct, since this is *ex hypothesi* irrelevant to what makes all correct utterances *correct*.

Is the demand for the 'right-making features' of all right actions similarly lacking in substance? The idea that it might be may seem startling, given that ethical theories have developed which take the idea seriously. It is relevant here, however, that these theories take the deontic notions to be basic.[38] Hence their starting-point rejects the approach of theories making virtue central, namely that the rightness of right actions is not basic, but merely a thin and uninformative way of gathering together virtuous actions performed along the whole scale from learner to truly virtuous. Here we should conclude that, even for theories of virtue in which it is not basic, but just central, there is a fundamental divergence of starting-points from theories in which right action is basic. Theories of virtue are, as we saw, concerned with virtuous action, and with right action only as a thin way of gathering together virtuous actions in an unspecific way. They do not share the assumption that there is a substantial but theory-independent answer to the question, what makes all right actions right? If we are clear about this we can see that many criticisms of theories in which virtue is central have missed the mark, because they have proceeded from assumptions not shared by the theories.

Some ethical theories start from the assumption that there *is* something substantial common to all actions that we call right, something which can be picked out, independently of any theory, as the 'right-making features' of right actions, indicating what makes them right actions (as opposed to brave, just actions and so forth). But an account of virtue of the kind discussed here rejects any such assumption; so unsurprisingly a virtue ethical theory in which it is central also rejects the idea that there is any such theory-independent demand as the one to give an account of the 'right-making features' of actions *just as right actions*, independently of the fuller account of them as virtuous actions.

Does this mean that the present account of virtue cannot serve as central in theories that claim to guide action? Clearly it cannot appeal to any 'criterion of right action' to guide the person uncertain of what to do, since it denies that there is anything ethically substantial in common to all right *actions, just as right actions*, and so no informative criterion that could pick them out just as right actions. But this is no disadvantage if we have no reason to suppose that there *is* any criterion of right action just as right action—unless, as we have seen, we are *already* committed to a theory which makes deontic notions basic, and does undertake to show what all right actions have in common. We can now already see one advantage of

---

[38] This is a broad claim, but not unreasonable; consequentialist theories see themselves as providing a criterion for right action.

an ethical theory in which an account of virtue like the present one is central: it allows us to explore practical thinking without having to commit our explorations in advance to fitting into the pattern of a 'theory of right action'.

What guidance do we get, then? We have what Hursthouse calls the 'v-rules': as we become more virtuous we learn to be honest, brave, and so on. This kind of direction is neither more nor less specific than that produced by 'rules for right action', such as 'act fairly' and the like. Suppose we press this: how do we get *guidance* in action by following directions to become honest and brave? A major theme of this work has already made the answer clear: this is like asking how we get guidance in communicating with Italians by learning Italian. Someone who has developed the disposition to be generous will thereby be able and motivated to act generously where this is appropriate. There is no shortcut to this other than by becoming generous, just as there is no shortcut to communicating with (monolingual) Italians other than by learning Italian. Just as we need to learn the subjunctive, we need to learn to be generous. There is no short cut through just doing what we are told to do (at least, no short cut to the right place). In not providing such a short cut, ethical theories employing an account of virtue like the present one give us guidance while treating us like adults.[39]

---

[39] In working on this difficult topic of virtue and action I have been greatly helped by Frans Svensson, Daniel Russell (especially in his 2009), and Liezl van Zyl, though each of these has their own different approach and is not at all responsible for the account I produce here. I am aware that the present account goes further, in rejecting the relevance to an ethics of virtue of a theory of right action, than many virtue ethicists, including Hursthouse, Swanton, and Russell.

4

The Scope of Virtue

The present account of virtue insists on the fact that virtue is understood in part by the way it is learnt, and that it is learnt always in an embedded context—a particular family, city, religion, and country. To become virtuous we need to learn how to act, and to learn we have to have initial trust in the teacher and the context. If this is to lead to virtue rather than mere habit, as has been repeatedly stressed, this has to be accompanied by the drive to aspire. This involves understanding what it is to be loyal or brave, becoming self-directed, recognizing for oneself what loyalty requires rather than copying one's model, and striving to improve; all this leads to actively becoming virtuous rather than acquiring a mere habit. Still, some may reasonably worry that the first point, about the trust required to learn in the first place, places constraints on the aspiration involved that are so strong that it is hard to see how the result could be virtue.

This worry sometimes takes the form of claiming that an ethics in which virtue is central will be committed to relativism. I learn to be brave in a society of soldiers; you learn to be brave in a society of pacifists. Surely there will be little or nothing in common between the contexts in which we learn what bravery is. Some of the contexts in which you exercise bravery—disregarding taunts about unwillingness to fight, for example—will be contexts in which soldiers would not be brave by acting that way. Are we really talking about the same thing?

Noting the difference between these two contexts of bravery, however, does not force us to hold that there is nothing to discuss, or no real disagreement. If the embeddedness of virtue encouraged relativism we would find that warriors thought of the pacifists' notion of bravery as so different from their own as to be simply irrelevant to it, and vice versa. This is not what we find. Pacifists have never denied that soldiers are brave, but have protested that their view of bravery and its point is too narrow.

Similarly soldiers have recognized the bravery of pacifists when the latter have endured hardships without abandoning their beliefs.[1] Rather than defusing disagreement, which relativism typically does, paying attention to the embeddedness of a virtue starts a discussion about what that virtue is, and this often leads from disagreement based on different contexts to agreement based on the common features which emerge in discussion.[2]

Nonetheless, it may still reasonably be felt that the need to learn may in fact so constrain the drive to aspire that people who become virtuous, on this account, will develop understanding of the virtues and what they require within the bounds of their own culture and society, but will not thereby achieve an understanding of virtue applicable to others whether or not these come from, and have been brought up within, their own embedded social and cultural context. Thinking in terms of the virtues, this objection goes, will be *parochial*. Our conceptions of the virtues will owe so much to the social and cultural contexts within which we have learned them that they will be effectively trapped within those contexts.

Hence, continues the objection, thinking in terms of the virtues will be essentially *conservative*. We may get as far as criticizing, from an internal point of view, the notion of fairness we have been brought up with, but this will not take us to a point where we will be able to criticize the social and cultural contexts themselves within which we have learned fairness. We will not be taken, by thinking in terms of virtue, to a point of view from which to criticize the contexts within which we learned what the virtues are. Slave-owners in a slave society, for example, may develop virtues within that society, being unquestionably fair and generous as they have learned to be by that society's lights, but never be led to reflect from a point of view applicable to all humans, free or slave, that the contexts within which they have learned those virtues rest on gross injustice. Hence they may never reflect that there may be something seriously inadequate, at best, about the ways in which they are fair and generous.

---

[1] Pacifists in the First World War often endured great hardship because of their refusal to fight, and this established that they were brave rather than cowardly in refusing, so that by the time of the Second World War they were treated more respectfully.

[2] This can be seen in The Virtues Project, often disregarded by philosophers because it aims at an early educational level. It claims that virtues are the best items to form an intercultural language, and this has been backed up by its success in places where there is a continuing need for intercultural understanding.

This is an important criticism. To meet it we should recall that it is the drive to aspire which leads us to the need to think in terms of reasons and explanation. We are not satisfied to have subrational habits of acting which solidify into routine; we need to go beyond mimicking the people we learn from, and to find out *why* they act as they do. This is what enables us to start the process of coming to understand what loyalty is, for example, as opposed to picking up a few habits of acting in ways conventionally considered loyal. It is the drive to 'give an account' of what we and others are doing, to ask for and give reasons, that enables us to become virtuous, rather than merely habituated to act in certain ways. Once we can reflect on the reasons we are given for acting in certain ways we can think for ourselves about them. Someone may come from a background where it is assumed that loyalty to one's country involves automatic respect for certain symbols, but there is no reflection about what the symbols stand for or why one's country is worthy of loyalty. This person may, by asking for reasons and thinking about the answers he gets, reflect for himself on loyalty to country, on what are good and bad reasons for it and good and bad ways of expressing it. The person will have come to understand more deeply what loyalty is, and will thereby have deepened his understanding of how various symbols express it (or fail to).

Reflection on reasons alone, however, cannot explain how people can come to criticize the social and cultural frameworks within which they have learned the virtues. For a start, not many of us actually do the latter; most people in a society do not start for themselves criticizing the social and cultural foundations of that society. We improve on what our parents did, but few of us think that radical change is called for. We need to explain, therefore, how people brought up to be virtuous in a given embedded context can come to be critical of that very context; to show how it is open to anyone to do this; and also to suggest why not many of us actually do it.

What is involved in acquiring a virtue? As we have seen, the learning involved is not a matter of just doing what we are told; it requires coming to understand what you are doing. This starts between teacher and learner, and expands among our peers and our experiences in our culture—in, for example, the figures put forward for admiration in movies and on TV. Learning to be brave or loyal takes place in and among people who are engaged in becoming brave, or loyal, and thus in learning to think, talk, and react in certain ways. It is useful to think of this in terms of becoming a member of a community. People becoming brave will share certain reasons, feelings, and attitudes in a way that renders them distinctive, and can be thought of as forming a community of the brave. This is not the obvious kind of community that is formed by family, friends, and the like. It is from the first an 'invisible' rather than a 'visible' community, to use Bradley's terms, one made up of people with whom what you share is not physical space, but rather common concerns and ideals.[3]

Once again the skill analogy is helpful. Learning to play the piano, ride a bicycle, skate, similarly makes you part of a community of people who are linked by commitment to doing these things. How much you feel a member of such a community depends on the seriousness of your commitment to the activity. If your interest in tennis, or art, is casual, your membership in the communities of tennis players or art lovers will fit in with your other commitments without strain. If you are serious about what you do, however, the claims of these communities may come into competition with those of other communities you belong to—family and school among others. At some point a decision may be needed as to how your time and effort will be spent, with your family or practising tennis, for example. Your tennis community may eventually be formed by people with whom you share more, in terms of activity, interest, and attitude, than you do with your family.

What is being picked out in the case of virtue from the skill analogy here is the shared community of activity and attitude. Learning to be honest is, at least, learning to do certain things and not to others, to be shocked and repelled by some actions and attracted to others. Learning to be honest is not, we have already seen, just learning to do what your family does. Indeed, learning to be honest may well at some point involve learning not to do what your family does and learning to be shocked by what your family does. When this happens, we can see the person as now belonging to two communities: the natural community of the family and the community formed by the honest, who think, act, and reason in ways that conflict with those of his own family. This is a simple example of how

<hr/>

[3] Bradley (1962: ch. 5). Contemporary examples of members of online communities linked by shared interests but not physically meeting one another indicate how people can be powerfully linked even without personal knowledge of one another. I have given a wide account of the community of the virtuous, since it will include people at all stages of the development of virtue.

learning to be virtuous can pull us away from our original contexts and communities. It does so by showing how we also, in learning to be virtuous, can be thought of as forming part of another community—that of the honest, with whom we share more by way of thinking, reasoning, response, and attitude than we do with our (*ex hypothesi*) dishonest family.

Learning to be honest, then, has, like learning to be a skater or a pianist, the potential to pull you away from your family and original contexts. I have used the idea of *community* here because it is important that this detachment from your original context is unlikely to be a purely individual achievement of reasoning; it is more plausibly an achievement of understanding what generosity, fairness, and bravery are in their application to you and others. We can think of a progressive enlargement of understanding as a progressive enlargement of the shared community. Thus, I may come to find, as I learn about honesty, that my family is dishonest. I may also discover that in my society this kind of dishonesty is taken for granted and not criticized. I may then find that the general opinion of my society, that this kind of dishonesty is unremarkable, is in conflict with my understanding of honesty, which is such that it applies both inside and outside my society. My understanding of honesty is now pulling me away not only from the context of my family but also from the community I share with my fellow citizens. I am not on my own, however, for I still share a community with the honest, with people who think and react as I do about honesty. This is a community wider than that of my society. It consists not only of (the perhaps few) people I know personally and can talk to, but people I read about in present and past history, people in my own culture and society and others beyond it. In being honest, I have more in common with them than I do with my own fellow citizens with whom I daily interact.[4]

There is nothing mysterious about the way in which thinking about virtue brings us into community with those who think and feel likewise, and can detach us from other communities like those of family and society. Indeed, it is so unmysterious that it is easily seen to be open to anyone who embarks on learning to be virtuous to begin with. It is simply a matter of

---

[4] We should not forget individual ethical trailblazers who had no support from their visible communities. But while this is certainly found occasionally, it is more common for people to gain support from invisible communities of people encountered in books, or in history or legend.

going on learning about virtue, rather than stopping. Unless we grow up in a perfect society and with perfect parents, we are bound at some point to find that we belong with the generous, brave, fair, or the like and thus not, in the relevant respect, with our teachers (sometimes, with our parents). Becoming virtuous has, to that extent, detached us from the community we form with those who have taught us. As Aristotle says in the passage I have quoted more than once, everyone seeks the good, not just what their parents did. Becoming virtuous starts the process by making it clear that the virtuous life cannot just be the life your parents lead. Anyone can come to realize this, and anyone can continue the progressive enlargement of understanding.

Why then do so few do so? This is not a problem particular to thinking in terms of virtue, since any ethical theory has to face the fact that most people do not live by it. The answer given by the present account is that while we are all capable of aspiring to become virtuous, most of us resist being pulled away from our familiar original contexts by becoming progressively more virtuous. Rather than deal with the fact that our family is dishonest, our country jingoistic, the values we have learnt inadequate, we make rationalizations, or simply refuse to face facts. We are unwilling to criticize the contexts and institutions within which we learned the virtues, because we are unwilling to be pulled away from those contexts in the way that would be required. The community of the family, or society, is a visible and tangible one, providing real comfort and support. The community of the honest (the brave, the open-minded, and so on) is an invisible one composed of all those who, past, present, and future, act, reason, and feel in certain ways; accessible only through thought and reflection, it offers less help in getting through the day.[5] If we think of community as a form of solidarity, pre-existing solidarities can make it hard to be detached from them.[6] To identify with the community of the just, rather than with your own fellow citizens, is often hard, for it requires

---

[5] Cf. Bradley (1962: ch. 5), where he makes the point that no actual context telling me 'my station and its duties' will satisfy me, since we all identify ethically with people outside our society, seeking an ethics that is 'cosmopolitan'. Hence our ideal of a good person can never be limited by the context of a particular society.

[6] While I cannot deal here with alternative theories, I think that this account of why so few of us manage to reach a high ethical level is intuitively more convincing than the Kantian claim that we tend to follow gratification rather than reason, or the consequentialist claim that we are too selfish.

detachment from the existing support you get from relations with your fellow-citizens. What requires explanation, then, is not so much the slackness of most people in developing the virtues, but the strength of the few in achieving them.

Thinking in terms of virtue, then, can enlarge our thinking, as our understanding of virtue and what it is becomes enlarged. If we think of this in terms of coming to see ourselves as belonging to communities larger than, and cutting across, our given communities of family and society, we can see that thinking in terms of virtue can lead us to a viewpoint where we see ourselves as forming a community with all other humans who are virtuous in a similar way, having something in common with people in other times, places, and cultures which we do not have in common with the people with whom we do share time and place. We have seen, however, that most people do not achieve this, because of the all too real pulls of the actual communities of family, job, society, and so on, and the narrowing of sympathies involved.

I will try to illustrate this so far abstract sketch by an extended example. Let us look more closely at the problem of virtue in a slave society, contrasting two cases.

Ancient Roman society was, like all societies in the ancient world, one in which slavery not only existed, but was basic to its structure. Whether or not you were a slave determined pretty much everything else about you in terms of social position, and nearly everyone either owned slaves or was a slave, there being very little free labour. Slavery was seen as not merely legal at present, but a matter of ageless tradition; nobody had any determinate idea of a society in which slavery was not fundamental.[7] As far as most people were concerned, there had always been slavery and there was no reason to think it would not always be there. Aristotle relies on this thought when he says that slavery is natural; something so ubiquitous must have some basis in nature.[8]

---

[7] Even in ancient utopian writings, such as Plato's *Republic* and *Laws*, and books 7 and 8 of Aristotle's *Politics*, there is no thought of abolishing slavery. A fragment of the Epicurean inscription from Oenoanda indicates that utopian thinking in Epicureanism was possibly an exception here.

[8] Aristotle takes a phenomenon to have a natural basis if it occurs 'always or for the most part' and its occurrence is not due to force. He fails to appreciate the level of force required to sustain large-scale slavery.

The Roman Stoics, however, came to disagree with Aristotle. Virtuous people, they hold, belong to the universal community of rational beings, and from this viewpoint can realize that slavery has no natural or ethical basis.[9] As rational beings interacting as members of a community of rational beings, owner and slave realize that the barriers between them are completely conventional. Whether someone is a slave is a matter of fortune, and does not affect his ability to become virtuous, to live as well in the conditions of his life as a free person does in his. Slaves are virtuous or vicious, depending on their character, just as free people are; the fact that a slave has to perform his duties does not prevent his doing so virtuously.[10]

How did the Stoics translate this into real life? Owners are told to bear in mind that the rights they have over slaves have no ethical basis, though they have society's backing. They cannot wish away the fact that the slave is working for them, but they should treat slaves as employees, refraining from exploiting their legal power to abuse them physically and sexually.[11] Slaves should be treated humanely not just out of self-interest, but in recognition of the fact that they are the owner's natural and ethical equals; the owner should treat the slave as he would wish to be treated if he were a slave.[12] Slaves are equally 'children of Zeus' as the owners, and should be treated as brothers and sisters.[13] Slaves are urged to remember that what matters in life is whether or not you live your life virtuously; slavery is a circumstance like others and what matters is what you make of it, living well or badly. Given that what matters is living virtuously, we find a recurring trope that 'true' freedom, the only sort that matters, is being in control of your own passions, while 'true' slavery is living in a way driven by them; an owner may thus be a 'true' slave and a slave a 'truly' free man.[14]

---

[9] I can't here spell out the large background of Stoic ethics (and ultimately Stoic philosophy as a whole) which grounds these thoughts (see Annas (1993) for a detailed account of these).

[10] Seneca, *Letter*, 47, and *On Favours*, III. 18–28, defends the idea that a slave can do favours for his owner. Limited scope of action does not preclude acting virtuously.

[11] Seneca, *On Favours*, III. 22, quotes Chrysippus' definition of a slave as 'an employee for life', so presumably this point was a Stoic one from the start. Ancient literature is full of injunctions to owners to refrain from cruelty to and sexual abuse of slaves, but often this is in the context of concern for the owner's character as much as or more than concern for the slave's welfare.

[12] Seneca, *Letter*, 47. 10–11.

[13] Epictetus, *Dissertationes*, I. 13. Owners who insist on the fact of legal ownership are told that they are looking to the laws of the dead rather than the laws of God.

[14] This can be supported by the thought that slavery affects the body only, leaving the mind free from any master (Seneca, *On Favours*, III. 20).

This is a remarkable ethical achievement on the part of people brought up in a slave society: it is demanding on the slave owner, and offers one of the few ancient recommendations that genuinely respects the slave's human dignity. Nonetheless, to moderns what stands out is that the Stoics never recommend trying to abolish or even reform the institution of slavery itself; they limit their recommendations to acting within it, whether as slave-owner or slave. Even Marcus Aurelius, who as a Stoic is very conscious that he should behave well towards slaves beyond anything legally required, never used his position as emperor to modify traditional legislation about slavery.[15]

Is this an indication that thinking in terms of virtues will trap you, at some level, within the social and cultural contexts in which you learned them? The Stoics achieved a universal viewpoint of ethical community on equal terms with the slave; but this is still within the institution they made no attempt to remove or reform. What, however, would have happened to someone who did try to attack the institution? Ancient slavery was profoundly embedded in every aspect of society. It was not open to a slave-owner, as it was later to an American slave-owner in the South, to free his slaves and adopt another approach; in the ancient world there was nowhere else to go, no way to opt out and move into a more just system.[16] A would-be reformer would have been silenced, either by ridicule or literally. (So if there were any would-be abolishers of ancient slavery, we will never know about them.) It is the circumstances of ancient society that limit the ways Stoics could act with regard to slavery, not the limitations of thinking in terms of virtue.

We can see this clearly if we contrast the movement in late eighteenth- and early nineteenth-century Britain to abolish slavery, which began by aiming to abolish the slave trade. At the time, the situation seemed just as hopeless as it did in the ancient world, and any attempt to change it just as quixotic. 'At the end of the eighteenth century, well over three quarters of all people alive were in bondage of one kind or another . . . of various systems of slavery or serfdom . . . This world of bondage seemed all the

---

[15] Studies of imperial legal rulings on slavery suggest that Marcus did not use opportunities to make slave legislation more humane. See Brunt (1998). In *Meditations*, I. 17, Marcus expresses gratitude 'that I did not touch Benedicta or Theodotus', which is generally, given its context, taken to refer to abstaining from an owner's power to abuse slaves sexually. At V. 31 slaves appear among those to whom Marcus thinks he should act rightly.

[16] In later antiquity entering a monastery offered one alternative.

more normal then, because anyone looking back in time would have seen little but other slave systems.'[17] Slavery seemed like a global fact that was there to stay. Among European powers with colonies where there was slavery only Britain developed an anti-slavery movement, and this case may have seemed among the most hopeless, given that the British political system, gravely in need of reform anyway, was dominated by powerful economic pro-slavery interests.

Still, some people did act, notably Thomas Clarkson, who dedicated his life to fighting the injustice of slavery. With help from the Quakers he organized the first sustained mass campaign in history aimed at abolishing injustice to other people—people, moreover, from whom the campaign organizers were separated by distance, culture, and race. The campaign was a huge success, getting a large number of people to lobby and protest in a number of ways. What motivated them was simply a desire for justice (and horror at cruelty); indeed, often the cause of abolition was contrary to the economic interests of the campaigners themselves. Working people in Sheffield petitioned against the slave trade even though they knew that abolition would hurt their own local economy.[18] Moreover, the movement finally succeeded. 'Looking back today, what is even more astonishing than the pervasiveness of slavery in the 1700s is how swiftly it died. By the end of the following century, slavery was, at least on paper, outlawed almost everywhere. The antislavery movement had achieved its goal in little more than one lifetime.'[19]

This unprecedented mass action was brought about by appeal simply to virtue, to ordinary people's efforts to be just and compassionate and thus to try to put a stop to injustice and cruelty. Because of greatly changed economic and political circumstances, including the growing globalization of trade, ordinary people now could do something meaningful to aid in the abolition of the slave trade—for example, they boycotted sugar grown on slave plantations in the West Indies.[20] No new way of thinking

---

[17] Hochschild (2005).

[18] Hochschild (ibid. 5), notes the bafflement of the pro-slavery lobbyists when petitions to Parliament came in from people 'stating no grievance or injury of any kind . . . affecting the Petitioners themselves'. They were faced by people trying to abolish a system on ethical grounds, against their own interests, and found this hard to understand.

[19] Ibid. 3.

[20] When Parliament rejected the first abolitionist proposal, the response was a widespread successful boycott of West Indian sugar. This was the first striking indication that the struggle was not limited to traditional political arenas such as Parliament.

about ethical matters was needed.[21] Opponents of abolition recognized this, being unable to mount any ethical campaign and having to limit themselves to the claim that human nature is too weak to put virtue above self-interest. We can see this in Thomas Love Peacock's satirical novel *Melincourt*, where the hero, Forester, is holding a large party to encourage people to pledge abstinence from slave-produced sugar. A cynical character claims that although of course everyone realizes that West Indian slavery is indefensible, and that consuming sugar supports it, humans are too feeble to give up pleasure, and go against custom, in order to oppose it. People get upset when told that their tea is sweetened with sugar from a slave plantation, but prefer to get over the feeling rather than do anything about the matter. The heroine, Anthelia, is given the following response: '[Y]ou do not render justice to the feelings of the company, nor is human nature so selfish and perverted as you seem to consider it . . . Many are the modes of evil—many the scenes of human suffering; but if the general condition of man is ever to be ameliorated, it can only be through the medium of BELIEF IN HUMAN VIRTUE.'[22] Earlier in the book a friend of the hero, Forester, says, a propos of the sugar boycott, 'The world is bad enough, I dare say; but it is not for you or me to mend it.' This gets the following reply: 'There is the keystone of the evil—mistrust of the influence of individual example . . . Yet the history of the world abounds with sudden and extraordinary revolutions in the opinions of mankind, which have been effected by single enthusiasts.'[23]

The abolitionist movement is also interesting here because it gives us a concrete illustration of the point made above in terms of communities. People concerned to stop the evil of slavery discovered that they formed part of a community of people reading the same books,[24] expressing the same thoughts and attitudes; as they moved to act they found themselves part of new communities of people working together for the cause. These new communities brought men used to political action together with people who were new to public activity and were not even represented in the political system—women, people of colour, workers from the new

---

[21] It is quite mistaken to think that a framework such as consequentialism is needed to think effectively about large-scale and global injustices, though this is sometimes asserted.

[22] Peacock (1948), capitals in original.

[23] Ibid. 123–4.

[24] Especially books by Olaudah Equiano, a well-known writer and speaker who was formerly a slave, and by Thomas Clarkson (the latter came to be a favourite of Jane Austen's).

industrial towns. In the case of women, the move to public activity was often found shocking by their families, and we find many cases where membership of a community bonded by commitment to acting virtuously did detach people from the traditional roles involved in their original contexts of family and culture.

Both the Roman Stoics, then, and eighteenth-century Britons were led by thinking in terms of virtue to see that slavery was ethically indefensible. The Stoics were limited to acting as best they could within the institution; by the eighteenth century thinking in terms of virtue could and did lead to effective action to abolish it. Do we then fault the ancient Stoics for not at least trying to abolish slavery? The rapidity with which abolition came about in the eighteenth and nineteenth centuries suggests that perhaps the Stoics could have achieved more than they thought they could. But in this kind of comparison it is always hard to know how much people are deserving of sympathy, rather than condemnation, if injustice was utterly fundamental to their society.[25]

This extended example illustrates the way in which thinking in terms of virtue can lead people to act virtuously in ways that condemn basic aspects of their society from a wider standpoint of justice. It is an illustration, not an argument, but it does at least undercut the claim that thinking in terms of virtue is bound to be weakly parochial and hence ethically conservative. Many people who are brought up to be virtuous in narrow patterns persist in thinking in ways still coloured by those patterns. But some do not. And sometimes the communities they form in rejecting these narrow patterns can influence society in the direction of changing those patterns.

In the last chapter we considered the point that we can think of an ancient Roman as doing the right thing by his slaves (especially if he is a Stoic), but not as being fully virtuous, only virtuous within the limits allowed by his unjust slave-owning society. If we think of particular ancient Romans as people we admire, we recognize that our admiration is limited by our recognition of the effects of living in a slave-owning society. That we can think of the ancient Roman as able to do the right thing, but as being virtuous only in a limited way should not, however, make us complacent. We should reflect that the ancient Roman attitude

---

[25] Cf. Hursthouse (1999a: 147–53, esp. 148): 'It is extraordinarily difficult to determine when someone is to count as having embraced the wicked beliefs of a society, or religion, or cult, and when they can count as just, so to speak, having been landed with them.'

to slavery is less like our attitude to slavery, which is now universally condemned, than it is to our attitude to global inequities between developed countries and the global South. We in developed countries recognize that globalization, especially in its recent forms, has produced patterns of dominance and exploitation which now benefit us in ways that cannot be ethically defended. What, however, can individual efforts do to improve such a large-scale situation? Our position is rather like that of the Roman Stoic convinced of the ethical untenability of slavery, but unable individually to do anything effective or to make any impact on the institution. Future generations will think of us in much the same way we think of the Roman Stoics, as doing the right thing (some of us) but as having a fundamentally compromised virtue.

These considerations may give rise to a troubling thought. On this account, does virtue not turn out to be too ideal? While we have seen that thinking in terms of virtue can lead people to act virtuously in ways that go beyond their own society and the ways of thinking they have grown up in, it might seem that even this will not render them fully virtuous. For they might be like the Roman Stoics, stuck with a society in which acting effectively in a fully virtuous way was not feasible. Our account allows that Roman Stoics were virtuous and could do the right thing, but they could not become fully virtuous. Now, however, it appears that the same is true of us and of members of any society structured in an unjust way. Even the abolitionists I have discussed, who did effectively protest against injustice, were not able to address all the injustices of their society—about gender and class, for example.

Is virtue then an ideal which we can never hope to attain because of the contingency of living in societies which are always in some respect unjust? Some have drawn this conclusion.[26] What has emerged is that being *fully* virtuous does seem to be an ideal that we aspire towards but can never achieve. At best we can be virtuous in a less than full way, one marred not only by our own deficiencies but by the point that the structures of our societies preclude us from being fully virtuous.

---

[26] e.g. Tessman (2005: 56) (disagreeing in this with Hursthouse, who thinks that few of her readers are 'steeped in vice') says, 'Given the pervasive injustice of oppression and given the high level of participation in maintaining structures of oppression and the difficulty of unlearning traits associated with domination even for those who become critical, I see unjust and other vicious people as fairly ordinary'.

This would be troubling if we insisted on a rigorist approach, such that a person either is virtuous or is not virtuous at all. This would have the result that only the fully virtuous person is virtuous, while none of us are virtuous at all. This is in fact the Stoic position, but it is a very awkward one, since it strictly allows for no difference between the mediocre non-virtuous and the horrendously vicious non-virtuous, and that difference has to be brought in again by allowing that there are degrees of progress towards virtue, though no degrees of virtue.

The present developmental account of virtue gives us a reasonable solution to the difficulties. Being truly (or perfectly) virtuous is indeed an ideal which none of us can exemplify. But it does not follow that none of us are brave, loyal, or generous. For we have seen that there are very different ways of being virtuous, ranging from the beginner to the truly virtuous, analogously to development in a practical skill. Suppose I have mediocre skill in skating and playing the piano; I can still honestly say that I am a skater and a pianist, though quite aware that I will never achieve ideal mastery of these skills.

Similarly with virtue. We preserve the distinction between the child learning to be brave and the adult who is already brave. We correctly say of 6-year-olds that Jane is kind and Tom is brave, though we realize that if we were to compare the children's dispositions to adult kindness and bravery we would find them very lacking; we are not led into confusion by using the same terms for the children and for adults. But once we reflect about what it is to be truly kind or brave, we realize that the adults' kindness or bravery too falls short of true or perfect kindness or bravery; if we are realistic we realize that the dispositions from which we act are always flawed in a number of ways, both by individual failures and by the way the virtues have been taught and learned in an imperfect society. But again there is no confusion in saying that ordinary people are kind or brave, as long as we are aware of the stage of development we are talking about, and the ways in which the imperfections and injustices of society can compromise even the most idealistic individual.

5

Virtue and Enjoyment

So far, the skill analogy has been helpful in thinking about virtue. There is a further important aspect of virtue, however, where it appears to offer a contrast. A skill can be exercised in independence of affective commitment; a skilled potter can produce pots, and a skilled plumber can fix leaks, in an unconcerned way. A virtuous person, by contrast, does not perform virtuous actions impassively and with lack of concern. The virtuous person not only does the right thing for the right reason, she has the right feelings about it. Someone handing out money, for example, but indifferent to the people receiving it and their responses, is not generous.

We should notice that examples that make this point persuasive tend to come from the productive skills; if the finished product is all right then it matters less what the expert's feelings were in producing it. It is less persuasive in the case of performance and sporting skills. Still, the point remains that at least in some clear cases of the kind of skill we are concerned with, the success of the skill rests on the excellence of the finished product whatever the affective state of the person producing it, whereas this is not true of virtue.

Is this a difficulty for the skill analogy? Not if we are careful in specifying the virtue case, and allow for the relevance of the developmental account. A learner, such as a child, can perform a just action because her parents tell her to, and without caring about being just, or even resenting the whole business. As she becomes more virtuous she learns to perform just actions for the right reasons. We expect the process to lead to her giving fair shares, not being unduly influenced in friends' favour and so on, easily and without effort; eventually she may give gladly. Suppose that this does not happen: she learns to give fair shares and be unbiased, but continues to resent having to do so. Such a person is not just; there is something lacking that a virtuous person would have.

Aristotle famously expresses this as the difference between the virtuous and the merely 'encratic' or continent person, who acts in the same way as the virtuous, but is not yet virtuous, because acting virtuously comes up against his feelings and attachments. Putting the difference in this way clearly expresses the idea that the encratic is someone who has not yet matured or grown up; there is something still missing in his development. There is at any rate clearly a difference between the person who gives gladly, not counting the money or the time, and the person who gives, but is secretly resenting this expenditure of time or money. The encratic's actions are not in tune with her feelings, so although she may do the virtuous act, she does not do it as the virtuous person would do it; she can do the right thing, but is virtuous only in the way that a learner is, and so cannot yet properly be called virtuous.

A distinction between the encratic and the virtuous is made by most theories that make virtue central. Aristotle's is the most celebrated, but even Kant recognizes the distinction, though in a less marked way.[1] Indeed, it is hard to think of a theory of virtue making virtue a matter of disposition and character which could fail to note the distinction in some form.

The encratic, then, does what is tactful, brave, or beneficent, but does not have the right feelings about it, whereas the virtuous person does. This point serves to emphasize the importance for virtue of having the right feelings. This can, however, easily seem mysterious. How do you learn to have the right feelings?[2]

This is a complex topic. One aspect of it has been touched on already, namely the point that the virtuous person is not someone who has learnt in a detachedly cognitive way what she should do, and then casts about for a motivation to prompt her to do it. As stressed, we come equipped with motivations, and the development of virtue is the education of these motivations in certain ways. An honest person will not only be honest in her own actions, she will feel disgusted by dishonesty. Kind people are appalled by cruelty; generous people are distressed by stinginess. Virtues

---

[1] See Hursthouse (1999a: ch. 4). It is a mistake to think that Kant's virtuous person is someone that Aristotle would regard as merely encratic.

[2] We have already seen that learning to have the right feelings is not a matter of discovering a new motivation but of forming and educating the motivations you already have. However, the specific issue here needs specific treatment.

involve a range of emotional feelings and expressions: not merely our thinking and reasoning but also our affective side. If we imagine someone giving time, energy, and money to a good cause, say helping the homeless, but doing so in complete emotional detachment, or even while having feelings of repulsion, we can see that while she is doing the right thing (which is certainly better than indifference or doing the wrong thing) she is not yet virtuous except in the way of a learner; she will not be virtuous until her feelings and emotions have been brought into harmony with her deliberations about what to do.

Just what is involved in the education of the emotions? There is little agreement among either philosophers or psychologists about what form this takes, for there is little agreement about what an emotion is.[3] Hence we find very different views about the role of emotions in the virtuous person's moral psychology.[4] It is easier, however, to find agreement at a more general level on the point that virtue requires harmony of the person's feelings with his reasoning and thinking. For anything short of this is the stage of the mere beginner, or the person who, whatever their age, has not got beyond the beginner's stage. The distinction is, as noted, hard to avoid in a theory in which virtue is a matter of disposition and character.[5]

So far we find a difference from skill. However, one aspect of the virtuous person's moral psychology, perhaps surprisingly, points us to another important analogy between skill and virtue. Aristotle famously comments that the virtuous person is distinguished by finding what he does *pleasant*: 'We must take as an indication of a person's states the pleasure or pain consequent on what he does, because the person who abstains from bodily pleasures and finds his enjoyment in doing just this is temperate, while the person who finds doing it oppressive is intemperate;

---

[3] See Damasio (1994), Elster (2009), Griffiths (1997), Nussbaum (2001), Oakley (1992), and Sherman (1989, 1997), for debates about the nature of the emotions and their role in character development.

[4] We find a basic difference between 'Aristotelian' theories, which think that our feelings and emotions can be so educated by our developing reason that they become wholly transformed, and 'Kantian' theories, which think of our feelings and emotions as never wholly educable and transformable, and thus always representing a potential threat to our acting as we reason to be best.

[5] However, in theories in which virtue is conceived as being less than this (merely an attitude, or a trait which can be unintegrated with the rest of the person's character) this demand is felt to be less pressing, and such theories require much less of the person's character.

and the person who enjoys facing up to danger, or at least does not find it painful to do so, is courageous, while he who does find it painful is a coward.'[6] The temperance example is not hard to understand. Someone resolving to give up meat, for example, will at first have to fight against temptation and will find the forbidden food attractive; but as they develop the relevant disposition to be vegetarian they cease to find it tempting. Eventually they take more pleasure in not eating what they now reject than they did when they ate it; the vegetarian finds it more enjoyable to be a vegetarian than she did being someone who enjoyed eating meat.[7]

The courage example is more complex. The courageous person is the person who does not have to fight down inclinations to run away when he should stand and fight. If, however, we think of him as someone who actually *enjoys* facing dangers, he sounds irresponsible at best. But Aristotle makes it clear that the pleasure taken in courageous activity is not pleasure in being wounded or exposed to danger, but rather pleasure in acting courageously, something which is not dependent on the circumstances or results of courageous activity.

How can we understand the idea that the virtuous person enjoys acting virtuously, and is not pained even when acting virtuously is difficult or makes great demands? Pleasure and enjoyment are notoriously difficult and problematic concepts, but in this connection I think that we can get useful help from the skill analogy in the light of some modern psychological study of enjoying activity.

Practical skills give us examples of enjoyment coming as a disposition develops. As we begin to learn a skill, we are held back by not being able to do it very well, and we tend to find it frustrating and unpleasant. As we get better at golfing, building, or speaking Italian, we enjoy doing it more, for we are less frustrated by inadequacies and failures in the ways we exercise the skill. Speaking Italian is painful and annoying as long as I have to consciously search for words, mentally check for gender and case and wonder if the construction I am using will require a subjunctive in the next clause. As these points become familiar and I do not have to consciously think about them, speaking Italian becomes more fluent—the expression of a unified understanding of the language. I come to enjoy the

---

[6] Aristotle (2000), *Nicomachean Ethics*, II. beginning of 3.

[7] This is not objectionably self-centred: what she enjoys is *being a vegetarian*, not *self-satisfaction at being a vegetarian*.

exercise of language mastery as it no longer requires conscious working-out but enables me to express my thoughts unimpededly.

This intuitive point has been strongly supported by the work of the psychologist Mihalyi Csikszentmihalyi, who has spent many decades studying what makes people find experience satisfying and enjoyable.[8] The results are significant for our understanding of skill, and also, on this account, for virtue, since this account of virtue makes such strong use of the skill analogy.

We tend to think, unreflectively, that we enjoy ourselves most, feel most satisfied, when we are relaxed and doing nothing, or at any rate nothing that requires effort. One of the most striking results of Csikszentmihalyi's research is to show that this is not true; rather, what he calls 'optimal experience' is experienced precisely when we are not only active, but engaged in our activity in an intelligent and concerned manner. We enjoy our activities when we can 'focus attention at will . . . be oblivious to distractions . . . concentrate for as long as it takes to achieve a goal, and not longer'.[9] We enjoy being engaged in complex activities such as puzzle-setting and problem-solving, whereas mere repetition and performing the same routine task leave us not relaxed but bored and frustrated.

Enjoyment is felt most when we are engaged in goal-directed activities, where achieving the goal typically involves responding to feed-back and picking up on new features created by solving the previous problem. However, enjoyment is threatened by frustration caused by new information that the person doesn't know how to deal with, especially as concerns achieving one goal at the cost of others. Enjoyment is most achieved, then, when all the person's relevant goals are harmoniously organized and sorted out, so that she is equipped to deal with feedback and new information without having to stop and figure out how it relates to the goal she is pursuing. 'Every piece of information we process gets evaluated for its bearings on the self. Does it threaten our goals, does it support them or is it neutral? . . . A new piece of information will either create disorder in consciousness . . . or it will reinforce our goals, thereby freeing up psychic

---

[8] Other scholars of ancient philosophy have seen the relevance of Csikszentmihalyi's work (I first encountered it through a paper by Naomi Reshotko) though they have connected it directly to happiness and flourishing, rather than to virtuous activity itself. In the growing field of happiness studies Csikszentmihalyi's work has been very influential.
[9] Csikszentmihalyi (1991: 31).

energy.' When a person's relevant goals are harmoniously structured and she is focusing on the achievement of a goal which requires engagement with the situation, 'attention can be freely invested to achieve a person's goals, because there is no disorder to straighten out, no threat for the self to defend against. We have called this state the *flow experience*.'[10]

Let us recall the earlier examples. When I drive to my parking garage this is mere routine. The driving is not something I give my attention to, and it goes on in a way sometimes independent of my actual deliberations. We are not tempted to describe my driving by the metaphor of flow, because for one thing it is not particularly enjoyable.[11] Contrast the playing of the accomplished pianist. Her skill has taken a lot of habituation to acquire, but it is far from routine; her playing of a piece expresses the intelligence of her interpretation of it. In this kind of performance we can see what Csikszentmihalyi means by the flow experience. 'Flow' may be a misleading metaphor if it suggests passively 'going with the flow', something suited to routine like my driving. Flow is rather what distinguishes the expert's enjoyable performance of activity which requires engagement and expertise, and the metaphor of a 'flow' experience is best taken to pick out the direct engagement with the task characteristic of expertise, unmediated by deliberation, something active rather than passive.

While Csikszentmihalyi does not explicitly limit his claims to exercises of skill, his examples are predominantly of skills, and this is not surprising, given that he is talking about the experience of engaging in goal-directed activity responsive to feedback, where the task is complex and involving rather than mere routine.[12] Much of his work is devoted to showing how, in several areas, boring routine work can be made more enjoyable by being transformed into a more complex piece of puzzle-solving or goal-achievement which requires skill, and thus engages the person more.

---

[10] Ibid. 39. Cf. p. 37: 'Whenever new information disrupts consciousness by threatening its goals we have a condition of inner disorder.'

[11] There are people who enjoy driving, but for them the experience is an exercise of skill rather than a mere habituated routine.

[12] 'By far the overwhelming proportion of optimal experiences are reported to occur within sequences of activities that are goal-directed and bounded by rules—activities that require the investment of psychic energy, and that could not be done without the appropriate skills. Why this should be so will become clearer as we go along; at this point it is sufficient to note that this seems to be universally the case' (1991: 49). I am grateful to Chris Freiman for bringing this passage to my attention.

The flow experience has two crucial features. One is that it is what is called 'autotelic': the activity is experienced as being its own end, and thus experienced as being enjoyable in itself. Even if it is undertaken to produce a further end, the person can experience it as enjoyable if it is treated as an end in itself regardless of whether the further end is produced. Sporting activities provide the best illustrations of this: the activity of trying to get a ball into a net can be experienced as enjoyable regardless of whether the ball does go into the net, but only if the person has developed their skill in the right way, so that it can be experienced as the specific physical activity it is, not just as a means to getting the ball in the net.

The other important feature is that the person engaged in the activity is not conscious of the self.[13] What this amounts to is that when I am engaged in this kind of activity I lose a sense of myself doing it. The pianist is not aware of hitting exactly these keys, of moving now into B flat. This is not a tuning-out or lapse into routine, as when I am not aware of driving to the parking garage. For the pianist is striking the keys in exactly the way she now wants to do, which reflects her intentions in playing the piece in a specific way. Nonetheless, there is often a loss of self-consciousness (and often also of the passage of time) while the person is fully and intensely engaged in the activity. Again, this is most easily illustrated from sporting activities, where athletes often report a sense of emptiness or 'loss of ego' as they are caught up in running, throwing the javelin, and so forth. It is the combination of intense focus with loss of self-consciousness which marks this off sharply from the loss of attention that we find in routine activity.

The flow experience, where activity is experienced as enjoyable and rewarding, results when a person whose relevant goals are harmoniously integrated engages in activity in which intelligent and focused attention is brought to bear on goal-directed activity in a way found intrinsically rewarding, independently of its instrumental value. For this to be the case, the intelligence and focus result from the development of a disposition with the structure of a skill.[14] The activity is experienced as unhindered, unselfconscious, and effortless.

---

[13] This has to be carefully specified. 'Loss of self-consciousness . . . [involves] . . . only a loss of consciousness *of* the self' (Csikszentmihalyi (1991: 64)).

[14] While I would not want to exclude the possibility of geniuses who experience flow without having to build up skill from experience, I suspect that it would be very difficult to produce convincing examples of this from types of practical expertise (it seems to occur with purely theoretical skills).

Obviously this is not the only way in which we experience enjoyment. We get pleasant feelings from eating, drinking, and sexual experience, for example. What is interesting about this account, however, is that it shows that we enjoy *activity*, enjoy *what we do*, when it involves the factors sketched above: we are engaged in an activity which is not simple enough to be routine, but not such as to require self-conscious figuring out what to do. We respond to the situation in a way that has already been educated by practice and so can be direct and unselfconscious, but is still intelligent in responding to feedback, and so consists of more than simple repetition. This is most easily seen in the exercise of skills, particularly performance skills and sports activities, where we can most easily see the difference between intelligent habituated response and mere routine, and can best appreciate the union of intense engagement and unselfconsciousness.

Can this feature of skills be carried over to virtue? Obviously some accounts of virtue can do little with it, but the present account, which has made heavy use of the skill analogy, can welcome it. Once again, we have a feature of virtue which appeared obvious to the ancients, who thought it obvious that a successful account of virtue should show that and how virtuous activity is pleasant. Aristotle gives us a convincing account of the pleasure in question: it is not pleasant feelings but what is experienced when the virtuous activity is unimpeded by frustration and inner conflict. But we can't just appeal to Aristotle; we have to do more work to spell out the ways in which we can agree that a good account of virtue will be like an account of skill in this respect.

As has been repeatedly stressed, virtue is a matter of habituation but not of routine. To become kind or just requires learning how to deal with experience of various kinds *for yourself* and not just copying what someone else, or a book, says. You have to start off trusting your teachers to develop kindness and justice in you, showing you the right contexts and situations and teaching you in the right way to pick up what is important in these. But because your learning is not just mimicking but involves the drive to aspire, what you develop is a disposition based on understanding (to some degree, of course) of what it is to be kind and just, such that you can respond to new and even unfamiliar situations in ways that express what you have learnt from familiar ones. Your actions will differ from the ones from which you learnt, but will do so in the service of expressing the understanding of kindness and justice that you have learnt. Virtuous activity thus involves ongoing selective and differential engagement with the world, not a repetition of a routine once learned and then safely relied on. This is one of the analogies with skill that has been most stressed, and it enables us to show that virtuous activity meets the condition that exercise of skill meets, namely that of involving the person in a response to a situation which is not one of simple routine.

Is virtuous activity, though, goal-directed in the way that skilled activity is? Here we must be careful not to think primarily in terms of the productive skills, where thinking is directed towards making a distinct product. Here the point is to have an excellent product, whose excellence is not dependent on the kind of reasoning by which it is produced. This seems the wrong pattern for virtue, where only the beginner is required to copy the teacher regardless of his own reasoning. However, if we think of performance and sporting skills we can see that the goal-directedness in question need not be that of producing a distinct object. The skilful dancer's performance is an expression of the skill, not a product distinct from it; judging its excellence cannot be pulled apart from judging the excellence of the way it is performed. Similarly virtuous activity is directed at the goal of acting generously or justly in a given situation; the resulting action is, like the performance, an expression of the virtue whose excellence (if it is excellent) has to be judged in a manner that includes the way it was brought about and the kind of reasoning that led to it.

The learner in virtue, as we have seen, has to figure out what to do, and to reflect self-consciously whether what he is doing is generous, or what a generous person would do; the person with more developed kindness or generosity will grasp what to do in a way that is direct and unmediated by deliberation about what he should do. This point has come up before in more than one connection; it is important here because we can see a real analogue to the way someone with mastery of a skill can perform actions which require application and intense engagement, yet perform them without self-consciousness. Virtuous activity, at least in those past the stage of the learner, exhibits the same combination of direct engagement and loss of self-consciousness that we find with skills. As we have seen, thoughts that are about virtue—thoughts about whether this is a virtuous action, or what a virtuous person would do, gradually efface themselves as the person progressively becomes kinder, fairer, or more generous.

What of the point that activity is experienced satisfyingly as 'flow' when all the person's relevant goals are in harmony? In the case of skill, this is obviously a local matter; someone might be a skilful skater while having all kind of unresolved issues in other areas of her life. In the case of virtue, the person's global state is what is relevant to the performance of the action. An action won't be performed easily and enjoyably if there is interference from attachment to goals that are in tension with what the person is doing in the action. An action will then not be fully generous, say, if accompanied by felt regrets about the money or time spent, and thoughts about how else the money or time might have been spent more gratifyingly. Virtuous activity requires overall commitment in the person to the goals of the actions performed; otherwise the virtuous activity is impeded and frustrated in its execution by awareness of alternatives passed up.

This aligns perfectly with the distinction, already seen, between virtue and continence or *enkrateia*. The merely continent person does the right thing, and is even guided to doing the right thing by developing virtue, but has other commitments and values that conflict with the exercise of virtue. Because of this, virtuous activity in her case has to be effortful and self-conscious. The mature honest person is aware of occasions for dishonesty, say, but it simply does not occur to her to take advantage of them. The person tempted by the rewards of dishonesty, in contrast, will have to rehearse to herself the reasons for honesty in order to act well. Honest actions will be experienced by the mature honest person in the 'flow' way; however complex and hard to navigate the circumstances are, there is no felt resistance to acting honestly, no interference with the direct having of honest responses.

Another feature stressed by Csikszentmihalyi is also clear in the case of virtuous activity, which is that it is valued for its own sake. The brave person values his brave activity for its own sake, and does not regret it even if it failed to achieve the objective.[15] Virtuous activity may well be valued instrumentally for what it enables the person to do, but if it is virtuous it is also valued for itself. (So far we have not examined this feature of virtue; we will look at it in the next chapter.) An analogy often drawn on here is from sport, where a sporting performance may be valued and admired in itself, even though it does not for some reason succeed in winning the prize.

---

[15] Stoic terminology gives us a clear way of making the distinction. I aim overall at the final end or *telos* of living virtuously (this being the way to achieve *eudaimonia*). I do so by aiming to achieve, virtuously, a variety of objectives (the singular form is *skopos*) such as earning a living, bringing up a family, and, where necessary, rescuing people in danger. I can fail to achieve a particular *skopos* without failing in my attempt at the overall *telos* (as long as the failure is due to circumstances beyond my control, and does not come from a character flaw in me).

So on this account of virtue the 'flow' model of skilled activity dovetails neatly with the relevant features of virtue. Moreover, it answers to our intuitions in many ways. It is very plausible that the enjoyment of virtuous activity does not consist in felt twinges of pleasure. It consists, rather, in the way the activity is done; this is not something extra to be added on but just is the ready and unselfconscious way the activity is performed, 'flowing' effortlessly from the person's overall harmoniously arranged goals unchecked by effortful self-questioning or conscious figuring-out. We recognize the difference between the encratic and the fully virtuous person, and can also appreciate that the virtuous person finds acting virtuously enjoyable; it is obvious, however, that this does not consist in the virtuous person's having perceptible feelings of pleasure that the encratic lacks.

It might be thought that an account of virtuous action as enjoyable, especially one making some appeal to the psychology of flow, makes acting virtuously sound too easy, as though the virtuous person just registers what is to be done and harmoniously goes along with this, no effort being required. What of occasions when acting virtuously requires what intuitively seems precisely like breaking the ongoing rhythm of what you are doing, stepping back to reflect about what to do? Perhaps you have to make a decision about someone's career where fairness demands that you step back and detach yourself. Continuing as usual would fall short of virtue.[16]

This is not an objection once we understand rightly what it is for virtuous action to be easy and enjoyable, understood in terms of the psychology of flow. It is a matter of being unimpeded in virtuous deliberation and action, and this is something which can well require detachment and reflection if it is not to lapse into routine. We can see this if we consider the difference between the virtuous person who takes a reflective step backwards unprompted, and the encratic or not yet virtuous person who has to be jolted, or pushed, into doing so. The virtuous person is not tempted by friendship to act unfairly, and so is not tempted to continue heedlessly on when the situation becomes such that continuing uncritically is likely to lead to unfairness. This is no more problematic that the fact that a practical expert will often pause to reflect while doing

---

[16] Justice and fairness provide the most obvious examples of this; the example comes from Walter Sinnott-Armstrong. I have found that this point is very often raised as an intuitive objection to the 'flow' view.

something which continued uncritically might lead to problems. A job that Csikszentmihalyi is 'built according to the blueprint of flow activities' is surgery.[17] Clearly surgeons do not engage fully with their work by 'going with the flow', switching off, or ignoring anything that could slow them down. This would be to lapse into routine. Activities in which flow is achieved involve paying attention to what is happening and responding appropriately to feedback, coming up with creative solutions where new problems occur. Engagement in a practical situation involves using your intelligence and imagination, one reason why the experience is often described as one of being in control.[18] In the same way a brave or just person acting intelligently will navigate difficulties and solve problems carefully and with attention to the details of the situation. The activity is harmonious in the sense that there is no disruption of intent, but it need not seem from the outside to consist of actions which progress particularly smoothly. Just as the exercise of an expert surgeon's activity might seem to an outsider to involve interruptions for thought, the exercise of a just person's activity might seem to an outsider to involve interruptions for thought. What matters is the kind of thought involved; there is no interruption in the exercise of surgical skill, or of the exercise of justice. What has to meet the conditions for flow is the exercise of skill or virtuous activity, and what that consists in may not be obvious, especially to someone who lacks the skill or virtue. If we know little about golf, we will not be good judges of whether someone's swing exhibits flow; similarly if we are biased we will not be good judges of the production of an unbiased response and how well this fits with the rest of the person's values and commitments.

There is a further point that needs to be met here, however. Even if we grant all the above, surely we have to realize that there are many occasions when even the most virtuous person will find acting virtuously difficult or stressful, not because of internal obstacles to responding and acting but because of the circumstances in which he or she has to act.[19] For example, a generous person might be faced with painful choices among possible

---

[17] Csikszentmihalyi (1991: 157; cf. 155–7). I am grateful to Chris Freiman for drawing the passage to my attention. Of course no job in itself guarantees flow; if the surgeon starts to regard his work as merely a means to a paycheck he will come to find it unrewarding.

[18] Ibid. 59ff., 201–13.

[19] The importance of this issue has been stressed by many people; I am grateful to one of the referees of this book for stating it most clearly and forcefully.

recipients of generosity: suppose that they are all appropriately situated but there are simply too many of them for her resources. A brave person might be able to rescue only one of several victims of a flood. A compassionate person might find himself forced to choose, among family members all of whom need full-time care, which can remain at home and which must go into institutional care. In cases like these, the response may still be direct, but hardly seems an example of an enjoyable activity, since a virtuous person would feel regret for the unmet needs rather than enjoying the recollection of her own virtuous activity as far as it went. There are cases, then, when even the most virtuous person would act virtuously, in an unimpeded way as far as internal factors went, but without anything like enjoyment, and with subsequent regrets about the limits of the way she was able to act in the situation.

In these cases, it is important to realize that the sources of struggle and regret lie not in the virtuous way the agent deals with the situation, but in the circumstances in which he finds himself. Virtue does not, of course, render us omnipotent, or even mildly in charge of the circumstances in which we find ourselves exercising it. Having to cope with overwhelming circumstances does produce difficulties for acting well and often regret for the imperfect way in which the person was able to deal with the situation. This is distinct, however, from struggle and regret whose sources are in the person's own character. A regret that I could not bring myself to be more generous is different from a regret that I had to choose among worthy recipients of limited resources. Where the virtuous person acts virtuously, but with hesitation and subsequent regret, it is crucial what the sources of this are. Perhaps he finds it difficult to act well because he is 'out of practice', as experts may be if they neglect to sustain their skill. Or perhaps he is not, but the circumstances are notably difficult, complicated, or overwhelming.

As simply stated here, the distinction between the way the virtuous person acts and deals with the circumstances, and the circumstances themselves, may sound merely like a (possibly ad hoc) answer to this problem. We shall see, however, that the distinction is an important one for an account of virtue in other contexts, and not at all ad hoc.[20]

---

[20] See Chs. 6 and 7 in particular.

Our results so far intuitively seem right. There is such a thing as enjoying the exercise of virtue. This is acting generously, say, gladly and readily, without regrets about the money or time spent. This contrasts with acting generously and finding it a nuisance and something you would rather not do—the latter is, as we say, finding it a pain to act generously. The contrast here, however, is not that the gladly generous person has a positive pleasant feeling and the reluctantly generous person has a painful feeling. Rather is is to be found in the fact that activity is experienced as pleasant and satisfying when it meets certain conditions, which virtuous activity fills. (It meets these conditions in the virtuous; we ordinary people have some idea of what it is like, unless we are hopelessly indifferent to virtue, but it is not a constant feature of the normal course of our lives.)

We enjoy exercising skill and exercising virtue; does this account make these too similar? We can enjoy exercising skills in a local way, without overall harmony of ends and commitments; pianists, plumbers, and golfers can experience flow from their respective activities without being virtuous.[21] Flow experience from virtuous activity easily exercised requires overall harmony of the person's goals and commitments. So far, not much has been said about this; the idea will be developed later.[22]

A big advantage of this account is that it shows how we can explain the point mentioned above, namely that the enjoyment we get from virtuous activity can often seem difficult or impossible to articulate. We may, indeed, at first resist the idea that virtuous activity is *enjoyable* at all, but this may come from ideas foreign to virtue ethics, such as the idea of ethics as a system of rules stopping you from doing what you want, or an emphasis on alleged irresistible *moral* obligations. The notion of virtuous activity as unimpeded and hence enjoyable is, however, when properly understood, as intuitive as the easily recognizable distinction between the virtuous and the encratic (indeed the two are obviously linked). This is something we recognize every day in ourselves and others, and so we may

---

[21] Indeed Csikszentmihalyi (1991: 209) himself holds that he is discussing what people enjoy in their lives generally, not studying virtuous people. Despite saying this, he shows interest in the idea of 'the autotelic personality', the person whose experience as a whole facilitates flow, and the way such a person can deal with misfortunes in an unforced and harmonious way. 'The "autotelic self" is one that easily translates potential threats into enjoyable challenges, and therefore maintains its inner harmony.'

[22] The account of flow, and the defence of the need for overall harmony, are mutually supporting; again, we do not have a foundational concept from which the others are derived.

readily be brought to see that the enjoyment of virtuous activity is not some implausible positive feeling but rather a matter of the performance being ready and in harmony with the person's other goals and commitments.

Even so an element of mystery persists. Just what is it that is enjoyable about virtue in general—being brave in rescuing people stranded after a flood, being generous in giving time to a good cause? These activities are completely diverse—what can there possibly be in common to make them both cases of enjoyable virtuous activity? What can we point to that the two cases have in common?

Moreover, something's being enjoyable is, other things equal, always a reason for doing it; but how do we explain to the reluctant warrior or the stingy person that if they become braver or more generous they will enjoy it? What can we point to in either case?

Our account enables us to see that these are just the same problems that arise with skills. How do we persuade the reluctant soccer player or pianist that when they get better at it they will enjoy it? What exactly can we point to in excellent soccer playing and piano playing which will appeal? And what is it that makes both good soccer playing and good piano playing enjoyable activities?

In the case of skills the answer is clear. We don't, and don't expect to, have any idea of what it is like to exercise a skill with mastery, and thus with enjoyment, unless we have some grounding in that skill. Watching a master potter, or sports star, gives no idea of what it is like for them to create pottery or score goals. Only if I can throw pots myself, or play soccer on the weekends, do I have a glimpse of the experience of mastering the skill and the enjoyment of doing so. We can recognize masters in various skills from the outside, but this is mostly via the prizes or praise they win from others who share the skill. As a result, although we do not doubt that there is something distinctive about the experience of Lang Lang when he plays the piano, or Tiger Woods when he tees off, those of us with no experience of the skills in question have no idea of it. Moreover, even those who do have some experience in the relevant skills find it very hard to convey to those who do not, what it is like to exercise the skills at all, never mind at a high level. We have not developed a vocabulary for doing this.[23]

---

[23] Sport has to some extent developed one, but not very far, and there are wide variations between sports as to how successfully it can be done.

There is, then, little that can be said to the reluctant soccer player or pianist other than the apparently unhelpful suggestion that as they get better at it they will enjoy it more and find it more rewarding. Moreover, as they find it more rewarding they will engage more with it and thus improve; a mutual bootstrapping will be set up. However, we know from experience that far from being unhelpful this is exactly on the right lines. We lack, however, a vocabulary for describing either what skill mastery is like in general or what it is like to be master in the distinct skills, and so we lack a vocabulary for explicating just what is enjoyable about the exercise of expertise.

The same holds for virtue. We all know that the only way to encourage genuine virtue, rather than behaviour done for reward, is to encourage the child to appreciate the rewards of virtuous activity itself. Sharing seems painful at first to the child who wants to play with *his* toys; after experience of various sorts of sharing he comes to find the rewarding nature of sharing toys and not regarding them as exclusively *his*. This experience cannot be conveyed to him any way than by his discovering it for himself as he becomes more generous. This is indeed one of the difficulties of teaching virtue: the parent can do little to convey to the selfish child why being generous is itself rewarding, other than by encouraging her to be generous and discover for herself that developing generosity is rewarding. We find ourselves in the slightly odd position of being able to discern that exercising virtue, on the part of the mature virtuous person, is enjoyable, without being able to say much if anything about what the enjoyableness consists in either in general or for the specific virtues. On an account that stresses the skill analogy, this position is no odder than the position we are in with regard to expertise and the enjoyableness of exercising it.

The nearest we can get to this is to give an account like that of 'flow', which captures something important. I can, after all, say *some* things about people who are more virtuous than I am. The way they act is less self-conscious than I am, more engaged with what they are doing. They are less fixated than I am on further goals that the virtuous activity will bring about. They are also less concerned about other goals which do or might create conflict or at least caution about doing the virtuous thing. Unlike me, they are ready for the challenge, and do not have to work out what is the just, or brave thing to do here. In all these ways virtuous people have their attention focused outwards on the action rather than inwards on themselves.

This is, interestingly, contrary to a common stereotype among philosophers of the virtuous person as more concerned with his or her self than with what it is right to do. Most of us are in fact concerned with ourselves when we act virtuously; for one thing, we do often need to deliberate self-consciously about what to do. So self-concern may be a feature of the learners and the mediocre in virtue. But this is not a problem with virtue; it is a problem with our imperfect achievement of it.

This account has left uncovered many important aspects of the virtuous person's affective side. My excuse here is that some of this, notably the issue of the role of the emotions, has been very fully discussed elsewhere. What I have tried to do here is to bring out the way in which the skill analogy points us not just to something important about the 'cognitive' side of virtue, the way that the virtuous person thinks, but also to something significant about the way the virtuous person feels. Like the master craftsperson the virtuous person experiences enjoyment and satisfaction in her activity and not just in the result. It is not a difficulty for this account that we can say very little about the actual experience either of the soccer player or of the brave person; this is something that you have to develop the skill or the virtue to experience for yourself, and there is very little other way of conveying it. This may be a practical difficulty in the teaching of virtue, but it reflects something important about the nature of virtue.

6

Virtues and the Unity
of Virtue

The last chapter introduced an idea which was not supported there, namely that the fully successful exercise of one virtue depends upon other aspects of the person's character. This is an important issue independently of the question, what virtues there are (an issue we will return to at the end of this chapter). An exercise of generosity will not be experienced as coming easily if there is friction between it and other commitments on the agent's part—an attitude of superiority or a desire to have one's time or money to oneself, for example. We may think that this leads to a problem; surely a virtue can develop relatively independently of whether the person has other virtues? We all know people who are fair but stingy, kind but cowardly, and so on. Will this get in the way of the person's developing a disposition to be fair, or kind, readily and directly? What *is* the role of virtues in the person's overall character?

Virtue, on the kind of account given here, cannot be properly understood without understanding how it comes about and develops. So it is useful to turn back to ethical development and to pick out some aspects of it which indicate the ways the virtues relate to one another and to the person's overall character.

One point already stressed is that we learn to find the virtues in a variety of very different situations and ways of life. We recognize generosity in billion-dollar funding and in a neighbour helping out with babysitting. We recognize courage in warriors and also in terminal patients,[1] journalists

---

[1] Surprisingly, Jacobson (2005) rejects this, denying that it is clear that the steadfastness shown by a terminal cancer patient should count as courage, and suggesting that the claim that it is may derive from the reluctance of contemporary intellectuals to recognize the martial virtues, apparently the proper location of courage. Plato, no despiser of the martial virtues, is closer to common sense when showing no doubt that courage is shown not only on the battlefield but 'in facing illness or poverty' (*Laches*, 191d).

tracking down a story, scholars putting forward a hypothesis, and many other situations. It is worth focusing on the point that we have no difficulty in doing this. Few if any of us could give a satisfying answer to the question of what makes all these kinds of activity generous or brave; so it can seem remarkable that we do learn to recognize generosity or bravery at all, still more that we learn to recognize them in the ready way that we do. One important point that this indicates is that right from the start a virtue involves more than the activity performed in the situations in which it is first learned: it involves something on the person's part (something we can recognize even before distinguishing a cognitive aspect and an affective aspect of it) which can also be shown in entirely different activity in a different context. From the start a virtue is not just a routine habit, which can be displayed and redisplayed only in the original context or one like it. It has an inner side which we can recognize in utterly different contexts, even without understanding much about it. Even learning about one virtue, then, requires some grasp of the way it figures in many different areas of one's life; we can't understand bravery in just one compartment of our life, but have to be able to exercise it over other areas in an uncompartmentalized way.

Another important indication of the nature of virtue comes from the point that we can't teach the virtues in isolation, one by one, since they can't be learnt that way. Generosity gives us a good example here. A child doesn't learn to be generous by just giving her things away, or sharing things whether they belong to her or not. Generosity involves considerations of fairness and justice. For, as Aristotle points out, generosity requires taking from the right sources as well as giving to the right people in the right way.[2] And 'giving in the right way' involves a great deal. Giving a gift which is indifferent to what the recipient wants is not generous. Generosity requires intelligence about what people both need and want, and also about appropriate ways, times, and manners of giving, avoiding obtrusiveness and condescension. Generosity thus requires, at the least, benevolence, a real interest in other people, their needs, and their wants. To get it right in giving, how to give, when and to whom, not to mention how much, you have to have an interest in the welfare of others beyond their role as your beneficiaries; otherwise you risk your giving becoming selfish

---

[2] *NE* 1119^{b}22–1121^{a}10.

showing-off. Generosity thus requires real benevolent concern for others, along with minor virtues such as tact. Obviously children don't get all of this at once, and even as adults we find we constantly need improvement; the point here is that we can all see, in the course of ethical development, that some virtues 'cluster'. This indicates something about the nature of virtue; it is not just a casual point, extraneous to an account of virtue, about how we learn to be virtuous.

Many other virtues are similar. It might be objected, though, that while virtues clump in this way, these clusters might remain relatively independent modules in a person's character. Different groups of virtues are prominent in different ways of life, for example. This is a point which requires a more theoretical response, which we will come to later.

There are some indications, then, that a virtue is not compartmentalized to a single area or context of life in its exercise, and that to learn how to exercise it is not compartmentalized from learning how to exercise other virtues. These two points come together in the idea that virtues are not mutually independent dispositions in a person's life; they imply one another, or 'reciprocate'. Aristotle's is the most famous argument for this position, called 'the reciprocity of the virtues': if you have one you have all the others (*All* the others? We will come to this), and so if you lack even one you don't have any. This claim is in contemporary discussions called the 'unity of virtue', so this is how I will refer to it.[3]

Aristotle's argument for the unity of virtue (understood in this way) is simple, and, perhaps for that reason, powerful.[4] The way our characters develop is to some extent a matter of natural endowment; some of us have traits 'by nature'—we will tend to act bravely or generously without having to learn to do so, or to think about it. This is 'natural virtue', which we have already encountered. Different people will have different natural virtues, and one person may be naturally endowed in one area of life but not others—naturally brave, for example, but not naturally generous. However, claims Aristotle, this can't be the whole story about virtue. For one thing, children and animals can have some of these traits,

---

[3] Strictly, the 'unity of virtue' thesis is the claim that all the virtues are really one single thing, practical reasoning exercised in different circumstances. For contemporary discussions of the reciprocity thesis (referred to as the unity thesis) see Badhwar (1996, 2009), Kent (1999), Watson (1984), and Wolf (2007).

[4] *Nicomachean Ethics*, VI. 13.

but in them they are not virtues. Further, these natural traits are harmful if not guided by 'the intellect', which in this context is specified as practical wisdom or practical intelligence (*phronesis*). Just as a powerfully built person will stumble and fall if he cannot see, so a natural tendency to bravery can stumble unseeingly into ethical disaster because the person has not learned to look out for crucial factors in the situation. Our natural practical traits need to be formed and educated in an intelligent way for them to develop as virtues; a natural trait may just proceed blindly on where virtue would respond selectively and in a way open to novel information and contexts.

This point should not be surprising if we bear in mind the crucial difference between virtuous habituation and routine. Obviously in our ethical life routine is dangerous; we need an open, learning attitude to develop bravery, fairness, and the like, since in merely repeating past responses lurks the danger of repeating past mistakes. Virtue requires (as well as habituation, and as well as the enjoyment that comes with greater mastery over one's activity) practical intelligence in both the formation and the exercise of the virtues.

Aristotle takes this to be the crucial point. We can now, he continues, meet the claim that the virtues can be separated from one another. This is possible with the natural virtues, but not the proper or real virtues. For to have even one of these you need practical intelligence, but when you have this you have all the virtues. Obviously here Aristotle is talking about *excellence* in practical intelligence; you don't acquire all the virtues just by beginning to think intelligently about your character traits, for clearly that's not enough to develop even one. The point here is that practical intelligence develops over your character as a whole, in a holistic way. You can't develop generosity in the absence of fairness and tact; you can develop *a* character trait, but it won't be generosity, since it will fail to get things right in action, and the result will be not generosity but extravagance or self-advertisement. To the extent that you are truly generous, you get everything right when acting generously, and to do this you have to get things right in other aspects of your character also. It isn't bravery that is shown in a risky and daring exploit that puts others at risk; the risky and daring action comes from a disposition which obviously shares a lot with bravery, but the truly brave person has a better and more intelligent grasp on what things are worth risk and daring and what are not. The truly brave person gets it right overall.

The important assumption here is clearly that practical intelligence itself is unified over the person's life. Why would we accept this (especially if we are leery of the conclusion it leads to, namely the unity of the virtues themselves)? Aristotle does not tell us. He is assuming the unacceptability of the alternative, which would be that each virtue had its own little practical intelligence, limited to the area of that virtue. This might be the case at the very start of learning about virtue, with young children, but it clearly does not work as a picture of the development of virtue. Life is not compartmentalized, and so learning to deal with the mixed situations that confront us is not a matter of getting ever better at extracting and then confronting the claims of different virtues. If this were the case, an initial assessment of the situation would be followed by more abstract comparison of different aspects of the situation, and then a conclusion delivered. But this is not a realistic picture of how we develop the virtues; for one thing, it would make the process completely opaque to us, since we have no idea of the basis on which the different practical intelligences located within different virtues could compare and assess their claims and so come to a mutually acceptable conclusion. Developing a virtue is not a matter of getting ever sharper at comparing and assessing different partial claims and then working out an overall decision on obscure grounds.

Once again the skill analogy is helpful; it points us in the direction of greater ease and directness of decision and action, with conscious deliberation effacing itself, thus leading to ready and unmediated action as the person becomes braver or more generous. The skill analogy and its application to virtue indicates that the practical intelligence involved is one which integrates and unifies all the relevant aspects of the situation from the start, rather than developing on separate tracks and then trying to tie the results together. The unification of the virtues is then no odder or more mysterious than the fact that a pianist does not develop one skill for fingering and another, quite separate skill for tempo, only subsequently wondering how to integrate the results.

The same point holds for the more contentious-looking claim that to possess even one virtue fully or properly you need to have them all. This looks excessive; why not stay at the point of recognizing that virtues tend to cluster, but hold that these clusters can remain relatively isolated in the person? Someone can certainly appear to be benevolent, kind, and compassionate and have a number of obviously linked virtues, but be deficient in other areas, such as courage. Why must we conclude that there is something lacking about the virtues where he appears to be successful? Surely we would need to appeal to far-fetched counterfactual situations where lack of bravery compromised the person's kindness?

Here also, though, we need to think about the unacceptability of the alternative picture that we would get if we allowed that within the person we had even two or three independent practical intelligences within distinct clusters of virtues. We do not need far-fetched thought experiments to grasp that the way we develop in one area of our lives can indeed have an impact on the way we develop in other parts. The compassionate person might well need courage to insist that a victim be treated properly, or to stand up to a bully on someone else's behalf. If he lacks courage, his compassion will be flawed too; victims can't rely on it, and others generally can't rely on him to be compassionate in appropriate circumstances. In general a virtue which is unreliable in its exercise because of facts about the person (rather than external circumstances) is a compromised virtue.

Further, we get the same problem as with single virtues if we look at the alternative to accepting that the virtues are linked by practical intelligence developing holistically, and rendering them mutually dependent. Rather than different practical intelligences within single virtues, we would just have different practical intelligences within each virtue cluster, with a picture of ethical development as a conversation and negotiation among different aspects of the person, both the methods and the conclusions being opaque to the person. This strikingly fails to produce an integrated view of the values in a person's life as a whole. Rather, it produces a person who is, and feels, stuck with potentially, and predictably actually conflicting, values and with no obvious resources available for dealing with the situation.

Sometimes we are tempted to make an exception in the case of people who occupy a role, particularly a professional role, within which certain virtues are developed which may not easily be integrated with the virtues the person develops in other aspects of her life. A trial lawyer, for example, may develop adversarial traits in the courtroom which, in the context of her family, would distress both her and her family, where the virtues she exercises are cooperative. Often it is not clear that both sets of traits are in fact virtues, but let us suppose that they are. The person is still living in a compartmentalized way, one with divisions and compromises always present, and one in which the values sought in one aspect of life may well be in conflict with those pursued in another. Moreover, the less the person sees it as her aim to live an integrated life, the more these conflicts will be both painful and hard for her to predict. This is hardly an ideal for a virtuous life. For one thing, it comes into sharp conflict with the aspect of virtue discussed in the last chapter—the point that the virtuous person finds her life enjoyable, in part because of lack of inner conflict or its threat.[5]

We find ourselves, then, with the position that full, proper virtue requires that our natural dispositions be formed and guided by practical intelligence, which functions holistically over the person's life, integrating lessons from the mixed and complex situations that we are standardly faced with, and developing a unified disposition to think, act, and feel, one which gets things right in action, thought, and feeling. Further reflection in this chapter and the next will develop the connections between these issues and those involved in finding things valuable in life.

One obvious objection, which occurs readily even to those sympathetic to the idea so far, is that this account makes virtue too *ideal*. Every account of virtue has to make some appeal to an ideal (such an account would scarcely be convincing if it concluded that we are all just fine the way we are). But in some accounts the ideal can appear too far from the reality of ordinary people's lives—too *hopelessly* ideal—and thus too demanding when we judge the characters of ourselves and others. How are we to deal with the point that however hard we and others try, none of us will ever actually be generous, brave, or fair, or have any virtue? Won't we despair of our own ethical progress, and be too hesitant to ascribe any virtue to others?

There is no real danger here, however, at least not to a developmental theory that insists that to understand the nature of virtue we must take into account the way virtues are taught and learnt. In everyday life we have no problem in using the virtue terms in the kinds of context in which we have learned them, in which bravery is shown in facing obvious danger, generosity in sharing toys or giving money, and the like. The process of advancing from this, which has been so much stressed in this book, need not leave us *confused* about our initial everyday application of the virtue terms. We are quite free to call someone brave or generous when they fulfil the conditions in which we learned what bravery and generosity are.

---

[5] For incisive comments on the idea that lawyers might be able to develop no-holds-barred adversarial traits while remaining 'good people' see Hursthouse (2008).

At the same time we are quite clear that they are not fully brave or generous; they do not indicate to us everything that these virtues involve. The only danger here would seem to come from the point that a lofty ideal might make us too hesitant to call people brave or generous who ⋅ have achieved far more than other people, on the grounds that they are not (yet) *fully* virtuous, since they still do not make clear to us everything that the relevant virtue involves. If nobody is really brave, should we be admiring, and possibly emulating, Alexander the Great for his bravery? It is salutary to remember here that too low a standard has dangers also. We often make heroes or celebrities of people for their virtues (not just their actions) in one area of their lives. Later we discover feet of clay in other areas of their lives, and we are disproportionately disillusioned. A new biography revealing hitherto unknown faults in some public figure's private life affects our view of the person as whole for the worse.[6] If we admire people for their virtue on the basis merely of one area of their lives, we risk being prematurely satisfied in our heroes and role models, and this will frequently lead to later disappointment, not just with the particular person but with the whole project of becoming brave, generous, or whatever.

The claim that the virtues are unified doesn't, then, prevent us from recognizing virtue at the everyday level, and respecting people for it, but it does require us not to be complacent or easily satisfied about our own or others' virtue, to expect our role models to have flaws and to respond to this maturely and without prematurely giving up on the idea of progress in virtue.

Another common objection is that the idea that virtues develop in a holistic way encourages a way of thinking of ourselves and others in terms of overall character rather than in more nuanced ways as having some virtues and lacking others. And classifying people in this way tends to lead, in familiar ways, to dividing the world up into the Good and the Bad. And if I think that I am one of the good guys, this can lead to complacency on my part, and premature rejection of others without regard for the complexity of their characters. It is even worse if I think of myself as one of the

---

[6] We may think of the effect on the reputation of Thomas Jefferson of the discovery that he probably had an unacknowledged family by one of his slaves. The poet Philip Larkin's posthumously published diaries, containing misogyny and racism, severely damaged his reputation.

bad guys; I may despair of myself as worthless, refusing to see anything good in myself because of some bad traits. But even if we don't fall into this way of thinking, we might find ourselves ignoring or forced to deny good aspects of someone who is on balance bad, or bad aspects of someone who is on balance good; an overall judgement of actual people seems bound to be simplistic.

We are not forced to this, however, by the idea that virtues are unified by practical intelligence (though we might be forced to it on some other conceptions of virtue). First, someone might quite well lack a *natural* trait or tendency, one that might indeed be quite isolated from other aspects of their character. Someone might well be patient and kind, yet lack the natural quality of boldness. Lacking the actual virtue of courage, in contrast, would mean a lack of practical intelligence in that area, so that the person would lack the ability to discern in a situation what kind of thing is worth defending and what is not. It is because situations are not compartmentalized as single-virtue situations that this failure would mean that the person's practical intelligence can't be relied on not to fail in other areas. Someone who cannot appreciate what is and what isn't worth incurring risks to defend has loyalty and honesty in similarly compromised forms, since neither can be relied on when courage is needed.

But even when we are dealing with failures of practical intelligence and not just natural virtue, we are not forced to any counterintuitive positions if we bear in mind the level at which we think that unification of the virtues is to be found. Whereas the first objection took the idea to make virtue too ideal, the present objection works only if we conflate the ideal with the actual. The ideal of unification is what we aim at, not what we have already achieved, and so we can happily admit that the world contains many people, including ourselves, who display a mixture of virtue, vice, and mediocrity. Indeed, bearing in mind the ideal role of the unified virtues leads us to avoid overall judgements of character when we are thinking of actual people. If we keep apart the ideal and the actual, we are led to caution when judging ourselves and others—the very opposite, in fact, of precipitate global judgements of character. The more we reflect on our possession and development of practical intelligence and on the many diverse ways in which different virtues contribute to decision and action in particular cases, the less likely it is that we will come to overall judgments of our and others' characters as being simply good or bad.

The third objection is the most important. How can the virtues be so unified by practical intelligence that they imply one another, when different people obviously lead different ways of life and need to exercise *different* virtues? A soldier needs one set of virtues, a caregiver to an Alzheimer's patient needs another set. Someone in a position of leadership will need a different set of virtues from the people being directed. We are faced by an apparent dilemma. On the one hand, if we are committed to holding that nobody can be fully virtuous unless they can exercise *all* the virtues, we seem committed to the absurd conclusion that to live a fully virtuous life you will have to live the life of a soldier *and* that of a caregiver (and many more besides). For if you have all the virtues, you must be able to exercise all the virtues, and it seems that you must live a life in which opportunities to exercise all the virtues are available to you. An addition to this claim can be made: to exercise a virtue will probably require fairly specialized knowledge. The virtue of compassion is not exercised by merely standing around wishing you could help: the compassionate person actually helps the wounded, aids the suicidal, and so on. But now it looks as though the fully virtuous person, in being omni-virtuous also has to be omni-competent, equipped to be, on demand, a doctor, psychiatrist, computer expert, plumber, and so on; which is even more absurd.

On the other hand, if we avoid these absurdities by responding that someone can be fully virtuous without having to live many different kinds of life, we have to say that all the virtues can be exercised in a single kind of life. And this looks implausibly limiting. On what grounds are we excluding some ways of living from the start from having a chance of being virtuously lived? It looks as though this way of thinking of virtue could appeal only to people who have a very narrow view of what human life is like, or even think that there can be only one fully virtuous way of life.[7] Though not absurd, this horn of the dilemma is also untenable.

Here we need a distinction which turns out to be important for much that follows. It is the distinction between *the circumstances of a life* and *the living of a life*. The circumstances of your life are the factors whose existence

---

[7] It is sometimes thought that Aristotle's account of virtue is meant to apply only to the lives of fourth-century BC elite males in Athens. This is astounding, given that Aristotle's account has been found relevant to utterly different ways of life even in the ancient world (to lives lived in Republican and Imperial Rome, for example) as well as the medieval period and the contemporary world.

in your life are not under your control. You are a particular age, with a particular genetic disposition, gender, height, etc; you have a particular nationality, culture, and language, have received a particular upbringing and education, have a particular family, employment, and so on. It's not that you can't do anything about these factors, but it's not up to you that they are there in your life. You can't bring it about that you are a different age or were born in a different place. You can alter your appearance, weight, language, culture, and so on, but you can't bring it about that you started with any but the original.

The living of your life is the way you deal with the circumstances of your life. You can't bring it about that you have a different genetic disposition from the one you do, but it's up to you how you respond to this, either refusing to think about it or working with it. You can't do anything about having the parents you do, but it's up to you how you deal with your relationship with them. You can't do anything about having been brought up in a particular culture, but it's up to you what you make of this, and what attitude you take to your culture and others. In the metaphor used in ancient ethical philosophy, the circumstances of your life are the material you have to work on, and living your life is working on these materials to make a product. Living your life well is doing this skilfully (the metaphor is one which brings the skill analogy to the fore); a life lived well is like the result of a skilful and intelligent formation of materials into a whole. The metaphor is suggestive: skill can be exercised on a wide variety of materials, and the same materials can be put to skilful, or to botched, use.

This distinction is not prominent in contemporary ethical theory. There are doubtless many reasons for this. One seems to be that we tend to think of ethical theories as entities to be fully developed first and only *then* applied to 'concrete situations' (as in much 'applied ethics'). But by the time I get to reflecting about my life, and how best to live it, I already *have* a life, as has been remarked more than once already: I am already embedded in particular contexts of society, culture, gender, education, and so on. The way I 'apply' theory will therefore of course have to be specific to my situation. But the theory will be applicable by others in very different situations and contexts. Because of respecting this distinction ethical theory turned out, in the ancient world, to be relevant to the lives of Romans as well as Greeks, slaves as well as emperors; because of this feature there is no problem of principle in finding ancient forms of ethical theory relevant to us in the contemporary world, despite the huge differences between our world and that of the ancient philosophers themselves.

With this distinction in mind we can see why the virtues can be unified by practical intelligence even though different virtues will be emphasized in different ways of life. For the virtues are not part of the circumstances of a life. An Aristotelian natural virtue might be; you could find that you are just stuck with a bold temperament, say, and have to think about how to deal with it. But you could not in that way find that you are stuck with being brave; you won't have *become* brave except by living your life in a certain way, a way in which you have developed a virtue by learning and aspiring in the way already sketched. The virtues are part of the way we *live* our lives, whatever the circumstances are; we don't discover the virtues in our lives, since we have to bring it about that they are there.

Virtues are thus always exercised within the circumstances of a given life. This point links with the point discussed above in Chs. 3 and 4, namely that the virtues are always both learned and exercised in a given embedded context. Since there are, obviously, many different ways of life, there will be many ways of living these ways of life virtuously, and no reason to think that there is any single recipe in terms of which virtues will always be needed, or any single hierarchy of which virtues will be most important. A soldier and a caregiver have very different ways of life. In the soldier's life, courage has to be prominent, since he or she will have to deal at many points with situations involving danger and risk. In the caregiver's life patience has to be prominent, since he or she has to deal with, say, an elderly Alzheimer's patient who is constantly demanding and incapable of real communication. It might at first seem that there is no overlap between the virtues these people need, since there is little or no overlap in the actual actions they perform on a daily basis. But the soldier will need patience as well as courage; he or she will need to be able to wait patiently for orders, or for the right moment to give orders, and be able to deal with long periods of inactivity without losing focus. And the caregiver will need courage to deal with the difficulties of his or her life, carrying on often without any encouragement or gratitude. Obviously both the prominence and the expression of the virtue will be different in the two lives, and so will be the way in which courage and patience will be related; still, both soldier and caregiver need both virtues, and need them to be integrated in their lives in ways that enable them to live their very different lives well. We find virtues unified in very different lives in different ways, because they need to be unified in ways appropriate to those lives; there is not likely to be any single degree of prominence or type of expression of either courage or patience which is equally appropriate in the lives of both soldier and caregiver.

What has been briefly illustrated for two virtues holds in the case of more, since the point is clearly a general one. There is no such thing as being virtuous in a way which will be appropriate to all kinds of lives, or one ideal balance of virtues such as courage and patience that could be got right once and for all for everybody. Virtue is not the kind of thing that can be specified in advance so as to be one size that fits all, precisely because practical intelligence gets things right in very diverse circumstances.

We now have a fresh perspective on the point that we develop virtue (to the extent that we do) in the embedded circumstances of particular cultures, languages, and so on. The virtues we develop will be those we need to deal *well* with those circumstances (in some cases dealing well with circumstances means trying to change them, as we saw in Ch. 4). How we do this may not depend on our natural virtues, which might indeed turn out to be ill suited to the kind of life we have to live; it depends on the development of our practical intelligence, the ability to understand and to do justice in particular circumstances to all the considerations that need to be addressed, and to produce decisions and actions which both express and confirm good character overall. Each of us needs to do different work to integrate the virtues we need to deal with the circumstances of our life as we aim to live well.[8]

If we return to the point made at the beginning of this chapter about ethical development, we can now see why we are able to pick out virtues so readily even when they are exercised in totally dissimilar contexts. It might seem remarkable just as a phenomenon, but it makes sense if we take it that we are implicitly distinguishing the circumstances of a life from the living of a life; we understand that exercising a virtue is doing something that can be done in very different circumstances. Underlying the way we think about the virtues is something that seldom becomes explicit: utterly different lives, in the sense of the circumstances or material

---

[8] As Watson (1984: 65) puts it, 'The unity thesis implies that if one has a particular virtue one must have them all; it does not imply that if one has a particular virtue one's life will allow for the manifestation of all the virtues equally. Which virtues will receive fuller expression will depend upon fortune, cultural context, and one's moral personality.'

of a life, can be lived, in the sense of the living of a life, bravely, patiently, generously (or not). Otherwise it would indeed be puzzling how we so readily discern the same virtues in totally unlike circumstances and actions.

Some accounts of the virtues do not make the link so stressed in this book, between the development of a virtue and the development of practical intelligence. For a variety of reasons, some approaches think of virtue in simpler ways, in which they are independent of one another. This answers to one everyday thought, namely that people can have some virtues while lacking others; we have seen, however, that this does not stand in the way of the kind of account developed here. One point of contrast is worth mentioning here. If the virtues are simply taken to be a number of distinct traits (generally, the admirable traits) of a person, then it would seem plausible that there would be a long list of virtues, since people have many character traits, and there are many reasons for finding a lot of these admirable. Hume, for example, and some contemporary ethics of virtue take virtues to be admirable traits which are independent of one another.[9]

One problem such accounts have is that of finding a plausible way of determining which traits are in fact virtues. Hume takes the virtues to be traits which are either useful or agreeable to the person him- or herself or to others.[10] How this will direct us to think of traits will obviously depend on what is agreeable and useful; and there are many ways in which this is both shifting and underdetermined. Does this matter? Perhaps not from many points of view, but it is likely that there will be cases where there is a question whether a trait is a virtue or just a conventional trait. Hume counts as virtues traits such as cleanliness, industriousness, and wittiness; these are virtues on Hume's criterion, but in these and other cases this merely makes us wonder if the criterion is the right one.

The present approach, which stresses the unified and holistically developing nature of the virtues, can provide a 'filter' to help us here, in a way which produces intuitive results which do not lead us immediately to question the correctness of the filter. Aristotle provides us with an excellent example here. When he discusses virtues in books III and IV of the *Nicomachean Ethics*, he sketches, among others, a virtue of 'magnificence'

---

[9] e.g. Swanton (2003), Adams (2006). But see Russell (2009: pt. II).

[10] This is, as it stands, far too inclusive, and Hume in fact relies on supplementary considerations; see Hursthouse (1999b).

(*megaloprepeia*). This is the virtue exercised by rich people in spending large sums of money on public goods. The rich in Athens, in the absence of an income tax, had periodically to use their wealth on public projects such as equipping a warship or financing a drama. This spending is what the rich had to do; 'magnificence' is the virtue of doing it well, neither spending too much on vulgar display nor spending too little and skimping the project; getting it right is a matter of taste and recognition of appropriateness, as well as just spending the right amount of money. Aristotle is quite explicit that this virtue can be exercised only by the rich, making it distinct from generosity, which anyone can exercise; a poor person trying to be magnificent would merely make himself ridiculous.[11] Is this highly context-dependent trait really a virtue? Aristotle himself runs right into this problem, though he does not face it. For, given the later passage in which, as we have seen earlier in this chapter, Aristotle argues seriously that the virtues imply one another, he is faced with an absurdity. If magnificence is really a virtue, then it will imply and be implied by other virtues such as courage and fairness. But obviously if you are truly courageous, and thus have all the virtues, you haven't miraculously acquired lots of money thereby, enabling you to be magnificent! Scholars differ on what Aristotle should do to repair the problem.[12]

We can see from this that the unity of the virtues (in the contemporary sense in which they reciprocate) enables us to 'filter' traits which may well be admirable, popular, valued, and more, but which are not virtues. They are not virtues because they do not imply and aren't implied by the group of virtues common to anyone's theory who aims to have a theory in which virtue is central. The ancient 'cardinal' virtues are courage, justice, 'temperance', and wisdom; a contemporary account would add at least benevolence, and would be more inclined to talk in terms of a larger group of more specific virtues, such as patience, generosity, fairness, and so on. They stand in intuitive contrast to Hume's purported virtues, and we can see why. Being generous, kind, etc. carries no implication that you will be clean, hard-working, or witty; and none of these traits implies that you will be generous or kind. It is obvious that you can be clean, hard-working, or witty in a generous or ungenerous, kind or unkind way. In

---

[11] *NE* 1122ª18–1123ª19.
[12] See Kraut and Irwin (1988), Gardiner (2005), and, for a thorough treatment, Russell (2009: ch. 7).

general, it is a good indication that a character trait is not a virtue if it neither implies nor is implied by central virtues, such as courage, but could be exercised in ways which are either courageous or cowardly, virtuous or vicious.

This is a way of working out which traits are *not* virtues; can the theory say anything useful about which traits *are*? Earlier I treated patience and generosity as virtues; on what grounds? They pass the 'filter' test of fitting in to the virtues thought of as unified by the holistic development of practical wisdom. Does this imply that they are really just forms of a more basic virtue such as benevolence? What would show that they are forms of a more basic virtue or distinct virtues?[13]

I am inclined to think that we don't at present have a good way of answering this question, but that it may not matter. We lack a good way of answering the question because the differences between generosity and benevolence are not like the differences between generosity and courage. We are not inclined to confuse the latter two, since they are distinct right from the beginning of our learning about them. We learn the application of the terms in different kinds of context, and the traits are from the start associated with different attitudes and feelings; generosity does not involve dealing with fear, for example. It is in fact extremely tempting to think that what have been routinely taken to be cardinal or basic virtues are distinguished by distinct clusters of feelings and concerns that we have as human beings (and thus as the basis of transculturally recognized virtues). Courage is the virtue we need for dealing with feelings of fear and situations of danger or difficulty; (some version of) temperance the virtue we need for organizing and regulating our desires in areas such as food, drink, and sex; justice and benevolence the virtues we need for dealing with our relations with others. Practical wisdom, where that is recognized as a distinct virtue in its own right, is the virtue we need for coping with the complexities of decision and action in varying and complicated situations. It is extremely plausible that there is a basis in human nature for at least some central virtues.[14]

---

[13] Russell (2009: pt. II) is a thorough treatment of important issues here.

[14] Many forms of virtue ethics make some version of this assumption. Examination of it in psychology has unfortunately been influenced by prematurely and implausibly definite claims such as those in the virtues list of Peterson and Seligman (2004), endorsed by Haidt (2006).

By the time we get to wondering about virtues such as generosity and benevolence, however, we are past this stage, and the question and its answer depend on more theoretical issues. It may not matter that we have no sharp theoretical lines distinguishing generosity from benevolence as either distinct or related to it. Whether it matters depends on the importance of this issue to the overall theory of virtue. It can be quite important for some theories of virtue, but from the perspective of the present one it matters less. Virtues which are distinct when we start to learn them turn out to be related, because they all involve the same practical intelligence, which operates over life as a whole, not in different ways in separate compartments of life. They are still distinct (we don't have to conclude that all virtues are really just the same thing) because different virtues will involve different paradigmatic contexts and different attitudes and feelings (a good example is that courage involves fear in a way not true of fairness or generosity). Yet we can see that different cultures carve virtues at different joints from the ways we do. Some virtues in other cultures seem to get lost in translation, so that we have to make up a word. Between the contexts of learning and the unification of virtues in overall character there are many different ways in which virtues can be distinguished, and it would be parochial to insist that we can now come up with the single correct way of doing this.[15]

This chapter has raised the issue of the relation of virtue to character as a whole, and thus to the person's life as a whole. It has introduced a distinction which will turn out to be important in discussing flourishing as well as in discussing virtue, namely that between the circumstances of your life and the living of your life. This is an intuitive, readily recognizable, and even mundane distinction, but one which turns out to be important in more than one context, and to bear a large amount of theoretical weight.

---

[15] Am I not just assuming that the virtues, at least central ones such as courage, are transculturally comprehensible? I think that the burden is on those who would claim that virtues are relative to cultures in such a way that one culture's virtues are simply opaque to another culture. This is implausible once we make the point that the same virtue can be realized in different contexts, something central to the learning of virtue even within one culture (as this chapter has underlined).

7

Virtue and Goodness

So far the account of virtue has built considerably on the skill analogy. We cannot, of course, just mechanically check off similarities between skill and virtue, but we can by now appreciate some major implications of the idea that the skill analogy helps us to understand virtue because both illustrate *the way we reason in practice*, reasoning expressed in doing and acting as contrasted with reasoning with no practical aim. The way we learn to reason, as we learn to do something skilled, offers resources for understanding the way we learn to reason in doing something virtuous. To state the obvious, this does not imply that all features of skill are features of virtue (we have already seen, for example, that skill can be practised in one area of your life without carryover to other areas, whereas this is not true of virtue). Nor does it imply that skill will provide us with the resources for understanding everything important about virtue. And, as already stressed, the skill analogy is important not for all accounts of virtue, but for an account of virtue like the present one, which foregrounds the role of practical reasoning in the development and exercise of virtue.

Skills, Virtue, and Commitment to Goodness

There is an important point about virtue which is not illuminated by the skill analogy, or by consideration of the role of practical reason in virtue. It emerges when we reflect that we admire people who have virtues, find them inspiring, and take them as ideals. We admire people for other things too, for example for being physically skilled, and also for other traits that we like to have in ourselves or to encounter in others—traits such as being witty, or tidy, or affable. The way we admire people for their virtues is distinctive, however, as we can see from what happens when a sports 'hero' turns out to have such vices as greed or cruelty; our view of him as a person changes, while the admiration for the sporting skill remains untouched. The same happens when we find ourselves ethically disillusioned by someone who is witty, tidy, and affable; our view of her as a person is revised, but we don't cease to find her witty, tidy, and affable, and our admiration for these traits in her, just as traits, is not necessarily thereby undermined.[1] Can we say anything more specific about the distinctive kind of admiration called forth by virtue?

The first answer is that in the case of the virtues our admiration is for the person's character: possession of virtues indicates something about what *the person* is like, whereas possession of traits such as tidiness or wittiness indicates only traits that the person has. Take someone who is characteristically tidy, who, noticing that his car has got messy, cleans it out. What does this tell us about his character? Very little. Let us suppose that the same person is characteristically brave, and that in the course of the subsequent drive he stops and courageously rescues passengers trapped in a crashed and burning car. This action, unlike the previous one, does indicate what kind of person he is. (We have to bear in mind, of course, that both actions are characteristic of the person; in real life we cannot draw conclusions so readily, since we frequently do not know whether an action is characteristic or not.) In our society appealing traits such wittiness and even physical skills may attract more attention and focus than virtues, and so they may be more salient, and encouraged, in the progress of our everyday lives; our approval of and admiration for them may be more vivid in our lives. But from the perspective of admiration for the person, virtues indicate character in a way that these traits do not. (I will shortly expand on this point.)

We might think at this point that the contrast here is not between virtues and other traits, but between virtues and vices on the one hand and other traits on the other. For surely, we think, vices indicate character as much as virtues do? This is true up to a point, and shows that virtues do more than merely indicate character. Suppose another person who sees the burning car, but pretends not to, and drives on. This is a cowardly act, and if it is characteristic of the person it does tell us something about him as a person, namely that he is a coward. But there is an important difference here, which can be brought out by the claim that the brave person is, by

<hr/>

[1] Some revelations, however, might well result in our reclassifying what we took to be tidiness as obsessiveness, what we took to be affability as indifference, and so on.

virtue of being brave, expressing a *commitment to goodness*, a commitment to *positive* value. Although this is a very general point, it is intuitive. The brave person's action reveals that he is committed to something valuable that is centrally important to him. He tries to save others from danger even when this puts at risk his own safety, perhaps his life. He is putting forward efforts to achieve an aim with value for his life as a whole: it is important for him to be brave in this kind of situation. The coward's actions, on the other hand, indicate that he fails to have this kind of aim. He will, of course, have an immediate aim—to ensure his own safety, avoid risk, and so on. But in being a coward he is not succeeding in an aim that he puts efforts towards. He cannot look back on his action in satisfaction, thinking that this cowardly act helped him in his overall aim of becoming a better coward. For there is no such thing as the aim to become a better coward. Cowards succeed only in becoming better at achieving their immediate aims—avoiding conflict, danger, and so on. There is no positive direction given to your life by the development of cowardice.[2]

Emerging here is an interesting asymmetry between virtues and vices: a virtue expresses a positive aim at some overall good way of developing, and so a commitment to goodness, while a vice does not express a corresponding positive aim at developing in a bad way, and so a commitment to badness. Cowardly, stingy, and envious people have immediate aims, of course: to save their life or get to safety, to minimize giving to others, to stop or spoil others' possession of something they themselves want and lack. But they are not aiming at becoming better cowards, misers, and gloaters. That is the way they are developing in the way they act, if it becomes characteristic, but it is not, so to say, their career aim. Cowards who are openly shown to be such can be proud of being cowardly only by trying to show that they really are aiming at something worthwhile.[3]

Why does a coward not explicitly aim to make himself cowardly, to learn to be a better coward? Obviously, because there is nothing *good* about being a coward, even if it is, in the circumstances, useful. Someone

---

[2] The distinction the Stoics make between our immediate objectives in acting (*skopoi*) and the overall aim of becoming a certain kind of person (*telos*) makes this point sharply. It is a pity that it has no resonance in contemporary discussion.

[3] Falstaff claims that others' notions of honour are mistaken. Parolles can find nothing good in his life overall; he says he will live 'safest in shame', but cannot go on living as he has done.

who cultivates cowardice does so as a means to other ends (sometimes through pressure of circumstances), but there is an internal problem in trying to aspire to, and be proud of, being a coward. Hence the coward who cares about the kind of person he is has to persuade himself that he is being prudent, thinking only of the usefulness of cowardice for other ends rather than cowardice as indicative of the kind of person he is. Similarly with the stingy person who persuades herself that she is being careful, and so on.

This is, I think, an intuitive and everyday way of thinking of the difference between virtues, vices, and neutral dispositions. Broadly, virtue is a successful commitment to goodness, vice a failure to commit to goodness, and dispositions which are neither, are neither virtues nor vices but just traits we have. The distinctions this enables us to make will converge, as we shall see, with those from the last chapter about the unification of the virtues in an integrated outlook on one's life as a whole.

Isn't this, however, a rather weak account of vice? Admitting that we don't aspire to be the kinds of people who are cowards, stingy and so on, still, surely people don't commit genocide or sadistic murders out of failure to become good? If we think of an intuitive list of bad people, we will come up with Hitler, Pol Pot, Ivan the Terrible, Genghis Khan, and others who don't seem like people incompetently aiming at goodness.

This overlooks the point that the nature of vice is not entirely to be discovered from whether the vicious person is committed to goodness or to badness. Some vices depend on weakness, but many do not. Many are both robustly terrible in themselves and productive of terrible results. Cruelty, for example, involves pleasure in other's suffering just for its own sake, and the cruel person is usually aware that her actions and disposition are destructive of other's good and of good aspects of herself. So any reasonable account of vice should not fail to take into account the point that many vices are deeply horrible, and express themselves in actively terrible ways. Only some express themselves in actions which are feeble or confused. We can see this simply from reflecting on the ways we learn about vices, which are like the ways we learn about virtues. Just as we come to find some of the good role models put forward for us compelling and others merely attractive, so we come to be *repelled* by some of the bad, as well as finding some of them merely despicable or regrettable.

104 VIRTUE AND GOODNESS

This is, however, quite distinct from the question of whether a vice could be like a virtue in involving a positive commitment to value—in the case of vice, badness rather than goodness. It does not affect the difficulty we have in seeing the vicious person as aiming at badness, doing actions precisely in order to become a bad person. It is this which is hard to make sense of. Milton's Satan says, 'Evil be thou my good,' and some have thought, with Robert Adams, that, '[t]he fascination of Milton's Satan is due in no small part to the fact that it does seem humanly possible, in bitter resentment and despair, to make it a life-principle to try to do great evils because they are evil.'[4] The pointlessly malicious seem to be those who are, as Adams says, so deeply disillusioned about goodness that they act out of resentment of it. This is a rather sophisticated state to be in with respect to goodness, which is presumably why devilish malice is less common in everyday life than thoughtlessness, insensitivity, and the like. But it is still problematic to see it as a positive attachment to badness.

The idea of vice as a failed or misguided commitment to goodness need not, then, lead us to underestimate the evil and nastiness that the vicious are capable of. Deliberate cruelty and malice come from a deep alienation from goodness, even if not a positive commitment to badness.[5] The idea that vice is some way of failing to be good does not imply, as is sometimes thought, that vice is not itself an extremely bad state,[6] nor that some vices are not energetically horrible. Nor is the idea that vice is a way of failing to be good so implausible when we read about criminal perpetrators of violent and horrible crimes; many of these people do not have any wicked aim or ideal, but are simply people who have allowed themselves to become strikingly selfish and insensitive to others, and often have failed to develop self-control.[7]

---

[4] Adams (2006: 41).

[5] See Haybron (2002), who talks in terms of the wicked person's failure to be aligned to the good.

[6] I say 'state' here rather than 'disposition', as might be expected from the treatment of virtue, because there is no reason to expect vice to be parallel to virtue in its internal structure. Since the vicious person does not aim at becoming cowardly, insensitive, and so on, vice does not exhibit the kind of progression in practical reasoning that characterizes the development of virtue, and so is not essentially dynamic in the way that virtue is. There is also no internal drive for the vices to become unified; a coward is not thereby motivated to become spiteful or unfair.

[7] 'Poor impulse control' is the de-moralized term for this.

Goodness and Kinds of Trait

So far we have only a very general characterization of what makes virtue admirable and inspiring as an ideal, namely commitment to goodness. But we can at least see something distinctive about virtue. Virtue is committed to goodness *because* it is good; the brave and generous do not merely have overall aims in their lives that turn out, as a matter of fact, to be good. Rather, they have an attitude to goodness which can be described as commitment: goodness attracts them in a way that the vicious are not attracted, and the mediocre are attracted only weakly.

What of the traits which are not vicious, but not virtues either—wittiness, tidiness, cleanliness, affability, and the like? As we saw at the end of the last chapter, dispositions such as these resemble virtues—they may be reliable dispositions to act, think, and feel in certain ways—but they are not virtues. We saw there that they are not integrated with the virtues: that someone is clean, hard-working, and witty is no guide as to whether he has virtues such as bravery or fairness (nor vice versa); these dispositions (as well as a range of talents) can be exercised either virtuously or viciously. We can now say something further as to why these dispositions are not virtues. A reason that wittiness, tidiness, and affability do not integrate with the virtues is because they do not express or indicate a commitment to goodness. This illuminates why they can be exercised just as well viciously as virtuously.

Wittiness, tidiness, and the like are thus not admirable in the distinctive way the virtues are. We do, of course, fairly frequently think of the person who has intelligently developed her disposition to be witty or affable as being admirable. This is, as we have seen, a recognizable sense of admirability, in which people can be found admirable just because they are amusing or agreeable to be with, or useful to others, for example, without being admirable for the kind of people they are. There is, however, a sharp as well as distinctive difference between our attitudes to virtues and these other dispositions, as emerges clearly from a brief comparison with Hume's very different account of virtues.

Hume defines a virtue as a disposition[8] which is useful and/or agreeable to the person whose disposition it is or to others. (On its own this is clearly

---

[8] He uses terms such as 'quality' and does not build reliability into his account of what a virtue is, but it is clear from his overall treatment that he does think a virtue is a reliable disposition.

inadequate, and it is supplemented elsewhere, but my point depends only on the present aspect of his account.[9]) The virtuous person, on this kind of account, will be the person whose dispositions (or 'qualities') are useful or agreeable to himself or to others. Hume gives us a description of a person, Cleanthes, presented as a perfect son-in-law.[10] 'Everyone, who has any intercourse with him, is sure of *fair* and *kind* treatment [qualities useful to others] . . . '[his] assiduous application to the study of the laws . . . quick penetration and early knowledge both of men and business, prognosticate the greatest honours and advancement' (qualities useful to himself). Cleanthes is also 'the life and soul' of the company: 'so much wit with good manners; so much gallantry without affectation; so much ingenious knowledge so genteelly delivered' (qualities immediately agreeable to others). Finally, he has 'greatness of mind' enabling him to be 'still superior' to past 'severe trials, misfortunes as well as dangers' (qualities immediately agreeable to the person himself). Everyone agrees that he is the perfect son-in-law for the writer. (The prospective wife's opinion is nowhere mentioned.)

'A philosopher', says Hume, 'might select this character as a model of perfect virtue'. It is always hard to be sure that we have got Hume's tone right, but if he is not being ironic here it is obvious that something is amiss. A yuppy lawyer who is great company at parties is a model of perfect virtue? Can this be serious? What has gone wrong here? We do not need to go into Hume's account of virtue in depth to discover it (one reason why the example is useful in the present connection). What the description of Cleanthes brings out is that someone may have a character that is useful and agreeable to himself and others, and still be utterly *uninspiring*, somebody that nobody could take an *ideal* of a *good* person to be.

Let us compare Cleanthes with someone who really is admirable and inspiring and has served as an ideal to countlessly many: Socrates.[11]

---

[9] See Hursthouse (1999*b*). Hume's account of virtue is to be found in book III of the *Treatise*, parts 2 and 3, and in the *Enquiry Concerning the Principles of Morals*.

[10] Hume (2006), *Enquiry*, IX. pt. 1. Hume's picture of virtue is thus quite explicitly limited to men, and does not transfer to women. This is not an accident, given that his account does not claim to go deeper than the level at which people find dispositions to be in fact useful or agreeable in their society; Hume is writing for a society in which men's usefulness, etc. is the default.

[11] Astonishingly, Hume does claim *en passant* that we admire Socrates, shortly before the notorious Cleanthes passage (*Enquiry*, VII. 16–17 (though here Socrates is raised above the merely human), VIII. 10 (where Socrates is praised for what we would call his robust

Socrates' dispositions were of course not at all useful to himself or his family: his commitment to searching for truth led him to neglect his own business affairs and reduce them all to poverty. Socrates' character was in fact useful to the Athenians, in stirring them to think about their values, but this was hardly clear to them, since they recognized this too late, after executing him. Also, Socrates' character may or may not have been agreeable to himself, but it was certainly very disagreeable to others. We can see from Plato's portrayal that he was relentless in showing up the confusions of others; in defending himself on a capital charge, in Plato's account he compares himself to a gadfly, a horrible stinging insect that nobody wants to have around, even if it stirs them into activity. Yet Socrates is a clear example of virtue; he has been talked about and studied for two thousand years, and even today serves as the paradigm of the philosopher refusing to compromise his values and commitments. Usefulness and agreeableness are clearly not even necessary for someone to be an example of virtue. We admire Socrates and take him as an ideal even while being perfectly aware that he was probably a complete pain to have around, and that following Socrates might well lead you to a result which is the opposite of what anybody else would consider useful. We inspire children with accounts and pictures of people like Socrates, not of successful lawyers and businessmen like Cleanthes.

For Cleanthes to be a real example of virtue, we would have to have some idea of whether he is characteristically committed to goodness—let us just say here, to simplify, to being a person of honesty and integrity. And we know nothing whatever about this just from knowing how useful and agreeable he is to himself and others. We assume from the passage (though it isn't explicitly said) that his practice in law and business is honest. But can he be guaranteed not to bend to pressure if threatened with ruin, if the government changes, if he suddenly finds himself a member of an unpopular minority? We can't say yes, for we have no idea how committed Cleanthes is to honesty and integrity, or whether he can be relied on to stick with honest dealings when this gets difficult or risky. His 'greatness of mind' is not presented as integrity or the courage to stand by commitments to others, only as the ability to stay tranquil through his own danger and

---

self-esteem)). But on Hume's own account it is utterly strange that we should do so. Hume does think that people are admirable for different virtues in different contexts, but it is hard to see how Socrates could ever be squeezed into the 'useful and agreeable' paradigm.

misfortune—and this quality contributes to virtue, we are told, in that it is 'immediately agreeable' *to Cleanthes!* The whole picture tells us nothing whatever about Cleanthes' character, or the kind of person he is; we learn nothing at all about how he would deal with other, less favourable, circumstances.

This is an illustration of what we have already seen, namely that a trait is not a virtue if it is not integrated with other virtues—and clearly it is irrelevant to this how useful and agreeable to anyone it is. We can now see, from considering cases such as those of Cleanthes, that pressing the issue of commitment to goodness also sorts out dispositions which are virtues from those that are useful and/or agreeable, but not virtues. (We also don't know whether Cleanthes would continue to be a great guest in bad circumstances, but this obviously does not matter in the way that his honesty does for the issue of whether he is really a virtuous person.)

This distinction between virtues and other dispositions also illuminates why we admire 'virtue in rags', as Hume puts it—virtuous people who meet with great misfortune. We admire Socrates condemned, Nelson Mandela in prison, Aung Sang Suu Kyi after fifteen years' house arrest (which she could have escaped at any point by abandoning her country). Hume's answer to the point that we admire people for their character in circumstances in which they are neither useful nor agreeable to anyone is that our esteem for virtue follows general rules and so somehow omits to take this failure into account.[12] Hume thinks that this is not very damaging, because we retain the idea that if virtue became more successful our admiration for it would no longer have to be so circumscribed.

This defence fails; it runs up against two points. We don't admire wittiness, tidiness, or affability 'in rags'. We feel sorry for witty, tidy, and affable people when they meet with misfortune, but so far there is no reason for us to admire them. And this is connected to the second point: we admire *virtue* in rags *precisely for* the commitment to virtue that led to virtue being in rags. What we admire, that is, is precisely what prevents the

---

[12] *Treatise,* III. iii. 1. Our esteem for virtue in rags is a special case of a general tendency we have to follow 'general rules'; 'where a character is in every respect fitted to be beneficial to society, the imagination passes easily from the cause to the effect, without considering that there are still some circumstances wanting to render the cause a compleat one'. So even in Hume's own terms our esteem for virtue in rags is at best carelessness.

virtuous person being, in the relevant bad circumstances, eithe
agreeable to herself or others.[13]

I have focused on Hume's example of the pedestrian
(although it does not of course show that Hume's account or virtue is
faulty in its own terms, since it differs from the present account at every
point), because it shows so clearly something which an account such as
Hume's cannot account for, whereas an account such as the present one
can. Virtues are dispositions which are not only admirable but which we
find *inspiring* and take as *ideals* to aspire to, precisely because of the
commitment to goodness which they embody. I take it that this is a
point which can be appreciated at an everyday level. We encourage
children in schools, by means of posters, lessons, and books, to admire
and aspire to be like some people and not others, and these are people
whose *characters* are admirable and inspiring because of their commitment
to goodness, regardless of whether in worldly terms they succeeded or
failed, or were useful and/or agreeable to themselves or to other people.
That is why it would be grotesque to have posters in elementary schools
depicting Donald Trump as a hero for the young, rather than people like
King, Gandhi, and Mandela.[14]

Kinds of Commitment to Goodness

Commitment to goodness is, then, a distinguishing factor in virtue, and
meshes with the results we have seen from considering the unity of the
virtues; it gives an account, at a general level, of what it is that unifies the
virtues and distinguishes them from the traits that cannot be integrated
with these. So far, though, the idea of commitment to goodness is still very
general. We now need to distinguish specific ways in which virtue can be
committed to goodness, for it turns out that there are many very different

[13] Note that we don't admire the witty person who ends 'in rags' precisely because of
commitment to wittiness; this just shows bad judgement (examples would be even more
bizarre for tidiness or affability). This reflects the view that these traits are not *worth* this kind of
commitment.

[14] Of course the admiration here may not translate into actually taking the person as any
kind of pattern for one's life; many parents who focus on the circumstances rather than the
living of a life pressure their children into taking Trump, rather than Mandela, as a model for
success, though not expecting posters of Trump in the classroom. Such a division of what is
admired and what is encouraged in a life often leads to inner conflict later on, or the withering
of admiration into lip-service.

such ways. These in turn distinguish different kinds of theory in which virtue figures, and I shall distinguish these, without discussing them in detail.

We can see already from the contrast with vice that it cannot be adequate to take virtue just to be a disposition which does in fact contribute to goodness. Why not? We can appreciate this by considering a particular kind of account of virtue, namely a consequentialist one, which takes as fundamental the point that right action is that which produces good (usually maximizing it, though there are variants). This kind of account thinks of virtues as dispositions to act (rather than as dispositions to act on certain kinds of reason). Acting rightly produces good (in the way favoured by the theory), and a disposition to act rightly will be a disposition that reliably produces good. A virtue, then, will be a disposition of character which produces good, since it is a disposition to act rightly. This has to be fine-tuned, of course: the disposition has to produce good systematically, not occasionally or by accident, and there are complications about the need to stipulate conditions under which the disposition will in fact produce good in the actual world.[15] An account of this sort holds that a disposition is a virtue if it systematically *does* produce good in our world (not, for example, if it would, but only under ideal circumstances). Obviously, whether generosity does actually produce good systematically in our world depends on a large number of factors, many of which are subject to change and modification as circumstances change. Thus, the issue of whether a disposition is a virtue will depend on actual consequences; which consequences it systematically produces will depend on circumstances, and a change in circumstances can alter the way it systematically produces good, perhaps bringing it about that it no longer does so. Changed circumstances, then, can turn a virtue into a neutral disposition or even a vice, even though the disposition itself remains unchanged.

This conflicts problematically with a number of central thoughts we have about virtue in everyday life. We think that virtue is its own reward, for example, since we deny virtue to those whose virtuous behaviour turns out to depend on ulterior motives.[16] We judge people not only on the

---

[15] See Driver (2001: ch. 4).

[16] Of course we are seldom in a position to judge this accurately. In our own case, however, our own judgements that we are generous, say, tend to be tentative at best, since we are aware of the difficulty of being certain about our reasons, motives, and feelings.

basis of what they do, and what that achieves, but on the basis of their character—the kind of person they are. We admire someone of good character even if their attempts to do good misfire because of unforeseeable circumstances. Our thought about virtue is centred on people and the way they are, rather than on their actions and the consequences of these. Moreover, we think of virtues as robust dispositions which can be compared across circumstances and even cultures, which makes it problematic to think that a disposition plastic enough to be pushed and pulled around by changing circumstances could be a virtue.

A consequentialist account can try to meet these problems. It can try, for example, to show that the theory does not have to deny the above points, which will involve reinterpreting many of the ideas. But it is anyway clear that any consequentialist account of virtue fails to account for the important point about a virtue which we are exploring here, namely that it involves a commitment to goodness *because* it is goodness. This is what marks virtues off from neutral dispositions and vices, and shows that what makes a disposition a virtue is not the results it produces but, broadly speaking, the attitude of the person who has the virtue. This is not, of course, a surprise to an account like the present one, which has emphasized the central role in virtue of the agent's own practical reasoning, not the results of having a virtue. An account of virtue which rejects this is left having to reject a number of very central aspects of our conception of virtue. Whether this is seen as a liability or not will depend on the theory's methodology. As I have several times underlined, the present account is one which aims to build upwards from our conceptions of virtue, rather than start on the level of abstract discussion of already developed theory. From this point of view losing such central aspects of virtue makes it at least unclear what the point is of having a theory of virtue at all. It should also be clear by this point that working from and with our pre-theoretical understanding of virtue goes with finding the *practicality* of virtue central, rather than looking for an account of virtue that does not make it clear how it relates to practice.

We need to appeal, then, not just to a virtue's ability to produce or promote goodness, but to the agent herself and the kind of commitment to goodness involved in her virtuous reasoning and attitude, not just her actions. As we start to specify kinds of goodness here we see different options. Something obvious, though not commented on so far, is that we should not expect all commitments to goodness to have the same form.

On one view, commonly called pluralism, we should not think of virtue as a *single* commitment to a single form of goodness. Virtue is just the virtues, a collection of distinct dispositions that we develop, committed to a range of different values, and thus to a range of *distinct* forms of goodness. On this kind of view, generosity expresses commitment to the value of helping others; patience, to the value of enduring difficulties calmly; bravery, to the value of being able to stand up against difficulties for what is worthwhile; and so on; but there will be no reason to think that these values are the same kind of value, that the same kind of goodness can be found in all of them. Someone with these virtues is committed to three *different* values, not to goodness in general, and so not to the idea of being a good person overall.

This kind of view can seem commonsensical, as long as we think of the virtues in isolation from one another. It is easy, as we have seen, to conceive of virtues as dispositions required to deal with different circumstances of life—a soldier needs courage while a caregiver needs patience; if we stop at this point it will indeed seem that the virtues have little if anything in common, and even that they will lead our energies in divergent directions. On this view different ways of life are focused on different values, and the virtues needed in different ways of life will tend in divergent directions, and in a single way of life may even conflict. The patient person's commitment may well conflict with that of the brave person; at any rate there is, on this view, no reason to think that their lives express commitment to the same value.

One kind of pluralist theory accepts this point about the virtues and holds that we should not go further in trying to unify them, for this will be a theoretical forcing of structure on dispositions which in actual life are disunified.[17] Nietzsche goes further in taking up the point that on this view virtues might conflict. Unsurprisingly, he holds that conflict among virtues is a fact not just to be recognized but to be welcomed as a healthy sign of development and psychological growth. Forcing unification on the virtues and aiming at a harmonious and settled character is, for Nietzsche, repression of aspects of the self in the interests of aiming at stasis, and this is unhealthy.[18] It is worth pointing out that whether we recognize plurality

---

[17] Swanton (2003) and Adams (2006) discuss the issues here.
[18] Nietzsche's view of virtues is affected by the point that he thinks that a properly scientific way of understanding them is simply as drives competing for the person's energy. See my (forthcoming).

or actually encourage conflict we lose what seems to be a central difference of virtue from skill, namely that skills are local. If virtues are plural in the sense of being committed to distinct and unrelated or even conflicting values, we lose any systematic way of contrasting virtues with local skills. This is visible, for example, in the way that Nietzsche's aggressive pluralism takes a healthy human life to exhibit artistic skills and abilities as much as, or more than, virtues.

Both these kinds of account—taking virtues to be dispositions which produce goodness independently of the person's reasoning, and taking virtues to aim at values which are mutually independent or even conflicting—assume that we can and should give an account of virtue which is independent of the virtuous person's overall aim in life, and so independent of their flourishing. Relatedly, on neither of these accounts does the practical reasoning which the person uses in becoming and being virtuous involve the person's life as a whole; it is not the business of practical reason, on these views, to integrate in a unified life all the different concerns that arise in the areas in which the different virtues are exercised.

The account of virtue developed here diverges from both these kinds of account; an adequate account of virtue does need to relate it to the person's flourishing (their happiness, as we shall shortly see). It's already clear that an account of virtue which stresses its practicality, and the relevance of the skill analogy, will reject consequentialist accounts, and we have already seen that the distinction between the circumstances of a life and the living of a life undercuts the main basis for a pluralist account of the virtues. This does not, of course, amount to an argued rejection of these kinds of theory; at the moment I am merely locating the present account with respect to virtue's commitment to goodness (and hence virtue's relation to the person's overall flourishing).

We need to consider, then, accounts of virtue in which they are unified, by the person's practical reasoning, over her life as a whole. It is worth noting that the previous kind of account, in which the virtues are considered in a pluralistic way, still needs the person's life to be integrated in some way (though Nietzschean versions might differ, preferring to think of a person's life as fluid rather than shaped overall). On such an account, however, the unification of the person's life will have to come from some source such as purely prudential reasoning, rather than being due to the practical reasoning involved in the development of the virtues themselves.

I shall go on to consider accounts where the person's life is conceived as unified, or at least integrated, in terms of a commitment to goodness in their life overall.

We can make a broad distinction here between two conceptions of goodness: goodness transcending a human life and goodness in the living of a human life. One version of the former is a Platonic theory, where we are motivated to aim at goodness that we can at best glimpse only partially and in an inadequate way in living a human life—in Plato's own case (in the *Republic* at least) the Form of the Good. In some versions of religious ethics this is the role of God.[19] On this view, the different kinds of goodness that the distinct virtues are committed to are seen as images or fragmentary reflections of a transcendent goodness that humans cannot aspire to achieve in anything like a complete or undistorted form in the living of a human life. The virtues we do have will be correspondingly fragmented and frail versions of commitment to goodness, as we do the best we can but are always frustrated by the limitations of human life and the conflicts and failures that it inevitably brings with it. Just how fragmented and frail will depend on how optimistic or pessimistic the account is about our abilities to get very far in our efforts to attain this transcendent goodness. Plato himself is generally quite pessimistic about this, and thus about our chances for unifying our own virtues, and so our own lives. Religious versions of this kind of account also differ greatly among themselves on this issue.

For accounts of virtue that hold the second conception of goodness, we do not need a good transcending human life as an ideal. Rather, the virtues can, and should in a good life, be unified by reference to something *in* human life. This is, familiarly, the approach of Aristotle, who rejects Plato's Form of the Good because it is not 'practical', not an aim that actually helps anyone to live their life better.[20] This kind of approach is often characterized as naturalistic, since it appeals to nothing beyond human nature as we find that in our ordinary lives, and it is familiar in

---

[19] See Adams (2006) for a theory of this kind (in this book the discussion is limited to virtue in living a human life). There are other forms of religious virtue ethics, which fall under the second conception of goodness, since they see the life of religious or spiritual achievement as to be achieved in living determinate kinds of life, observing certain practices, and so on.

[20] *NE* I. 6 (1096^a11–1097^a14).

contemporary ethical philosophy.[21] On this view, although in exercising different virtues the virtuous person is directed towards different values, the different virtues can, and should in a good life, be unified by the person's living their life in accordance with a unified conception of goodness, one to be discovered and exercised by the person's practical reasoning, which unifies the acquisition and expression of the virtues. The virtues are, then, unified into an integrated commitment to goodness and are exercised in the living of a good, flourishing life.

This idea, of living a virtuous life, can in turn be understood in two very different ways. One is a *circumstantial* understanding of a virtuous life, one which specifies it in terms of a particular set of circumstances. There are some passages in Plato, and some in Aristotle, in which they extol the life of theoretical reasoning (sometimes called the life of contemplation) as the life the virtuous person will lead. In both cases it is controversial. In part this is because of its content: there have always been people to whom the idea of a life devoted to contemplation seems inadequate to, or inappropriate, for humans.[22] More important is the point that to think that one way of life, specified in terms of its circumstances, is what can unify the practice of different virtues is to neglect the difference, already stressed several times, between the living of a life and the circumstances of a life. History is full of people telling us that the virtuous life can be lived only in some particular set of circumstances; sometimes, like Plato and Aristotle in these passages, they provide arguments for this, sometimes they merely try to impose it on other people. All such attempts meet reasonable resistance as serious accounts of the virtuous life, because they don't distinguish between the circumstances of a life and the living of a life, and so are merely accounts of one kind of good life, not accounts of what would be a good way for everyone to live their lives.

The second conception of living a virtuous life is one in which the distinction between the circumstances of a life and the living of the life is

---

[21] This does not make it naturalistic in one of its contemporary senses, a narrower sense in which an account is naturalistic only if its methods conform to those of the contemporary sciences. Some accounts accept this narrower sense while others do not.

[22] Aristotle's *Nicomachean Ethics* contains such a specification, as half of what we read as book X; it is clearly irreconcilable with the passage we read as book I, despite vast amounts of ingenuity spent trying to make them look like parts of the same work. Plato in some passages presents the aim of the virtuous person as flight from this world and becoming like God (who has no human virtues); on the difficulties involved in this see my (1999: ch. III).

respected, so that the understanding of a virtuous life is *non-circumstantial*. The different kinds of goodness to which exercise of the different virtues commits the virtuous person are unified, simply, in the person's life's being lived *well*. The life is thus unified in being lived virtuously, but this life can be lived in a variety of circumstances and ways of life, and so implies none of them in particular—not a life of contemplation, nor one of political engagement, military ambition, or whatever. We have already seen that and how a virtuous life can be lived in very disparate circumstances. There is no one circumstantially specified good life in which the virtues have to be exercised. Many different specific kinds of life, in different circumstances, can be lived virtuously. This is the kind of account that has been developed here.

The virtues are not just admirable but inspire us as an ideal, whether or not they are useful and agreeable. They are inspiring, not just useful or agreeable, because exercising virtue is a commitment on the part of the virtuous person to goodness because it is goodness: goodness is not just an outcome. The different virtues appear to be focused on different values, but the virtuous life consists in the living of a life, not its circumstances, and so the diversity of ways of life and the values they focus on is not a barrier to the unification of the virtues, and thus an aspiration to a good life overall. Moreover, the account of practical reasoning that we have seen developed actually leads, as we have seen, to the unification of the virtues.

The *ideal* and aspirational side of the virtues has now been brought out several times, from different angles, and it is clear how important it is.[23] Together with the unification of the virtues, it leads us towards a deeper understanding of the idea that virtue involves a commitment to goodness, an idea that can be fully grasped only by the study of the many diverging ways that lives can be lived. The route by which we have come to this conclusion illustrates the way I have aimed to build up an account of virtue from our understandings of it, giving it the appropriate contours without forcing or deforming it. Accounts of virtue which begin from definitions based on more abstract grounds produce tidier accounts, but, I suggest, ones which risk missing some of the ways in which virtue is part of our lives and also directs the way we live them.

---

[23] To repeat: this is not to be confused with any form of perfectionism, in which we know beforehand what the ideal achievements are that we are to attain. The ideal aspect of virtue leads us to aspire continually, not to get the prize and then retire.

We can see from the above that there is a sense in which virtue, in an account of the present kind (not all accounts, nor even, as we have seen, all the ones in which virtue is committed to goodness) gives a life what we can call a positive directionality. The life is pointed in a positive direction by the fact that the aims and values the person pursues form a whole which is marked by absence of conflict and increasing cooperation of the sources of energy. This is not like the kind of direction given to a life by the exclusive pursuit of money, say, or of fame. The kind of direction given to a life by virtue is a direction of overall aim in the *way the life is lived*—in the aim to live *well*, to live a *good* life—not a direction given by a specific objective such as wealth or fame, which can be pursued either virtuously or viciously.

Contrast a life in which wealth is pursued honestly, with rejection of corruption and greed, and a life in which wealth is pursued dishonestly, with every means to increase wealth sought regardless of honesty or dishonesty. The vicious life may well display more outwardly discernible direction in being relentlessly focused on achieving one kind of object, namely wealth, and can be made sense of in these terms. The direction of the virtuous life is less obvious from external observation, and may be clear only when we can take into account the person's reasons and feelings as well as his actions. (Something which almost none of us is in a position to do; but we have a partial idea of this from the way in which a biography revealing a person's values may revise our estimate of the kind of life they led.) The virtuous life, then, may not appear to have the kind of strong direction given by the pursuit of a single objective (and so it may not appear a success from a point of view that values the achievement of this objective). Both its unity and its positive direction· can only become apparent when we know something about the person and his character, not just what she does and what she aims at in what she does. Only then can we appreciate the direction given to the person's life by their commitment to living it in a way that is brave rather than cowardly, generous rather than stingy, and so on.

We have had from several different angles what I hope is a reasonably full picture of virtue, something often oversimplified. The account of virtue I am presenting and defending is one in which practical reasoning is central (this is clear from the extensive usefulness of the skill analogy) and which covers a fairly specific range of positions on the ways in which virtue involves a commitment to goodness. The account I have presented is Aristotelian in one respect, namely in stressing the importance of practical reasoning in the acquisition and exercise of the virtues. In another respect, namely in being open to a quite wide variety of ways in which virtue can express a commitment to goodness, it is much wider than Aristotle's own account, which commits itself to a version of naturalism (and in this has been followed by the Aristotelian tradition).

We now come to the second theme of this book, namely that virtue constitutes (at least in part) the person's flourishing or happiness. Thus we come to happiness after, rather than before, an examination of virtue. Contemporaries often still find it puzzling that the virtuous life could turn out so much as to have anything to do with the happy life. Virtue and happiness are often discussed in different theoretical contexts, and attempts to bring them together seem forced and implausible. I shall argue first that we have, and are familiar with, a certain conception of happiness, and that, although it is not the only one we have, it is central for us. I will then argue that this conception of happiness enables us to make sense of the idea that virtue constitutes, at least in part, the happy life, and to see the force of arguments for even stronger positions.

8

Living Happily

The very idea that virtue might have any role in flourishing or happiness has seemed, for about two hundred years, deeply unlikely. Philosophers in that period have been among the most robust in insisting that the whole idea of thinking that virtue could lead to happiness is absurd. Bentham says of the idea that virtue is sufficient for happiness, 'What benefit, in any shape, could be derived from impregnating the memory with such non-sense? What instruction from a self-contradictory proposition?'[1] Nietzsche is even more dismissive. 'Such assertions and promises as those of the antique philosophers concerning the unity of virtue and happiness or the Christian, "But seek ye first the kingdom of God, and his righteousness, and all these things shall be added unto you" have never been made with total honesty and yet always without a bad conscience: one has advanced such propositions, which one very much desires to be true, boldly as to the truth in the face of appearance.'[2] This idea, that there is some kind of naive wish-fulfilment or over-optimism in the claim that the virtuous are happy, lingers more effectively than actual arguments. Up to this point I have used the interim term 'flourishing' rather than happiness, but this has not been intended to avoid the issue stated brutally by Bentham and Nietzsche, and I shall now talk in terms of happiness.

We should begin by reflecting that there is an oddity here. It is common to find this assumption, that there must *of course* be a conceptual gulf between virtue and happiness or flourishing, making it problematic or even absurd to think that happiness could require being virtuous. And yet

---

[1] Bentham (1983: 300). This is his response to Cicero's *Tusculan Disputations*, whose last book argues that virtue is sufficient for happiness. Bentham does not mention that he chose this book to study for his final examination at Oxford, boasting to his father about how well he performed (presumably not by venting the above response).

[2] Nietzsche (1997: 456).

few of us have any half-way definite account to give either of what virtue is or of what happiness is. Where does the assurance come from that virtue and happiness *must* come into conflict when there is so little agreement (general or among philosophers) about what either is? The assurance may partly come from other sources,[3] but it is likely to come at least in part from confusion about what virtue and happiness are. The revival of ethical thought which gives a role to virtue has helped us to get clearer about virtue, but the same can't be said for the recent surge of work on happiness in a number of academic areas as well as in popular culture. We have recovered the thought that happiness is an important concept for ethics, but there has never been a greater cacophony of voices from different directions on the topic of what happiness is.[4]

As with virtue, I think that we can be helped here by looking at the resources we can find in traditions of ethical enquiry preceding the era in which thinkers as different as Bentham and Nietzsche could be equally at a loss when thinking of virtuous flourishing lives. I shall therefore start by looking at flourishing or happiness as that figures in eudaimonist accounts. I shall claim that it is not only viable but natural for us to think of happiness in the way these theories develop it. (This account will not be complete until the next chapter, which brings it together with the present account of virtue.) I will then look at the major competing claims as to what happiness is which I can extract from a (necessarily very selective) survey of current views, asking about the extent to which these might suggest modifications to a eudaimonist account.

Eudaimonism

What is a eudaimonist account? An account of how to live, one in which happiness, *eudaimonia*, is central. While *eudaimonia* just means 'happiness' in the ancient world, it is obviously, for us, to be understood in terms of the role it plays in a eudaimonist account. Here, happiness is a central concept (not, and this is important, the basic or foundational concept), but

---

[3] e.g. identifying virtue with morality, and assuming uncritically that morality is about others' interests and happiness about your own, making it appear problematic that one should seek one's own interests in a way that gives a more than instrumental role to those of others.

[4] See Haybron (2008), Kraut (1979), Layard (2005), Myers (1992), Seligman (2002), Tiberius (2008). Accounts of virtue vary widely, as we've seen, but with happiness there is even less agreement.

it is not the first concept that we encounter. Rather, the entry point for ethical reflection[5] is thinking about how your life is going, thinking that can only arise in people who already are, or are becoming, adult, and who are aware that everything in their life is not satisfactory. Nearly all of us engage in this reflection, since it is exceptionally rare for our lives to be completely satisfactory and to give us no basis for reflection on how they are going. Some people do seem never to be led to step back from their lives and reflect on them; usually this is because their lives have been fortunate and they have never had to question the relative importance in their lives of fortune and of the way they live their lives.

So you step back from the ongoing happenings of your life, and wonder about how and in what direction it is going. This at once reveals a fundamental difference between two ways in which you can regard your life. One perspective is the everyday one, in which you do one thing after another, one action following another chronologically. You get up, go to work and so on, one thing after another until eventually it comes to an end when your life does. This is the linear way of thinking of your life, and it is important as you get through the day, and in many other ways. But reflection reveals another way in which your life enters your thoughts about it. We can call this the structured way of thinking of your life.

Take the action you are now doing or have just done. You can think of it in the linear way, as coming after the previous action and going on to (perhaps giving rise to) the next one. But you can also ask yourself about it, *why* am I doing this action (and not another one)? With very trivial actions there may be no substantive answer to this, but with most actions there is. Why are you doing exercises?—To keep fit. Why are you keeping fit?—To be healthy. Why are you aiming to be healthy? Or: why are you reading that book?—To learn how to make a software program. Why are you aiming to make a software program? – To become a computer expert. – Why are you aiming to become a computer expert?—To have a good career. Why are you aiming at having a good career? These ways of following through the question 'Why?' indicate what you are aiming at in what you do, not just now but in your life more broadly. Actions are related, then, not just chronologically but also by the relation of one being

---

[5] This is how I characterize the starting-point for ethical theory in the ancient world in Annas (1993); I have come (in large part through teaching) to think it still available, and compelling as a starting-point, in the contemporary world.

for the sake of another, and as you think of them in this way in your own life, it reveals what you are aiming at in doing what you are doing. One point that emerges rapidly is that the goals we have in life are *nested*: the answers to the question about reading the book become ever more general, each smaller goal turning out to be for the sake of a broader one. Your actions fit into structured patterns in your life; a snapshot of what you are doing at one time turns out to reveal, when we think about these structures, what your broader aims and goals in life are.

Thus from reflecting about things I do every day I come to find that I have several broader and long-term goals. I want to be healthy, to have a good career, to have a good family life, to take a safe and simple example. Do we end there? At first it may seem reasonable to do so. I have several long-term goals; what is wrong with that? A life with any degree of complexity will surely have several larger goals within which smaller everyday goals are nested. But in fact once the structured way of thinking about our actions gets going, it turns out to have a unifying tendency which has us thinking about the goals revealed in our lives. First, the goals I have need to be compatible, since I don't stay statically at the stage of wanting, for example, a good career and a good family life. In some circumstances I can aim at both without worrying about possible conflicts, but in many I will have to give some thought to conflicts in achieving these jointly. My partner may want to move just at the point that my career is taking off in a place favourable to it. This sort of consideration comes up all the time with our various goals, and so the thinking that makes clear to me what my goals are in the way I am acting and living my life is also thinking that raises the question of how these goals are to be made consistent. In everyday life we do this all the time without thinking much about it when the answers are obvious: we stop working for a degree once we decide that we no longer value the having of the degree, or need a different degree, for example. But when our goals are such that there is a built-in conflict among them, or one or more are confused or self-undermining, reflection brings these issues to the surface and gets us thinking about how to adjust, modify, or reorganize the goals so that they can be achieved in a consistent way.

Reflection thus both triggers and then furthers thinking about how to achieve the goals I have in the light of the constraints I have (time, money, energy) and their mutual achievability. This thinking is unifying about the goals because they are all *my* goals, and I need to have an integrated and unifying way of achieving them because I have only one life, the life I am living. What is activated is not thinking in the abstract about types of goal and how they could fit together, but thinking about how *I* can achieve the goals I have in the life I have. It is thinking about my life and how it is going. It is *practical* thinking, thinking about my life and how I should structure it.[6]

Thus the original everyday thinking about the way one thing I do is for the sake of another thing I do leads seamlessly into thinking about my life as a whole in a structured way. This is a *global* way of thinking about my life: I come to see that I have various goals that I aim at, and that in the one life I have, and which I am already living, these goals need to be structured in a *unifying* way in order for me to achieve them. It is also an *active* kind of thinking: the way I organize my goals *shapes* my life and the way I act; it does not just record them. When I think of my actions in the linear way I can just observe the way I am living, but when I think of them in the structured way the result is that I am faced with a *task*, namely, the task of organizing the goals I am working towards, and shaping my life as a whole.

It is this—the idea of what my life as a whole is aimed at—which in ancient ethical theories is called the *telos* or overall goal of life. If we think in a contemporary way about the idea that my life has a goal that it works towards, our response may be that it is implausible that everything I do is a contribution to a single goal or aim. But this is to make a fundamental mistake, namely, to think of the overall aim as something already given in a determinate way, as though I already know that my life is aimed at achieving a specific goal and all I have to do is to work out how to achieve that. This way of thinking of one's life can be found, but only in a very few people, usually those who from an early age have a vocation for art, or politics, or spirituality. Most of us have nothing like this specific grasp of what our lives are working towards achieving. We have only the vaguest idea of what we are aiming for in life as a whole.

This is exactly what eudaimonism holds: we have at best a vague and possibly muddled idea of what our 'final end' is; it is most likely to be only the indeterminate and in itself unhelpful idea of 'a good life' or 'a life lived well'. This supports, rather than undermines, eudaimonism, for few of us have a determinate idea of what we are aiming at in our life as a whole at

---

[6] It does not conform to the contemporary dogma that the results of thinking can be *either* descriptive *or* normative but never both.

the *start* of ethical reflection. If we did, we would have no need of ethical reflection or theory; our aims would already be clear and the only problems we would have would lie in actually achieving them. What we find in fact is that nearly everyone (every moderately thoughtful person, in any case) is already living a life in which he or she is to some degree actively unifying the aims they have by working out what exactly those aims are and what form they should take. The final end, then, is the indeterminate notion of what I am aiming at in my life as a whole. And the role of ethical thinking is to get us to think more determinately about it, to do a better and more intelligently ordered job of what we are already doing anyway.

Can we say anything more specific about it? At this point Aristotle says that everyone agrees on something more determinate that we can say about it: it is happiness (*eudaimonia*); but that this does not get us a lot further, since people disagree about what happiness is. This is the point at which contemporaries get restive about the notion of happiness; I will return to this, but for the moment I shall make the point that Aristotle is bringing happiness in here merely as the only answer people can give, at the common-sense level, to the questions about why you are doing what you are doing, and how you can have all the goals that you have. That is, at the common-sense level, what is being appealed to is the idea that happiness always puts a stop to these questions. I may want to be healthy, to have a career, to have a family, as part of being happy, but I don't want to be happy as part of or a means to something further. It's just what I want; a terminus to my other goals.

Happiness is, however, still a fairly indeterminate notion, though less so than that of our final end; we can see this from the fact that Aristotle at once goes on to remark that people differ about what makes for happiness not just at the everyday level (some think it's prosperity, others status and fame) but at the theoretical level (some think it is constituted by pleasure, some by virtue). Aristotle himself devotes a large part of his ethical writings to his own answer to the question of what happiness consists in. This answer is dominated by his concern about getting right the relation between what, in a happy life, is up to the agent to develop and what she needs to have as material to work on; arguably it is not as successful an answer as those developed later on by the Stoics and others.[7] Here I am not

---

[7] For the development of these debates see Annas (1993: pt. IV), and Russell (forthcoming).

concerned with Aristotle's own answer, but with the point that happiness in eudaimonist thinking plays a mediating role between the very vague and indeterminate notion we have of the direction in which our lives are going overall, and specific answers on both the everyday and theoretical levels ('money', 'pleasure', 'virtue', and so on). Happiness is what we all want as a general aim in life, one which brings into focus the unspecific idea of having an overall aim in life, but it is still sufficiently unspecific that people have radically differing views of what it consists in and thus how to go about achieving it.

This role for happiness is extremely useful in ethical theory. At the common-sense level people disagree about what is worth aiming for in life, but all agree that, whether they are going for money-making, fame and fortune, or serving others, they are all aiming for happiness. Happiness thus forms the point at which common sense agrees on a notion which forms the starting-point for ethical theory. Aristotle, the Epicureans, the Stoics, and later Platonist and Christian theories all offer competing hypotheses of what happiness is when you think carefully and rigorously about it. All these theories, however technical, are immediately available to ordinary people as more rigorous answers to questions they ask themselves. Starting to do ethical theory does not require throwing out all or most of everyday thinking about ethics (even though the theories themselves may produce results which are very counter-intuitive). Ethical theory helps us to improve what we are already doing—thinking about how are lives are going and how we can do better.

Of course contemporary eudaimonist theories won't be the same, in structure or in results, as the ancient theories, since, to state the obvious, ethical theories must answer to the concerns of their time and place. However, eudaimonist theories, ancient or contemporary, give happiness the central role of the intersection of everyday ethical thinking and ethical theory. One advantage of this is that we don't find what we do with some ethical theories: just at the point where ethical theory tries to solve the problems whose felt pressure in our concepts and ways of thinking led to the need for theory, it tells us to replace those concepts and ways of thinking with others imported from the theory, whose relevance to our problems is not clear. Eudaimonism does not have this top-down feature.

In eudaimonist thinking we are seeking happiness whether or not we explicitly think to ourselves that we are, because we are all implicitly working out how to adjust our goals, as we live the one life we have.

Happiness has the role of being, for each person, *your* happiness, the way *you* achieve living your life well. It is not some plan imposed on you from outside, or a demand made by some theory which has not arisen from your own thoughts about your life. At the same time it is not just anything you want it to be. There are better and worse ways of seeking happiness, for there are clearly better and worse ways of organizing your goals and aims in life, and of seeking to live a life that achieves them overall.

One important point is that, in the development of the role of happiness as my overall end, the distinction between *my interests* and *the interests of others* is so far irrelevant. Happiness is my overall end because I am, obviously, the one living my life. There is no reason to believe that happiness is my overall end because I either cannot, or will not, take into account the interests or concerns of people other than myself. There is no source in eudaimonist thinking from which to get this idea. (This has not stopped objections that eudaimonism is egoistic; we will return to these in the next chapter.)

Eudaimonism and Happiness

Is happiness in this role in eudaimonist thinking happiness as we understand it?

This issue is sometimes posed as the issue of whether *eudaimonia* is happiness as we understand it.[8] In one respect there is a divergence. Aristotle, and everyone who discusses the issue in the ancient world, treats it as completely obvious and undeniable that we all seek *eudaimonia* in everything we do, and this is not comparably obvious to us with happiness; some people find it obvious, some agree but don't find it obvious, and others deny it. One reason for this is that our idea of happiness is much more determinately specified (often in fairly rigid ways) than happiness in the eudaimonist tradition. Some people, for example, will robustly deny that they seek happiness in everything that they do. They are understanding happiness as an end whose content is already firmly determined, maintaining that while they may seek happiness they also seek other ends as well. It is the prior determinateness of such an end which forms

---

[8] Sometimes a distinction is drawn between happiness and well-being, but this distinction, at least where it rests on the idea that happiness is 'subjective' and well-being 'objective', does not answer to anything in eudaimonism.

the problem here. It is difficult for us not to feel some influence from this idea, and so it is not just obvious for us now, as it used to be, that happiness is, at a general level, what we are aiming at in everything we do.[9]

This point is not insuperable, however. It is a mistake to remain fixated on the point that happiness often has the role, in contemporary discourse, of an already determinate rather than unspecified end. For a start, we have thoughts about happiness which do line it up with happiness in eudaimonist thinking. Take an everyday dispute about whether a colleague did or did not ruin her life when she lost her job as a result of acting in accordance with her values. (She may have blown the whistle on corrupt practices, say.) One person says that she has ruined her happiness, for now she is unemployable, and all her training and ambition will go to waste. The other person responds that if she had failed to act her life would have been infected with dishonesty and hypocrisy, so that she would never have been happy. This is a substantive dispute about happiness of a recognizable kind. The two disputants are arguing about what their colleague's happiness consists in, and they are both doing so on the assumption that each of them has in mind a different specification of what that is. Does happiness require material prosperity, or is being an honest person more important for being happy? If we all agreed on an account of happiness whose content was already fixed, such discussions would never take place. It would just be obvious, from what happened, whether the person had ruined her happiness or not.

One source of our tendency to assume that the content of happiness must be already fixed is the amount of work done on happiness in the social sciences, work which proceeds on the assumption that it is, for if it were not, it could not be measured, and examined in experiments according to the methodology of those sciences. As it is, large amounts of data have been gathered about happiness by psychologists, economists, and others who are measuring something identified as happiness.[10] I will not

---

[9] We shall see in the next chapter that it is this assumption about determinateness which lies at the bottom of many of the arguments that claim that happiness must in some way be egoistic as an end.

[10] See The World Database of Happiness, run by Ruut Veenhoven, <http://worlddatebaseofhappiness.eur.nl>, accessed 26 Nov. 2010. Sometimes the methodology of identifying happiness is startlingly unsubtle. See Layard (2005: 6): 'Happiness is feeling good, and misery is feeling bad.' Layard then proposes measuring happiness by tracing people's brain waves (although the 'science' of happiness he has in mind is economics).

here deal with the issue, whether this kind of research has an appropriate grasp of happiness (obviously, on the eudaimonist approach, it hasn't, but this cannot be followed up here). I merely point out here that the notion of happiness employed in the social sciences is not obviously the appropriate one for an individual to use when thinking of his or her own life. In eudaimonist thinking, the entry point for ethical reflection is reflection on how your life is going. However useful, or not, to the social sciences are specific items that can be measured and assessed, this does not seem the appropriate or useful notion of happiness when you are thinking about your own life and how best to live it. The reflection that gets going when each of us thinks about our own life is rather linked to the idea that happiness is something we are already aiming at in a vaguely specified way, and that the task of reflection is to guide us to more specific ways in which we can achieve that.

There is one influential criticism of any account of happiness in eudaimonist thinking. Answering it helps to indicate an important feature of happiness. Grant that we all aim for *something* in our lives overall, vaguely and without being able to specify it beforehand. Grant also that this is happiness, understood as a very general aim which we can achieve in a number of ways. Still, happiness is the point where ordinary thought meets theory: to achieve happiness we have to reflect about what we are doing to achieve it, and how this could be improved. (Assuming that few people think that their lives are, as they stand, completely well-ordered, with well-structured goals.) Different ethical theories offer us different options at this point as to how best to achieve happiness. But this presupposes, as already recognized, that there are better and worse ways to go about achieving happiness, and that different ethical theories are giving us competing answers. But—don't we now find that some people can come up with better answers to this than others? And if so, aren't they in a position to tell other people how to be happy, since the second lot of people would be well advised to listen to what they say? Yet surely it is both intuitively repugnant, and at the level of theory objectionably paternalist, for some people to be in a position to tell others how to be happy. Some philosophers recoil at this point, seeing a spectre emerging from eudaimonism: some people imposing their own vision of the good life on others.

This objection rests on failure to distinguish the circumstances of a life from the living of that life. As we've seen, this is a crucial distinction needed to avoid confusion about the virtues and the way that these are integrated in a life overall. It is not surprising that we need to keep in mind the same distinction to avoid confusion about happiness in eudaimonist thinking, since this also concerns your life as a whole overall. Some aspects of your life are factors whose existence in your life is not under your control; virtue, as we saw, is not among these, but is to be found rather in the way you live your life, the way you deal with these various factors which you can modify or cope with, but not ignore.

In eudaimonist thinking, happiness is likewise a matter of how you live your life, how you deal with the material of your life. Happiness is not a matter of the stuff you have, or whether you are beautiful, healthy, powerful, or rich. A happy life is not one in which you just have these things—after all, plenty of people have all these things but in no way live happily. A happy life is one in which you deal well with these things that you have—and cope well with illness, poverty, and loss of status, if these things happen to you. Accounts of happiness in this way of thinking are telling us how to live our lives, not urging us either to keep or to change the circumstances of our lives. Thus they are not saying that to have a happy life we need to be healthy, have a lot of money, be educated, or the like. They are telling us that, whatever our circumstances, whether we are healthy or unhealthy, rich or poor, educated or uneducated, we should think about our lives and try to live them well, rather than just continuing on with the way we have hitherto been coping with the circumstances of our lives. It is worth noting that in this they contrast with some recommendations from contemporary theories in the social sciences to the effect that if you want to be happy you would be well advised to be married, go to church, etc. on the grounds that married, churchgoing etc. people are statistically happier than the unmarried and the unchurched. Clearly this confuses the circumstances of a life with the way that life is lived. If you are emotionally unstable, for example, it is usually a very bad idea from the viewpoint of happiness, as well as others, to get married, and probably to become a churchgoer, and an even worse idea to do either *in order to* become happy.

Theories of happiness will correspondingly give us guidance as to how best to live our lives in whatever our circumstances are. A hedonist will tell us that, whether we are rich or poor, educated or uneducated, we should live our lives so as to achieve pleasure from the way we do whatever we do. Aristotle tells us that we should live our lives, whatever these are, virtuously, that is, bravely, temperately, justly, and intelligently; but he does put some constraints on the circumstances, insisting that we cannot live virtuously in very reduced circumstances. The Stoics deny this, saying that we can live virtuously in any circumstance whatever, however elevated or reduced. These are contrasting views of what we need to do in order to live happily, but none of them force any particular way of life on us (getting married, becoming a churchgoer, etc.) since they are talking about happiness as living your life, not giving us advice about the circumstances of your life. We can follow these theories today just as people could in ancient Greek city-states, the Roman Empire, and Christian, Jewish, and Moslem states in the Middle Ages. It is irrelevant that Aristotle himself, for example, was writing for people in a very specific set of circumstances.[11] Happiness is *active*: it is a matter of how you do whatever it is you do, how you live your life in whatever circumstances you find yourself as you start to reflect about your life. When I start to reflect ethically there is much about my life which I have to recognize as the material I have to work on. The first ethical move is not to abstract from my individual context, still less to discount it, but rather to understand what it consists in, to achieve self-knowledge as far as I can, and then to think about how best to live my life in these circumstances. Only then will I be in a good position to consider the various options offered to me by different ethical theories.

It is clear even from these brief remarks that different theories of happiness in the eudaimonist tradition can take different attitudes to the circumstances of our life. Aristotle thinks that they put constraints on the scope of happiness. Other theories think that they matter, but in different ways. Perhaps good circumstances (money, health, etc.) cannot make us happy in their own right, being in their own right merely so much material; but maybe they can make a good life better? Perhaps they have a different kind of value from the value of living well and being happy? Ancient theories developed these alternatives in rich and sophisticated ways. Contemporary theories are only just beginning to broach these

---

[11] That Aristotle was teaching elite male Athenian citizens in the fourth century BC tells us about the circumstances of life for and within which he was thinking about happiness. (This explains, for example, why he considers only men, and why he considers some activities that only fairly rich people could do.) It does not, however, determine the way he thinks of happiness, and virtue, in terms of *living your life*, which is why his ethical theory has been found relevant by both women and men in a wide variety of different historical and cultural circumstances.

issues, particularly the issue of whether virtue is necessary or sufficient[12] for happiness. But it is at least clear that it is crucial to draw the distinction between the circumstances and the living of a life if we are to get at all clear about what happiness is, and hence what the relation is between happiness and virtue.

So far I have drawn the outlines of a eudaimonist account without drawing attention to what is an important point about happiness. A happy life is one you enjoy, one you find pleasant, want to continue with, find sustaining. An unhappy life is one in which you are miserable, one you avoid if you can, one in which there is little or no enjoyment. Happiness, in other words, seems to imply some connection with *pleasure*. A eudaimonist account doesn't deny this: as Aristotle says, everyone 'weaves pleasure into' their account of happiness.[13] It is clear, though, that on this account happiness will not turn out just to *be* pleasure, because it can't—pleasure is at the wrong level to be the end unifying all our aims and values. This end, recall, is initially unspecific, and different theories give us guidance how to live by specifying it in different ways. A hedonist will tell us that happiness just is pleasure, so that we will live our lives best by going for pleasure, in some way, in everything that we do. But this is an alternative theory to those that tell us that we should be aiming at a virtuous life, with or without certain constraints. Happiness is the indeterminate end; pleasure is just one suggested specification.

Pleasure and Happiness

Contemporary accounts of happiness often make a different connection between happiness and pleasure, one which has been available only since the late eighteenth century. Happiness on this account is just *identified* with pleasure, where pleasure is understood as a feeling. 'Happiness is feeling good', as the recent author of a book on happiness claims.[14] Happiness is taken to be primarily a matter of having feelings or episodes of feelings, and only secondarily, if at all, a life containing such feelings. This particular way of thinking of happiness has become quite common; when asked if we are happy out of the blue, with no context, we may well first think

---

[12] Strictly, necessary and sufficient.
[13] *Nicomachean Ethics*, 1153^{b}14–15.
[14] Layard (2005); see n. 10 above.

about feeling happy, and turn to longer-term ideas of happiness only subsequently. We have acquired a notion of happiness which, far from obviously applying long-term to our lives overall, has come to be associated with short-term episodes or feelings.[15] It is remarkable that this has occurred, and it may be to some extent an accident of history and language; there are languages where there is no single term for both overall happiness and feelings, and even in English the term 'happiness' seems to have been applied to feelings only from the late eighteenth century. It has become part of the way we think about happiness, however, and we have to take account of it.

Could feelings of pleasure be the right kind of item to form the basis of a happy life? This sounds dubious right from the start. It's nice to have feelings of pleasure when eating a good meal, and to enjoy activities such as walking or reading, but these feelings vanish when their object does: the pleasure of eating, and the pleasure taken in walking or reading ceases when the eating, walking, or reading does. This can hardly be what matters to us when we think seriously about how to live our lives.[16] Pleasure is too trivial an item in life to be the most important thing in it, or the goal round which life is organized. Imagine being told of someone that they think that the most important thing in their life is pleasure, and that this is their overriding aim. We would conclude that this was an adult with the mentality of a spoiled 2-year-old, and wonder how they proposed to survive in the real world. (Even spoiled 2-year-olds do not do very well; trying to make a child happy by always aiming to give her pleasure does not in fact succeed in its own terms, as any book on bringing up children will point out.)

Saying anything negative about pleasure is often wrongly thought to indicate puritanism. It is worth meeting this point by reflecting on the role of pleasure in the kind of life we want our children to lead. Suppose I am, *ex hypothesi*, not a puritan, and want my child to lead a happy life. I will want my child to enjoy her activities and have feelings of pleasure. But could this be what makes her life a happy one? This strikes two wrong notes. I will scarcely think that my wish has been granted if my child lives a

---

[15] In some psychological work 'happiness' is even used for an emotion, on a par with anger, envy, and the like. Presumably it is taken to be a state of feeling good.

[16] I am not dealing with theoretical kinds of hedonism here, but with the appeal, or lack of it, that pleasure has when we are asking about the role of happiness in our lives.

life enjoying activities which are degraded or addictive.[17] And even if an activity is a serious one, something has gone wrong if the person's life is made a happy one not by the activity but by the feelings of enjoyment she gets from it. Any parent would be disconcerted to find that their child had grown up to regard her life as happy because of the enjoyment she got from, say, helping others, but would unhesitatingly drop helping others the minute she ceased to enjoy it. This is, once again, not an adult attitude. And this seems right even before we are in a position to explain *why* something has gone wrong.

One factor helping to explain why it goes wrong is the point that pleasure lacks the right kind of relation to the rest of our moral psychology. This has been called lack of 'causal depth'.[18] If we think of happiness as just feeling good, we cannot, for example, distinguish between the different kinds of impact on a person of unwelcome events. In a revealing example from Daniel Haybron, take two scenarios, in one of which I have pleasant feelings and am feeling good, and then get a flat tyre, while in the other I am feeling good, but then my child dies.[19] If happiness is just having pleasant feelings, the impact of these two events would appear to be the same: first I have pleasant feelings, then I don't, having painful ones instead. Since it is absurd for a theory not to be able to distinguish between these two ways of no longer feeling good, a supporter of pleasure has to say that my loss of pleasant feelings will be much more intense in the second case than in the first. But this plainly fails to give us the right distinction.[20] The real difference lies in the wider impacts and ramifications of the second event; what is bad about it for me is not the intensity of loss of good feeling and occurrence of painful feelings, but the wide and connected effects in all areas of my life of this loss. Nothing like this happens with the flat tyre, which puts a stop to pleasant feeling but without wide or deep impact on my life.

The idea that happiness might just consist in feelings of pleasure or the enjoyment of activities is not very plausible, once we bear in mind the role of happiness as our final end, something in the achieving of which we

---

[17] Kraut (1979) has influentially made a similar point.

[18] The point, and the term, are from Haybron (2001). See also Haybron (2008: ch. 4).

[19] The example is Haybron's; the idea can be explored with a variety of examples.

[20] As do hedonist moves such as saying that losing a child is losing *more* pleasure than having a flat tyre, the difference being one of degree, not kind.

shape our lives. Pleasure is just not the right kind of item to play this role. It becomes clear that if happiness is construed as feelings of pleasure we have produced a conception of happiness which is not only radically different from the eudaimonist one, but strikingly trivialized.

Happiness and Desires

A more plausible candidate emerges when we follow up the thought that happiness surely has to do with getting what you want, rather than suffering frustration from not getting what you want. This is what seems to matter to young children, for example. We all have desires, and so it can readily seem that the happy person is the person whose desires are fulfilled. Hence the desire-satisfaction kind of account of happiness, a step up from the idea that it is just the having of pleasant feelings.

The desire-satisfaction kind of account appeals to people who are impressed by the fact that we can be happy living very different kinds of life. If we take this seriously, it will seem hopeless to require any particular specific content to the happy life. How can we come up with a content acceptable to everyone? If we think that the happy life must be tranquil we at once think of people happy in lives of physical activity or political engagement; if we think that happiness must require the meeting of challenges we think of the even lives of contemplatives; and so on. The idea that happiness is having your desires fulfilled seems suitably neutral on the content of the happy life; whatever your desires are, if you are getting what you desire you are happy. We've seen, on different grounds, that it is a mistake to try to come up with a single contentful, circumstantial account of happiness to apply to everyone's life, so this may appear a promising idea to develop.

One problem arising at once is that on this account, precisely because of this neutrality, people can be happy if their desires are fulfilled whatever the content of those desires, and some people's desires are evil, or disgusting. Do we really want to call these people happy? We might respond that this is not a problem for the account, since any criticism of these desires will be deflected onto other facts about them (whatever it is about them that renders them evil and/or disgusting), not the point that satisfying them makes us happy. More serious is the point that desires are notoriously malleable. People with low expectations in a certain area of their life, or even their life as a whole, come to have correspondingly muted desires. The force of social pressure brings it about that many girls come to desire less for themselves than for their brothers, and come to find themselves satisfied by a way of life in which they are valued less, given fewer opportunities, and sometimes even fed less. (This is still true in large parts of the world, if no longer in the West.) When their opportunities are expanded and their expectations raised, they come to be dissatisfied with what previously fulfilled their desires. It is thus notoriously dangerous to rely on the desires that people have at a given time, even when honestly expressed, as indicators of happiness; we should be made uncomfortable by conclusions such as that women in traditional societies, with adjusted modest desires, have less need to be happy than do women in developed societies. Desires can also be manipulated and corrupted in ways that are impossible or at least not easy to reverse, for example by addictions; we are hardly comfortable with the idea that heroin addicts are living happy lives as long as they can get their fix. (Though of course they can have happy *feelings* from time to time in what are usually wrecked and miserable lives.)

Another problem with the desire-satisfaction kind of account is less obvious. We normally get pleasure from the satisfaction of a desire because the desire arises from a perceived need. We enjoy eating when we are hungry, and drinking when we are thirsty. Eating and drinking when we are already satisfied doesn't result in enjoyment; it may be actively unpleasant. In so far as they relate to happiness, then, desires rest on our having needs that are being perceived as needs. We find, then, that a life in which we are happy by having our desires fulfilled is a life in which happiness is built on our having needs that are perceived as needs. And we might wonder if happiness is really linked in this way with *neediness*. This is a point first made by Plato when he describes people seeking happiness by fulfilling desires as constantly trying to fill leaky jars.[21] Humans are, of course, needy creatures; we have natural recurring needs such as hunger and thirst, and as a result of our enculturation we have a number of other needs, such as need for status, money, and so on. Can happiness really just be what we have as we meet these needs? Many of them are bound to recur whatever we do, particularly those that are the least culture-dependent, such as hunger and thirst, and so the leaky jar idea

---

[21] *Gorgias*, 493d–495b.

starts to sound distressingly apt. If we are to be happy by fulfilling our desires, and these depend on the existence of needs whose nature it is to recur as often as they are met, then trying to be happy appears to be a hopeless task: whatever we do the jar will never get filled.

It can be responded that the problem here is not really human neediness but only the problems we encounter as we try to fulfil our needs. It's not the recurring nature of hunger and thirst which makes them problematic, but the fact that we have to meet these needs from resources that are often scarce and troublesome to find. Further, needs that arise in society, such as needs for money and power, involve competition between people, and are troublesome for that reason, not just because of our neediness itself. To the extent that happiness seems compromised if it rests on neediness, then, this is because of our problems in fulfilling our needs, not the nature of neediness itself.

In a very idealized world, we might think, we could fulfil all our perceived needs without creating any further needs or other problems. Our jar is full of holes, but we could be happy if we could overcome the problems in filling it up; meet our needs, that is, and enjoy doing so, in ways that did not depend on or lead to further neediness. This is an interesting idea, which has influenced some accounts of happiness.

But it turns out to be problematic to remove neediness as an essential aspect of human nature.[22] The author Julian Barnes, in a brilliant piece of writing, brings this point out. In one of his works he describes a man who finds himself in heaven, or rather in 'New Heaven', an up-to-date version of heaven which is non-judgemental, and where you get everything you want, effortlessly and without any adverse consequences. The food is always exactly as you like it, and produces no fullness, indigestion, obesity, or the like. When you play golf, you always win; you excel in any sport or skill you take up. Your favourite soccer teams win; you meet any famous person you like. Your world conforms to what you want it to be, so that all your desires are fulfilled without any of the problems that arise from normal human neediness. What could possibly be the downside to such a life? None appears for a while, but eventually the narrator realizes that he,

---

[22] When Socrates suggests the idea that a happy life might be one that is not needy, his interlocutor Callicles responds that if that were happiness then stones and corpses would be supremely happy (*Gorgias*, 492e). (This is not the end of the story for Plato, but that would take us far afield.)

and all the other happy people in New Heaven, will ultimately get bored with being able to satisfy any desire they have, with no bad effects, however they ring the changes. And then they will have nothing left to keep them going. When this becomes apparent to a person, he or she willingly goes out of existence. A life of having all your desires fulfilled without the problems created by human neediness leaves humans with nothing to live *for*, nothing to propel them onwards.[23] A life of complete desire-satisfaction, even without the problems involved in having needs, turns out to be essentially backward-looking, and leaves out anything that could get us to move forward with our lives. We recognize, even without any theory about it, that something is deeply lacking in an account of happiness that leaves us nothing to live for once our needs are met in a way that leaves no further neediness.

Happiness and Life-Satisfaction

Not surprisingly, problems with the desire-satisfaction account have led many people studying happiness to a more plausible account, that of *life*-satisfaction. This kind of account takes happiness to be, not a local attitude had when desires are satisfied, but an attitude of global satisfaction with one's life as a whole. This is an improvement on the desire-satisfaction kind of account, since it involves not just a positive feeling but some kind of overall judgement about one's life as a whole, and thus some kind of evaluation of how one's life as a whole is going. If you are studying happiness in the social sciences, this is the obvious item to try to study, since we can ask people what their overall evaluation of their life is, and record answers, whereas asking people about their feelings or whether their desires are satisfied does not lend itself to measurement. Hence we find that, in the social sciences, numerous students of happiness in sociology and psychology departments study self-reports of life satisfaction, and

do you feel satisfied w\ your life ?

---

[23] Barnes (1989: ch. 10). The narrator is someone with very simple and basic desires, and so comes to the point of 'deciding that he's had enough' quite soon. People with more complex wants last longer. Gratifyingly for intellectuals, these are lawyers and scholarly people who 'like sitting around reading all the books there are. And then they love arguing about them' (p. 304). (The people who actually write the books don't last as long.) Still, eventually everyone has had enough of getting what they want, and with nothing else to live for, they go out of existence. A related idea is treated in Janáček's opera *The Makropoulos Case*, on which see Williams (1973).

this often leads to the assumption that life satisfaction is just what happiness is. This is the assumption behind the World Database of Happiness, which over a period of twenty years has amassed the results of questionaires on life satisfaction and come up with numerous conclusions about happiness both in and between different nations.[24]

There are obvious problems with this approach. One is that people can be expected to have a variety of views as to what it is to be satisfied with their lives. Some may respond that they have an affirmative attitude to their life as a whole because they have attained their major goals in life, even though emotionally they feel flat or even distressed. Others may respond affirmatively about their lives because they are feeling happy at the time they are asked, even though they have failed to attain, or lost, the things they have spent their lives attaining. Some may think that individual achievement matters for being positive about one's life; others may value family ties and connections more. It is thus quite unclear that people asked at a given time about satisfaction with their lives are answering the same question; and this obviously renders uncertain what is achieved by collecting the answers. In several forms of questionnaire, for example, subjects are asked to answer the question as to how happy their life is (where this is taken to be a measure of life satisfaction) by picking a face on a single line of simplified faces from very smiley to very frowning. Some may be picking the face that corresponds to the way they feel at the moment; others may be picking the face that corresponds best to the way they think their life is going in terms of actually achieving their goals. Interestingly, it is completely unclear how subjects are supposed to pick a face on a single scale when two or more ways in which they think of their life as satisfactory conflict. For example: I have achieved my life's goals, but my family has just been killed in an accident. Or: I have achieved my life's goals, but in ways that I now regret and leave me miserable about them. Or: I have never achieved much of what I aimed at, but late in life have found a warm family life. In this kind of case no answer can be right: neither picking the face at either end nor picking the one in the middle, as though you could split the difference between these kinds of factor.

Not only are there these problems about a person's response at a given time, we might also wonder how we are supposed to take into account the fact that our estimations of how our lives are going tend to change in various ways. They change over time. As I struggle unsuccessfully as a young architect, with unfulfilled commissions, I rate my life negatively; in later years I may rate it more positively, either because I got commissions or because I came to terms with the fact that I had limited talent or bad luck. They also alter in response to taking different perspectives. On a weekday I might rate my life negatively because of the stress my work involves. On a weekend I might rate it more positively, and again for a variety of reasons. I may now appreciate the material goods my job enables me to get. Or I might appreciate the contrast between weekend leisure and weekday work. Or I might go to church or synagogue and appreciate the wider view of my life I get there.

Thus, although I am taking a view of how positive or negative my attitude is to my life as a whole, I am necessarily taking this view from a particular perspective, which is of course influenced by where, in my life, I am, and the many factors that hence come to be salient. This is an obvious enough point, but important to bear in mind when considering the use made of life-satisfaction questionnaires in the social sciences, and the kind of conclusions that can reasonably be drawn from them.[25] And it is even more important when considering the usefulness of life-satisfaction surveys for the question of what happiness is. The many ways in which answers to questions about life-satisfaction can vary, depending on the person's position in their life-narrative, the importance they attach to different factors in their lives, and the adoption of different perspectives, show that if we were to take life-satisfaction accounts to be accounts of happiness, we would have to conclude that a person's happiness, the positive or negative attitude they have to their lives, varies over time and depends on which factors the person thinks important, and which perspectives (not to mention pressures of various kinds) are salient and important to them at the moment. But clearly we are not entitled to conclude this. What we can conclude is that people's *opinions about their happiness* vary over time and according to the factors that are important to

---

[25] One example of such a use made of the World Database of Happiness (which I remember from a conference) was a claim that people think that having children will make their lives happier, but are not in fact made happier by having children. No account was apparently taken of the age of the children when the second report was made. Of course parents of small children will typically report that their lives have worsened in many ways; the outlook is very different years later.

them at the time. But this is not news. It was not news to Aristotle: '[T]he masses think [happiness] is something straightforward and obvious, like pleasure, wealth or honour, some thinking it to be one thing, others another. Often the same person can give different accounts: when he is ill, it is health, when he is poor, it is wealth.'[26] People have varied, shifting, and often confused ideas about what happiness consists in. This does not show that happiness itself is varied, shifting, or confused.

We should notice that evaluation of your life as a whole may tell us a lot about the person doing the evaluating, and in this respect prove useful for studying the evaluation side, as it were. Recent studies in the area of mental health have discovered the limits of self-report about how people are feeling about their lives, reports which track their feelings of pleasure; but this has indicated the importance of a different kind of self-report, namely reporting on how you are *functioning* in life. Corey Keyes, who has pioneered this kind of study, has shown how this distinguishes between people who are *flourishing*, in his terminology, and people who are *languishing*. Flourishing and languishing are overall conditions of effective or ineffective functioning, which correlate in a surprisingly weak way with absence or presence of mental illness.[27] Studies of flourishing and languishing indicate how important it is for us that we take seriously our overall assessment of how well we are functioning in life, in whatever our cultural and social context is, and not just how we feel about our life. The former, but not the latter, holds out some hope for helpful social policies directed at happiness.

Subjective and Objective

This kind of flourishing, in terms of good functioning in various areas of your life, obviously has a great deal in common with the notion of happiness that we find in eudaimonism; whether you have a positive attitude to your life is surely part of, or at very least relevant to, the issue of whether you are happy. There are dangers, however, in taking any

---

[26]   *Nicomachean Ethics*, 1095ª22–5.

[27]   See e.g. Keyes (2007). Traditional psychology has paid little or no attention to such overall states, focusing more on specific types of mental illness, and has also overwhelmingly focused on psychological problems and defects, rather than on ways in which we can encourage positive conditions. On this conception of flourishing and Aristotle see Keyes and Annas (2009).

positive attitude, even one more complex than feeling good, to be what happiness is, at least as we are concerned with happiness in eudaimonist thinking. A positive attitude—approving, feeling positive about, endorsing, and so on, your life—depends on me, and so it depends on me whether I am happy, since it depends on me, and the condition I am in, whether I approve, feel positive, endorse, and so on, my life. I can be wrong about important features of my life, but if I approve, feel positive, endorse it, then on this view I am happy. The point here can be well brought out by an example.[28] Susan thinks of her life as a happy one; she is married with children, and all is well except that her husband is frequently away on business. She discovers that in fact these absences were spent with a second family, and that he has divided his time between the two families for some years. Uncontroversially, Susan evaluated her life positively before the discovery, and no longer did so after the discovery. The question is: before the discovery, was her life happy or not? If positive evaluation of your life is what happiness is, then Susan had a happy life until the discovery. But this runs into the problem that we are also inclined to say that after the discovery Susan discovered that her life never was a happy one; she was deceived into thinking that it was. Our responses are divided: we see the force of the point that her life was not a happy one even when she wrongly thought it was, and also the force of the point that her own attitude to her life is important for her positive evaluation of it. At any rate, we do not have unambiguous responses to the effect that Susan is happy just when she thinks she is.

In modern debates this is often seen as a conflict between 'subjective' and 'objective' views of happiness. The terms 'subjective' and 'objective' are used in very many different ways, some of which are defined in terms of specific theories, but here we need consider them only in relation to the different responses to the Susan example and others like it. The view that happiness is a positive evaluation of your life turns out to be, in these terms, a subjective theory of what happiness is: Susan is happy if and when she thinks she is, so she is happy during all the years her husband was deceiving her and their children. If this sounds wrong, as it does to many people, it may appear that there is a straightforward alternative: an objective theory. On an objective theory of what happiness is, Susan is not happy once her

---

[28] The example is from Sumner (2003). I have frequently used it in classes, and found that response to it is generally divided.

husband starts producing another family and lying to her about it, whether she knows about it or not. This gives us what many see as the acceptable answer about Susan, and it matches a number of our other intuitions also.

If we accept an objective theory in these terms (taken from our responses to the Susan story) we seem to get into difficulties too. It's obvious what is wrong with Susan's situation, but once we accept that you can be unhappy even though you think you are happy, we face the task of coming up with a systematic account of what things count as making someone happy rather than unhappy when they think they are happy; and so we are led to find a list of things you need to have, or aspects of your life that need to go well, for you to be happy regardless of the way you feel. This is sometimes called an 'objective list' theory. And attempts to come up with such a list are doomed to failure, for they are all liable to convincing counterexamples. We might think that nobody can be happy if they are chronically ill or desperately poor, but we can find examples of lives lived in these conditions which it would be unreasonable not to call happy. If we insist that people can't be happy if they are ill, or poor, we at once seem to be imposing on their lives requirements that the healthy and prosperous take to be necessary; but why are we privileged in our accounts of happiness just because we happen to be healthy and/or prosperous?

Moreover, another kind of problem looms. It sounds plausible to say that to be happy people need health, energy, good attachments, and the like; but what of the person who *rejects* one or more of these but none the less consistently claims to be happy? Some people have rejected prosperous lifestyles and even put their health at risk in order to live lives they find worthwhile; again, it is far from obvious that the prosperous and healthy are right when they say that such lives can't be happy. It soon emerges, then, that we can find convincing counterexamples to both the subjective and the objective accounts of happiness.[29]

This very fact, though, is an indication that we have a false choice here, and that it would be unpromising to follow up either alternative. We have, as Aristotle would put it, ended up in *aporia*; we seem to have to choose

---

[29] To repeat: I am not canvassing the literature on subjective and objective accounts, which would require going further than I can in the present work into the many different distinctions coming under these terms. I am simply dealing with responses to the Susan story, which does divide people between views of happiness, views which they often characterize as subjective and objective.

between two alternatives, but not only are both unacceptable, we have run out of resources for solving the problem as long as we stay within the terms of debate which presented us with these alternatives. This strongly suggests that this whole approach to thinking of happiness is systematically unpromising.

Eudaimonism Again

I have indicated the kind of thing which goes wrong with accounts of happiness as feelings of pleasure, having your desires satisfied and having a positive evaluation of your life. The first two have been the objects of much academic philosophical discussion, but have not been rescued from the objections of principle I mention here. The third is more prominent in the social sciences; it has also recently been discussed by Haybron.[30] Contemporary discussions of happiness focus on these three alternatives (outside philosophy, some of the authors seem unaware even that there are these alternatives). Even the most subtle of them, the third, ends up unable to make progress beyond a dilemma that it lacks the resources to reject.

This does not amount, of course, to a complete argument in favour of a eudaimonist account, but it does lay out the main lines on which such an argument will have to go. Contemporary discussions of happiness often start from the idea that happiness just is having pleasant feelings or getting what you want, or having a positive attitude to your life overall, sometimes without being aware that there is anything problematic in any of these conceptions, or that they are very different conceptions, or that there is a powerful alternative in the eudaimonist conception of happiness. Happiness in eudaimonist thinking does not exclude pleasure, but it excludes the idea that happiness could just *be* pleasure. It answers to our thoughts that happiness must in some way have pleasures 'woven into it', as Aristotle says, as something which is involved in it and not just accidentally attached,[31] but makes it clear that pleasure is the wrong kind of item to be happiness—unless we become convinced by hedonist arguments. But

[30] Haybron (2008). Haybron's own account, though rich and sophisticated, does not escape the problems of a 'feelings' account. See Lebar and Russell (forthcoming).

[31] Aristotle's other interesting metaphor for the relation of pleasure and happiness is that happiness does not bring along pleasure just as a removable attachment, like a necklace (probably with an amulet) hung round the neck (*Nicomachean Ethics*, 1099ª15–16).

in this framework hedonists have a hard time convincing people that happiness could just be constituted by pleasure, since in a eudaimonistic framework this requires both allowing that happiness is less active than we conceive it as being, and also reconfiguring the idea of pleasure in quite extreme ways till we can think of it as an overall end for our lives.[32]

Happiness in a eudaimonist account is what I come to when I start asking about my life, how it is going and how I can achieve better. Happiness is _my happiness_, the way I live my life; only I can achieve my happiness, because only I can live my life, and happiness won't result from some plan imposed on me from outside my own reflections. This answers to some of the thoughts behind contemporary insistence that happiness is 'subjective'. However, it is not exposed to many of the objections raised against such 'subjective' theories. Happiness on this account is not a matter of my feelings, or something to be achieved without reference to other people. We are all seeking happiness, explicitly or not, because we are all working on our lives; there is more to achieving happiness than just feeling a certain way, or getting what you want, and there are better and worse ways of living your life. Happiness in a eudaimonist account answers in these ways to some of the thoughts behind contemporary 'objective' accounts of happiness. However, it is not exposed to many objections to these accounts; it does not require a list of objectively valuable components of a life, and is not committed to the idea that we can give one-size-fits-all requirements for everyone to live a happy life.[33] This account of happiness thus does justice to considerations which have led many to think that happiness must be either 'subjective' or 'objective', while not getting committed to the view that we must take one of these options and that they form a dilemma; as we've seen, this leads to a dead end.

Having argued for an account of virtue, I have now argued for an account of happiness. In both cases there are alternatives, both ancient and modern, and I have done no more than bring out the strengths of the

[32] In the ancient world the hedonist Epicurus is notorious both for having a final end which is too 'passive' (since it is pleasure) and for insisting that in so far as it can form our happiness pleasure has to be thought of as tranquillity, a move generally found to be forced. See Annas (1993: chs. 7, 11 s. 2, and 16). Mill's struggles to find a place for virtue and the _telos_ in a utilitarian framework are well known.

[33] These would turn out to be rather one-size-fits-none, since we have already seen that the circumstances of people's lives are so diverse that there is not going to be a single way of living which deals well with all of them.

views I defend. This would be of little interest if either of these accounts were ones that are alien to us, but by this point I hope that this is not the case for either of them. The account of virtue has emerged from everyday thoughts about reasoning and acting. The account of happiness has emerged from reflecting on a conception of happiness which is now only one of the conceptions of happiness that we have. The recent resurgence of eudaimonist versions of virtue ethics indicates that it is readily available for our thoughts and deliberations.[34] The problem is rather to give a proper place in it to pleasure, while distinguishing it from the view identifying happiness with pleasure which we have inherited from the late eighteenth century. The accounts both of virtue and of happiness will be further filled out in the next chapter, which discusses their relationship.

[34] Anecdotally: my own experience in teaching over many years is that eudaimonism strikes most people as a natural and obvious way to think about their lives, and that when introduced to it as an option in ethical theory they frequently find it both more powerful and more plausible than consequentialism and/or deontology.

9

Living Virtuously, Living Happily

Virtue and Happiness

It will be no surprise that the account of virtue and the account of happiness presented here enable us to make good sense of the idea that living virtuously is a good way of living happily, even perhaps the only way. It is not meant to be a surprise at this stage; a large part of the point of this work is to show how these accounts of virtue and happiness fit together.

Is virtue even a starter as a candidate for making you happy? By now it's obvious that the answer is: probably not, on contemporary accounts of happiness as feeling good, getting what you want, and feeling satisfied with your life. But we've seen that we don't have to think of happiness this way. If happiness is the overall end you aim to achieve by living your life well, then virtue does look like a very obvious starter, for it looks like a better idea to be loyal and sincere than to be disloyal and deceptive. It is absurd to think that we really have no more reason to acquire the virtues than not when we are thinking about how best to live. Rosalind Hursthouse has made the point forcefully:[1] we want our children to grow up honest and brave, rather than shifty and cowardly, and we bring them up to have these virtues (as far as we can) not just for our own sake, in order to be able to rely on them in pursuing our own interests, but for their sake, because we think that they will live better lives being honest and brave rather than being shifty and cowardly.

When we are thinking of a happy life, then, it is just common sense that we want ourselves and our children to have the virtues. This doesn't show

[1] Hursthouse (1999a: 174–6).

that the virtues are either necessary, or sufficient, for living happily, but it does show that we think that it is, at weakest, reasonably to be expected that living virtuously will in at least in part constitute living happily. We need further argument to convince us of stronger claims such as necessity or sufficiency, but this is reasonable, and in tune with many ordinary responses to changes in circumstances. We reject bringing our children up to be vicious, but when bad things happen to a good person our reactions tend to be confused. Has the person lost their happiness when they suddenly lose all their money, or their house, or their health? Or does their happiness depend on the ways in which they can cope, or not, with these losses? Our intuitions go both ways, and we struggle in the way that Aristotle does between the thought that bad enough changes of circumstances can affect happiness, and the thought that even bad circumstances don't themselves compel you; it's always up to you to deal well with bad situations.[2]

I am not in this work arguing that virtue is necessary (or sufficient) for a happy life. More modestly here, I am showing how, given the present accounts of virtue and of happiness, these issues arise naturally as issues of philosophical argument from the ways we think about our lives. They are not, as they appear on some rival accounts, alien imports from high-minded theory that we can barely make sense of.

The intuitive place to start is the ordinary, commonplace assumption that a person's life will, to put it generally, *go better* if they have the virtues—if they are generous and brave, for example—than if they don't. Before reflecting on any of these issues, we want to be talented, beautiful, successful—and also to be good people: loyal, honest, dependable. We get this far before we even raise the issue of the kind of value the virtues have in relation to other factors such as beauty and success. Does this kind of thinking reasonably fit thoughts about *happiness*?

Here, as emphasized, we moderns have come to have a problematic conception of happiness. On the one hand, we think of it as an overall end to be achieved in living a happy life, and to this extent we can make ready sense of the idea that living a good life is a way of living a happy life. It at once becomes natural to argue whether it is the best way of doing so, or

---

[2] *NE* I. 8–10 (1098^{b}9–1101^{a}21). Aristotle uses evocative metaphors: the good person in difficulties will be like the general making the best use of the troops he has, and the shoemaker making the best shoes he can out of the leather that he has.

perhaps the only way, or whether it is merely one way, and perhaps not even reliable. These arguments all develop within the assumption that living virtuously is, intuitively, a way of living happily, where that is not itself something that needs to be argued for.

But on the other hand we also have another, more passive notion of happiness—the more recent idea that happiness is pleasant feeling, or getting what you want, or being satisfied with your life. Apart from the internal problems that each of these recent conceptions of happiness brings with it (problems we have looked at) they all make it difficult to think of virtue as even a starter candidate for either contributing to, or constituting, the happy life. The pleasure-view of happiness brings this about in several ways. First, feelings of pleasure and states of desire-satisfaction and life-satisfaction are all determinate states of the person. At any given time I have feelings of pleasure (or not) and am in a state of having my desires satisfied (or not) or being satisfied with my life (or not). On this view, how can my having the disposition to be brave, or loyal, contribute to my having these feelings or being in this state? Perhaps the answer is that it does so by way of the brave and loyal actions I perform, brave and loyal thoughts I have, and so on. But the mystery does not lessen: how do virtuous actions and thoughts lead to my having feelings of pleasure, or being in a satisfied state, any more than virtuous dispositions do? On this view, we are forced into making large and unconvincing assumptions, such as the assumption that virtuous actions will predictably put me in a position to have feelings of pleasure, or states of satisfaction. Small surprise that philosophers who think of happiness this way have generally had little to do with virtue, thinking of it as alien to their framework and likely to import implausible claims.

Thinking of happiness as feelings of pleasure or states of satisfaction imports another problem: pleasure is a static way of thinking about something essentially dynamic. Thinking of my life in terms of being pleased or getting what I want is, as we have seen in the last chapter, essentially a backward-looking way of thinking about it; there is nothing in these accounts answering to the central point that happiness is forward-looking, an *aim* we have that propels us forward. As ancient authors point out, it doesn't make sense to ask why you aim to be happy, in the way it certainly makes sense to ask why you aim to have pleasant feelings or to have desires satisfied, rather than choosing to have some other aims. Living happily is essentially an overall *aim*, in eudaimonist thinking, and this gives it the right place in our lives. Living happily is not feeling good, getting what you want, or feeling satisfied with your life. How could any of these serve as an aim, inspire you to *do* anything? When we aim at living happily we are aiming at going forward in certain ways, getting somewhere in what we are doing. Hence the static conception of happiness which takes it to be pleasure is ill situated to make sense of any connection with virtue, which is itself essentially dynamic and forward-looking. Again, it is no surprise that philosophers with a static conception of happiness have seen little connection of that with virtue. Why ever would becoming a virtuous person, aiming at doing virtuous actions (for the right kinds of reason and with the right kinds of attitude) land you in a state of pleasant feeling?

Possibly the most significant problem about virtue's relation to happiness imported by thinking of the latter in terms of pleasant feelings or satisfaction is that it leads us to confuse the circumstances of a life with the living of it. We have seen this confusion with virtue;[3] but it happens with happiness too. Feeling pleased is essentially a passive part of my life. I can be active in bringing it about: eating appropriate food when hungry, engaging in activities that appeal to me. But feeling pleased, like any feeling, is not itself part of the way I live my life. As with other circumstances of my life, it is not up to me whether feelings of pleasure or satisfaction come from experiences, including the satisfaction of desires; it is only up to me to manage this in so far as I can. Pleasure thought of as feeling or satisfaction is essentially passive, part of the materials making up my life but hardly part of actively living it. Hence pleasant feelings or satisfaction come to be thought of, on a 'feelings' view of happiness, as episodes in my life. But then they are just part of the circumstances of my life. Aiming at pleasure, understood as a way of living my life, will come, on this view, to nothing more than manipulating other circumstances so that I get as many of these episodes as I can.

If we think of happiness this way we will see no plausible connection with virtue. Indeed, *virtue* comes to be seen as just one item in the life I am leading, with nothing to encourage me even to see it as crucial in my life. This is perhaps the position some people find themselves in who want to be good, but also want to be rich and successful, and then ask why virtue should be a more important item in their lives than money or success.

---

[3] See the end of Ch. 6.

If we are not clear that virtue is part of the living of my life, rather than the circumstances of it, we will be hard put to it to find any reason for systematically preferring virtue to pleasure (or, come to that, pleasure to virtue) as we live our lives. The decision between them will come to appear a matter of personal preference, or even arbitrary. I prefer virtue to pleasure; you prefer the opposite. This fails to take virtue seriously, and shows the importance of being clear about the distinction between the circumstances and the living of a life.

On the eudaimonist approach, none of these problems arise. Neither virtue nor happiness is a matter of the circumstances of my life. (This is consistent with the point that that these circumstances might put constraints on happiness.) Both living virtuously and living happily are ways of living my life, dealing with the materials I have to hand, making the best of the life I have led up to now. Problems about their relation are problems as to the relations between ways of living my life. If I ask, about my life, how best I can live happily from now on, this is a practical question, to which answers will take the form: living honestly, say, or living dishonestly. Which I choose will make a difference to whether I live happily; it will make a difference, for example, to how I earn my living. 'Earning my living' is not itself an answer to how best to live happily: earning a living is part of the material to be given a shape by honesty or dishonesty. More-over, happiness, taken as living happily is clearly an ongoing activity, not a static condition to be achieved and then rested in. And happiness as living happily is not a determinate, any more than a static condition. Virtue doesn't makes me happy by getting me to an already clearly defined goal, as I might be given feelings of pleasure by winning a game or a prize.

How then does it make me happy? At any given time in my life I already have a life; I am living the life I have, which presents itself to me in large part formed by the way I have already lived it, given the circumstances of my life. How I live my life is greatly due to my character, the way I am dispositionally, my tendencies to act, reason, and feel in various areas of life in accordance with the values I have. Since life is always ongoing and we are always developing in various ways, both as a result of reflection and in response to changing factors in our circumstances, my character is not fixed; I am always maintaining the way I am, whether sustaining or protecting formed dispositions or actively trying to change myself in some respect. How I progess, or regress, to or away from being a virtuous person will depend on a number of factors: for example, the way

I was brought up and the extent to which I have reflectively gone along with that and built on it, or rejected or modified its effects in myself; the frequency and depth with which I examine myself and ask about the way I am living; the extent to which my ways of thinking about myself and others are infused with either theory or more imaginative and empirical reasoning, or all of them. Although I have not emphasized it, an important part of how I think about myself will come from how I have responded to books, movies, and the like as well as more intellectual fare.

The virtues, as we've seen, are a matter of character: the different virtues (and vices!) make up my character in various areas of life. Happiness, on a eudaimonist view, is the way I live my life overall. In any life there will, then, always be a dynamic interplay between the virtues (or vices!) and happiness. Whether I live happily will depend at least in part on the dispositions I have developed as I have lived my life, the way these are maintained or decay, and their mutual interrelations. Our intuitive view of our lives takes this much for granted; it's then a matter of philosophical argument *how* important these dispositions are for the living of a happy life.

What, after all, is the alternative? How could it be just the circumstances of our lives that make us happy, or not? How can stuff make you happy? As we constantly discover, a big house, a car, money, holidays, don't make us happy if we cannot make the right use of them in our lives. On their own they do nothing for us; how can they? A shop flyer I saw gets *something* right: 'Money doesn't make you happy—shopping does.' Stuff is irrelevant for happiness until you *do* something with it, even shopping.

This much is true of any reasonable account of happiness, though the point tends to be ignored by 'happiness studies' which tell us that we are more likely to be happy if we have money, education, a spouse, and so on, as though this could possibly be advice for everyone to follow.[4] Given that so much in contemporary work on happiness searches for happiness in the circumstances of our lives, it bears repeating that money, health, beauty,

---

[4] Myers (1992: 206–7) lists things that 'enable happiness': 'fit and healthy bodies, realistic goals and aspirations, positive self-esteem, feelings of control, optimism, outgoingness, supportive friendships that enable companionship and confiding, a socially intimate, sexually warm, equitable marriage, challenging work and active leisure, punctuated by adequate rest and retreat, a faith that entails communal support, purpose, acceptance, outward focus and hope.' Myers adds that his book is 'like *Consumer Reports*', which gives us useful information when making choices; we are envisioned as picking from the list of approved items to suit our own choices about happiness.

even relationships don't make us happy; our happiness comes at least in part from the way we do or don't actively live our lives, doing something with them or acting in relation to them. Happiness is at least in part *activity*. If we fully take this on board, putting the feel-good accounts of happiness on one side, it becomes clearer why what makes us happy couldn't just be stuff sitting there in our lives, or passive states of feeling or satisfaction. To live happily we require something with as much dynamism and internal drive as happiness itself has, and the virtues provide this.

Happiness and Egoism

Any eudaimonist account of virtue has to meet the challenge of showing that eudaimonism is not committed to egoism.[5] This is a charge which comes in several philosophical variations, but they all answer to an intuitive worry that we contemporaries feel, though it has no traction in traditions in which eudaimonism is central. We have come to have a vague feeling that morality, or ethics, is essentially about the interests and concerns of others, and that concern with myself, whatever form it may take, can't be moral or ethical. Since the virtuous person, in a eudaimonist account, is concerned with making herself a virtuous person, this can alert the vague feeling that something must be wrong about the whole idea. It is beyond the scope of this work to get to the roots of this vague feeling and the way we have retained it from a tradition in which morality has been assumed to have a form into which eudaimonism does not fit.[6] Here I will merely take on specific objections to accounts of virtue in a eudaimonist framework, on the grounds that virtue is here egoistic. The relevant construal of egoism here is ethical egoism, the idea that my own good is the source of my reasons for what is right for me to do, the dispositions I should have and the kind of person I should be.

These objections do not hold for consequentialist accounts of virtue, where what makes a trait a virtue are the good consequences it systematically

---

[5] Egoistic forms of eudaimonism are of course possible (Epicurus, for example), but eudaimonism is not as such egoistic.

[6] Since MacIntyre (1985) it has been clear that the ethical options open to us have increased since the late twentieth century. (This is partly due to increased awareness of the history of ethics.) There has been less awareness of this than there should be in metaethics, where theories featuring virtue and happiness are still often misunderstood and forced into anachronistic moulds.

produces; these are obviously indifferent to my attitude to my and others' concerns, since they depend on the state of the world independent of me, and might benefit me or others indifferently. Nor do they hold for pluralist accounts of virtue, in which I should cultivate the virtues because they are valuable, and further various values, in a number of ways which cannot be reduced to a single one. In these accounts, living virtuously is cultivating the various virtues, but without the claim that this will *benefit* me. Indeed, although living virtuously will be living admirably, there is no inner drive in the theory to take this to be living happily. Thinkers such as Nietzsche, who take the virtues to lead to conflict and disturbance in a single life, are (as we saw in the quotation at the start of Ch. 8) quite scornful of the suggestion that living according to the virtues might benefit you, make you happy, or even lead to your advantage. If we accept this thought, we might conclude that we should live virtuously and accept that it will not make us happy; or we might take the more Nietzschean path and reject the whole idea of seeking happiness as a pathetic aim anyway.

Eudaimonist accounts of virtue do, however, face the egoism objection. For living virtuously is valuable, it seems, because it will constitute, in part, my happiness; isn't this selfish? Even when we clear the ground and make it patent that my happiness is not pleasure but *eudaimonia*, my final end, this does not get rid of the point. This is *my* final end, not yours, so it looks as though it is my good (interests, concerns) which gives me reasons for my acquisition and exercise of the virtues. (Henceforth in this argument I will just refer to happiness.)

Two mistaken views of the objection, and meeting them, will help clear the ground further. It might be thought that if my reason for having the virtues is that they will benefit me, then I will act on the wrong reasons, for I will be favouring my own interests, and I will have the wrong kind of motivation for acting. Both charges fail to take into account that this is an account of *virtues*, not traits which bend to fit the aims of the person who has acquired and exercised them. Someone acting for reasons of self-interest, or only out of self-interest, is not virtuous. The egoism charge is focused rather on the person who genuinely has the virtues, and also thinks in a eudaimonist framework, and the aim is to show that there are internal problems in this combination. The basic charge is that if a person has developed the virtues and thinks in virtuous ways, and also thinks that living virtuously is, even in part, constitutive of her happiness, then her reasons for acting, feeling, and so in, in virtuous ways, will ultimately come from, and be motivated by, concern for her happiness. And this is egoistic, however virtuous the person.

A familiar way of putting this objection, in part because of a well-known proponent of it, is in terms of the claim that such an account of virtue is 'foundationally egoistic'. Happiness in a eudaimonistic theory is said to be the 'foundation' or 'basis' for virtuous motivation, which is 'derived from' it and 'defined in terms of it'.[7] Such attacks fail against an account like the present one, which is avowedly not foundational but holistic; they are imposing a Procrustean framework on accounts like the present one.

This point does not dispose of the objection, however. Even if happiness is not foundational in the account, you might still be disconcerted to find that your reasons and motivation for acting virtuously and acquiring and exercising the virtues come from concern for your happiness (even if not 'derived' from it). Surely, you might think, your reasons for acting virtuously and being virtuous come from what you were taught they came from: this is the best way to act, and to be, in this area of your life. Virtue involves a commitment to goodness because it is goodness. And surely your happiness is a different concern from this. This gets the worry going even for people who do not already accept a 'foundational' framework for ethics and who do not think that any eudaimonist account of virtue must squeeze into a framework where one part of the theory is 'derived' from another.[8]

The alleged objection, as articulated by contemporary critics, goes thus. If the account is eudaimonist, then happiness must be one's overall aim in living. And if the account is a virtue-centred account, then one is also aiming to be living virtuously. But one has to give some account of how these two aims fit together. In acting virtuously and aiming to become a virtuous person, my reasons for doing this are either aimed at achieving happiness or not. But either option is troublesome. However worthy may be my aim of acting virtuously and becoming a virtuous person (worthy as opposed to an aim of having a good time, or getting rich), I am still aiming

---

[7] Cf. Hurka (2001: ch. 8). I have criticized this aspect of Hurka's attack, and some other points of his, at greater length in Annas (2007).

[8] There is also the assumption, in Hurka and many others, that any ethical theory will produce some kind of decision procedure telling everyone what to do. See Ch. 3.

at *my happiness*. And this, it is claimed, is inconsistent with a proper account of virtue; virtue implies a commitment to the good, and whatever account we give of what the good is, if I am virtuous my good surely can't be my own happiness. So it looks as though I am driven to say that in acting virtuously and aiming to become virtuous I am not aiming at achieving my own happiness. I am aiming at the proper aim of the virtuous, which is the good (whatever account we give of that). But then is the account any longer eudaimonist? It seems that it could only be so if eudaimonism were what is now called a self-effacing theory—that is, a theory which tells us to achieve the aim of the theory not by aiming at it but precisely by *not* aiming at it, by not doing what it bids and by not becoming the kind of person it recommends, but doing, and aiming at being, something entirely different.

The first horn of the alleged dilemma first: acting virtuously and being a good person is not being focused on yourself—yet the eudaimonist virtuous person's reasons for acting virtuously and becoming a virtuous person do have reference to her own happiness. We can by now see that this charge loses any force it appeared to have as soon as we clarify what happiness is here. Critics often assume that the only viable conceptions of happiness must be of the pleasure or desire- or life-satisfaction kinds, and clearly any of these would create a problem for the virtuous person. On this view, the objection fails as soon as we point out the difference between such conceptions and happiness in eudaimonist thinking.

At this point, though, the objection can be reformulated: even if happiness can be thought of as flourishing, for example, it's still an end that virtue appears to be a means to attaining, and virtue still seems threatened with merely instrumental status. This can be rejected when we recall that happiness is not an end which is defined or characterized in a circumstantial way—that is, in terms of specific circumstances—independently of virtue. The objection holds only against people who hold that being virtuous is a good (or possibly the best) way of achieving happiness where happiness is *already* defined in a determinate and circumstantial way independently of whether you are virtuous or not. Examples of such definitions might be: having a successful career, making lots of money, being a movie star, and the like. But it is so obvious that virtue is not a good, still less the best, way of achieving ends like these that as an actual position this would be hard to find, held only by naive people (before they become disillusioned).

Happiness in eudaimonist thinking, as we have seen in Ch. 8, is not this kind of end at all, and there is actually no excuse for thinking that it is, since we have a two-thousand-year tradition of kinds of eudaimonist theories none of which take this form.[9] Happiness is the unspecific overall aim that we find that we have in mind in some form in what we are doing. What we take it determinately to consist in is not given in advance of our becoming virtuous. (If it is, then becoming virtuous is likely to change it, as someone might be brought up to think happiness simply consists in being rich, but alters this view as he becomes a better person.) Our final end *becomes* more determinate as we live and develop our characters. It is as we develop our characters that we come to form our views that happiness is being a good person with a reasonable level of material goods, or just being a good person, or perhaps that it is just having a good time, or being rich or famous. Virtue cannot be assessed as a means to an already agreed-upon and determinately formed end.

A last gasp form of this objection takes it that virtue must be a means to happiness as a determinate and circumstantial end because happiness, whatever we take it to consist in, is a state of the agent. This fails because, as we have seen, happiness is precisely not a state; it consists in activity, because it is dynamic rather than static. It is activity in my life—and a last desperate version of the objection might claim that it's my life, not yours, so there is at bottom something egoistic about it. But my happiness is my living happily, and what life can I live other than mine? It would be absurd as well as objectionable for me to try to live your life. Eudaimonist accounts, then, will not have some people trying to live others' lives by imposing values and priorities on them. We have already seen a reason for this in the distinction between the living of my (and your) life and the circumstances of them. I can aid you to live your life by improving your circumstances, but it must always be up to you to live your life in those circumstances.

What of the second horn of the alleged dilemma? Strictly we need not consider it, since the first horn fails, but following up the issue of self-effacingness turns out to be illuminating about the present account of virtue. We can start by asking, What is *wrong* with self-effacingness? It seems an odd feature for a theory to have, but why should it discredit it?

---

[9] A possible exception is Epicurus.

We will get clarification here if we consider how self-effacingness arises for the theory in which it is most notorious, namely consequentialism. I am not here presenting an attack on consequentialism, merely pointing out a familiar feature of it, in the interests simply of making clear how and why self-effacingness is a problem for one kind of theory, so that I can then point out in contrast why it is not a problem for the kind of account of virtue I am sketching, either in itself or in the context of eudaimonism.

As has been recognized by consequentialists themselves for a century and a half, if our end should be to maximize some good consequence,[10] it will soon become patent that if everyone tries to employ a method so remote from our practical thinking, the result will not only not be good, it will actually be worse, from the theory's point of view, than the result would be if we did not employ the theory's method. So it looks as though the theory's aim is best achieved by its being aimed for not directly but indirectly, in a way that precludes its being achieved directly by everyone's using the theory's method.

This at once forces the issue, *by whom* is the theory's aim to be achieved? Answers have to divide into two the source from which the theory's inventors hope its achievement is to come. One scenario is that some people do have a clear view of the theory's aim,[11] and they achieve the theory's aim by manipulating others into achieving it. They do this by either withholding information or by misleading them into having motivations which have no reference to the theory's aim, but whose presence helps to bring it about. This unattractive scenario, which in its pure form has been mostly avoided, has aptly been called the 'Government House' version.[12]

Commoner is a scenario which at least takes into account the point that the theory is supposed to apply to everyone, and so assumes that, at least in principle, each individual can understand the consequentialists' aim, and also the point that our practical reasoning will not bring it about.[13] Hence

---

[10] It makes no difference here what the consequence is taken to be—pleasure, welfare, or whatever.

[11] Though *ex hypothesi* there will be a mystery how they, but not the rest of us, can acquire this clear view.

[12] The term comes from Bernard Williams. The colonials deem it impossible to enlighten the natives, so they manipulate them into achieving aims that the colonials deem enlightened.

[13] Given any normal methodology, this would amount to good reason for rejecting the theory. That defenders of the theory persist is an indication that, although it is taken as a

they are taken to understand that most of the time they should forget about the theory and follow reasons whose effect, but not their content, conforms to the theory. From time to time they are allowed to reflect on the theory itself directly, but most of the time they are achieving it indirectly, through following reasons whose content the theory rejects, but whose presence helps to achieve its aim. Thus the person's practical reasoning is quite explicitly split. Part of it is engaged in manipulating the other part into following reasons the following of which, though not the content, will further consequentialist aims. What of the unfortunate other part? Either it is too stupid to notice, or it somehow dumbs itself down into forgetting, or ceasing to mind, that it is being manipulated.

This split in the agent's practical reasoning is not in the least like a division to which it is often compared. This is what happens when we from time to time step back 'in a cool hour', detach ourselves from our ongoing reasonings and reflect about the ways we have been reasoning in our crowded and often hurried lives; we may criticize our ongoing reasoning from the point of view of a more detached and reflective van-tage-point. These, however, are cases where reflection is prompted by felt difficulties at the everyday level of experience; it is the stress of everyday reasoning which triggers reflection that leads to solutions. This is nothing like the situation where the everyday level thinks that it is doing fine, and discerns no problem, but alleged problems, and their alleged solutions, are *imported* by the external reflection. In this case the external reflection does not solve or clarify the everyday reasoning's problems; it simply rejects everyday reasoning without arguing with it on its own terms.

The major problem created when a theory is self-effacing in this way is obvious enough: it renders impossible a unified account of practical reasoning. Since the theory promotes my acting on reasons whose content it rejects, I am all right as long as I act on those reasons in innocence of the theory (though innocence might be dangerous in the first scenario). But as soon as I discover the theory, there is no way I can unite the reasons it endorses and the reasons it directs me to act on. The problem with a theory's being self-effacing (at least an ethical theory with claims to guide the way we act) is that it can give no coherent account of the way we

source of directives as to what we should do, the theory is not thought of as one we can put into practice. We are owed an account of how we can still understand it as an *ethical* theory.

should reason when we act. And, for a theory aiming to guide practice, this is an outstanding flaw.[14]

To return to the alleged dilemma for eudaimonist virtue accounts: self-effacingness is a serious problem for a theory of the above form. However, while eudaimonist virtue accounts do require a *kind* of self-effacingness, it is entirely harmless. It comes in at two stages, in fact.

First, there is a way in which virtue comes to efface itself from the virtuous person's motivation; thoughts about virtue will no longer have an explicit place in the thoughts that lead the virtuous person to virtuous action. A beginner in virtue (usually a young person) will have to try to become virtuous, and to perform virtuous actions. His deliberations will explicitly include such thoughts as that *this* is what a virtuous (brave, etc.) person would do, or that *that* would be a virtuous (brave, etc.) action. By the time he has developed to being a truly virtuous person, he will not have to, and won't, think explicitly about being brave or doing a brave action. Rather he will, as a result of his experience, reflection, and habituation simply respond to the situation, 'from a disposition', because he thinks that people are in danger and need help. Thoughts about bravery or the brave person are no longer needed. We could say that they have effaced themselves. But they have not evaporated. They could be recovered if needed—if, for example, the person needs to explain what he did afterwards, say to a child who is being taught to be brave. In fact, if someone does brave actions but, when asked about them, can say absolutely nothing relevant, we might doubt whether he was really brave. If he can convey nothing as to why some dangers are worth running and others not, his actions don't determine whether he was brave or just foolhardy.[15]

It's obvious by now that this point is illuminated by the skill analogy. We merely need to recall the way in which the learning of virtue was introduced via illustrations of practical skill, and the way that virtue displays many of the same features. We do not find anything problematic in the fact that a skilled plumber, pianist, or marathon runner will respond to

---

[14] I am of course aware of the numerous moves that consequentialists make, in particular the move of insulating the truth of a supposedly applicable theory from the issue of its applicability. (Familiarity with these moves seems to have rendered many philosophers unworried by the bizarre nature of an ethical theory that precludes itself from being generally put into practice.) These moves fall outside the scope of this discussion.

[15] None of this presumes that others are always or indeed often in a position to determine this.

a challenge directly, without explicit thoughts about good plumbing, playing, or running. These are not needed, as they are in the apprentices, who need them in order to develop the expertise that will be exercised without reference to them. In everyday life nothing is more familiar or commonplace than this point about the development of a practical skill. On the present account of virtue we can see that and why it is not problematic for virtue either. We need, again, to remember that there is no all-purpose 'virtuous person'; there are learners and those who are like the experts, and virtue is always a matter of development, and will be different in the beginner and in the person in whom it has developed.

Second, however, what of the virtuous person's thoughts about happiness? Does she even need to have any? This may seem unlikely given the initial indeterminacy of happiness that has been so much insisted on. But here again we need to think in terms of development. When we learn to be brave and to be fair, there seems at first little or no reason to connect the two; the areas of life in which they are displayed, and the feelings and attitudes with which they deal, have little in common. Pluralist accounts of virtue maintain that we never get further than this in terms of connecting the virtues overall in a single life. We have seen, in Ch. 6, reasons for rejecting this view, reasons which rely on the centrality of practical reasoning in the development of the virtues. Here we need to focus on ways in which this development of overall practical reasoning applies to happiness.

We can bring this out even at the level of the individual virtues. Take someone who is learning to be brave, but who has no thoughts about happiness. He learns, that is, to stand up to bullying, to put forward an unpopular opinion, and to endure hardship and difficulty when this is needed to achieve an aim. In so far as he is learning to be *brave*, rather than merely stubborn, what he is learning must involve learning which aims are *worth* enduring hardship for, what the difference is between circumstances that do require you to stand up for an unpopular opinion and those in which it would be merely tactless or showing-off. And so on, as we have seen. He is learning about the value of acting bravely and being a brave person. How is this compatible with his having *no* views about his overall happiness? How could he have learnt these points about value, acting, responding, and feeling, and have had no thoughts at all about their implications for how he lives his life? If he really has no views on his life overall and which aims are worthwhile, to that extent he seems not to have a virtue, but merely an inculcated routine habit, localized in his life without his drawing any implications from it, obvious though these may be.

Similarly if he does have views about happiness, but these are clearly misguided (in the present case, this need only mean that they would clearly be considered misguided by a reasonable range of ethical theories). Suppose he holds, for example, that what matters most in life is having a good time. If he really holds this, then again we can't think that the character he has developed is really that of a brave person; for bravery often requires that you forgo having a good time, and so the person who really holds this view, and so is committed to the having of good times, will just not notice many of the ways in which bravery should be called forth. Again, we look to have local routinized habit, not a virtue. For this person to develop in such a way as genuinely to become brave, the first thing he would have to do would be to think again about what *matters* in his life and what his view is of his happiness.

We can see from this that the virtuous person does have thoughts about happiness, and that they become more determinate as the person becomes more virtuous. To become brave requires you to accept that some things, and not others, are valuable in your life and, to that extent, your life has acquired a shape it did not have before your character developed in this way. This has been presented as a point about the development of virtue, but if we accept the point that we are always developing—as we live our lives, our work is never done—it is clear that there is always a dynamic relationship between the development of virtues and the person's conception of their happiness. Sometimes this can be very dramatic, as with people whose values undergo a radical conversion. As somebody arrogant becomes modest, say, the development of modesty, with the required revisions in her opinions of the respect due to other people, will go along with the development of a different conception of the kind of life she aims at living, the kind of person she now aims to be. Discovering respect for other people and their views goes hand in hand with developing a view of your life in which you now rebuke yourself for not taking account of the views of others, actively aspire to do, and be, what you despised before, and so on.

This is even more marked if we think not just of single virtues but of the development of virtue as a whole. As your character as a whole develops, in so far as it develops towards a more integrated overall structure, your view of happiness will likewise become more integrated; commitment to conflicting values will weaken to the extent that your character develops connections among the virtues related to those values. The ideal development produces a unified view of what is worthwhile and worth pursuing in your life, a determinate conception of your happiness which both encourages and is encouraged by a unified development of your character. This is, of course, an ideal, one that we are always some distance from. (And, to repeat, this is unification of happiness in relation to *virtue*, to the *living* of your life; it does not imply that you either should, or should not, always try to remove conflict in the circumstances of your life.)

The virtuous person will, then, have thoughts about happiness as she develops in virtue, and these will make her conception of happiness increasingly determinate as her character develops. Does this give us something which opens the present account to the charge that virtue must be self-effacing in a problematic way? Clearly not; for the same account will obviously be given as we saw above for virtue. As you become more virtuous (brave, or whatever) your thoughts about happiness become more determinate, but they also need to play less of an explicit role in your deliberations, for just the same reasons as thoughts about doing the brave thing, or being a brave person, do. And this is because, as we have just seen, your conception of happiness develops along with, and corresponding to, your thoughts about first individual virtues and, increasingly, character as a whole. So explicit thoughts about happiness gradually become effaced from explicit deliberations, along with explicit thoughts about virtue, but can be recalled and reactivated if required, for explanation and teaching. Nothing in this gives any opening for a split in the self, or a problem for unified deliberation.

So we find that we have the resources to break the alleged dilemma. When we reflect about the relation of virtue and happiness, we find that both are central to the way we think about our lives. As we develop the virtues, we may begin to do so for reasons that come from happiness; but even where this is the case it does not give rise either to defensible charges of egoism, or to charges that the theory requires a damaging way in which thoughts about virtue and happiness come to efface themselves in the person's deliberations.

We should bear in mind at this point that eudaimonist accounts come in many different kinds. They differ over the relation of virtue to happiness (partly constitutive, necessary, sufficient) and they also differ, as we have seen, in the account they give of the way the virtues express a commitment to goodness and to the kind of goodness that is committed to. The above remarks therefore stay at a very high level of generality, given the different accounts of virtue and of the relation of virtue to happiness. It is possible for a eudaimonist account of virtue to be egoistic, as Epicurus' account arguably is; but we can see from the above that this implies that there is going to be something controversial in the account of virtue.

The Skill Analogy Revisited

Exploration of the way that virtue and happiness fit together in a eudaimonist account of virtue has shown us the strengths and resources of the skill analogy. We have just seen that it is the fact that virtue is 'self-effacing' in the way that practical skills are (that is, that explicit reasons in terms of virtue cease to be explicitly present in the person's deliberations) that enables us to see how virtue in a eudaimonist account is not egoistic in any way. It also enables us to see how natural it is for us to come to think of living virtuously as (at least partly) constituting living happily. Our conception of happiness becomes more determinate as we become more virtuous; as our character develops, we come to have a more integrated view of what is worth having and doing in life, and again this happens in a way which ceases to be explicit in our deliberations, but is still present in a way that can be recalled if required.

Another strength of the skill analogy is the way that it makes us foreground teaching and learning when we are thinking of a virtue. It encourages us to realize that we do not have an adequate account of a virtue until we have an account of how it is taught and learned; and this in turn encourages us not to develop an account which focuses exclusively on mature adults. Theories which do this tend to ignore the idea that the development of a virtue might actually be an essential part of the account of a virtue. We have seen how, if we take the developmental aspect seriously, we can give their proper roles to a number of points about virtue. One is the point about aspiration; virtue is always an ideal that we aspire to, and so we are always developing towards or away from it. Connected is the point that virtue is essentially dynamic, not a static condition of the person but an aspect of him or her that is always developing for the better or the worse. Our work, in living virtuously, is never done. (We may find this point inspiring, or depressing, depending on temperament.) Moreover, in a eudaimonist account we are now able to give substance to the idea that happiness is something to be achieved in activity rather than a passive experience.

Moreover, the skill analogy, with its emphasis on development, enables us to avoid problems that arise if we think solely of 'the virtuous person', forgetting that we are always dealing with people at various stages of development. This helps us to see why we should not expect the account to deliver a single one-size-fits-all decision procedure, of any kind, which would tell everyone what to do, whatever their circumstances and stage of virtuous development. And this in turn connects with realizing that this kind of theory will not deliver a 'theory of right action' or an account of 'the right thing to do' independent of the virtuous thing to do, or a decision-procedure telling everyone what to do. It is the aspects of virtue illuminated by the skill analogy which enable us to allow fully for the embeddedness of the way that virtues are acquired and exercised, while not falling into danger of relativism; for we do not lose sight of virtue as an ideal that we aspire to in a way that crosses communities and cultures. In all these ways we find that we have an account of virtue which makes it natural and fruitful to think of living virtuously as being (at least partly) constitutive of living happily.

All these points give us an attractive picture of the happy life. On this account it is not a fun state that we struggle to achieve and then relax, as though we were working at an uncongenial job in order to retire and forget about the work we did to get there. Rather happiness, living happily, is always an ongoing activity. It is an ongoing project, and so very different to accounts in terms of feeling good or getting what you want or being satisfied. This is an account of happiness which emphasizes activity and engagement rather than passive experiences.

Virtue, Goodness, and Living Happily

So far in this chapter there has been less emphasis than the reader might expect on the points about virtue explored in Ch. 7, points which do not stem from the skill analogy. This is because the present account is comprehensive about ways in which virtue involves commitment to goodness, and hence discussion of this point has to stay at a high level of generality.

As discussed in Ch. 7, living virtuously can involve commitment to a conception of the good which transcends human life, often religious or spiritual. It can also involve commitment to a conception of good to be achieved in living a human life, and this naturalistic kind of theory can in turn take a circumstantial or non-circumstantial form. The present eudaimonist account of virtue thus covers a range of different accounts of the virtuous life currently on offer, both secular and religious, and of their relation to living happily. I take it that this level of comprehensiveness is an advantage in an account like the present one, which aims to work out the general lines of a eudaimonist account of virtue, rather than to present and to argue for one specific version. Each variant will need its own arguments and evidence, but their conflicts occur within a framework that they share. In this they all differ radically from theories of a consequentialist and Kantian kind, and cannot be considered mere variants of one or other of these. We have a distinct family of theories that needs to be understood in its own terms rather than being bent out of shape in analyses which fit only consequentialist and Kantian theories.

But Is It Happiness?

But is it *happiness*? Is it enjoyable? By now we do not need to point out yet again that we are concerned with happiness as *eudaimonia*, not with pleasant feelings and desire-satisfaction. But once we have thoroughly cleared these passive conceptions out of the way, what do we still need? What is lacking? Happiness is (at least in part) constituted by virtuous activity, and it is itself, as has been stressed, activity; and we have seen how this is itself enjoyable. A final way in which the skill analogy helps us to understand both virtue and happiness lies in the way in which we find that enjoyment lies in active engagement with what we are doing and how we are living, rather than in waiting around for pleasant feelings.

The virtuous person is happy living their life, in so far as that is virtuous; and this is not a far-fetched and ridiculously high-minded idea we have no reason to accept, but a view of life which develops readily from the way we think about virtue and happiness, if we start from the perspective we have which illuminates them. Our perspective is one in which we start by thinking about how we act in the world in ways that we can do better and worse—the perspective of practical expertise. It is not blank 'know-how' but skill in which we can become experts. This idea of developing skill is, as we have seen, surprisingly complex to untangle, and we have seen how it corresponds closely to virtue, since after all virtue is, among other things, an example of how we act in the world in ways that we can do better and worse.[16]

Throughout these two chapters I have insisted that living happily is '(at least in part)' living virtuously, and this constant qualification may have seemed coy. I have insisted on it because I think that this is the position that emerges from our conceptions of virtue and happiness when we explore them. We want to be good people, and we want our children to be good people also, because this will be better for us, and for them. But we also want to be successful, attractive, popular, wealthy, and many other things. Most of us do not succeed in working out an overall consistent view among these many things we want until we start reflecting seriously. So for most of us the happy life is enjoyable because it consists in part in virtuous activity, and this is enjoyable. But it also contains enjoyment from other sources. Someone living this kind of life is likely to feel satisfaction when they look back and reflect on the way they have lived. But most of us also take some of the circumstances of our lives to be parts of our living happily. We enjoy having money, security, and status, and feel that we would not continue to live happily without these. Hence we think that items such as money and status are also needed for happiness, as well as living well. These things do matter to most of us also in themselves and not only as circumstances enabling us to live virtuous lives. (It remains a mistake, of course, to think that these kinds of thing on their own could make us happy—a less common mistake.)[17]

So we find that the ordinary view of virtue and happiness is a mixed one. Many of us implicitly take happiness to require both being a good person *and also* (in their own right) some amount of money, security, status, and so on. This is the point at which philosophical debate starts. Can you be made happy by aiming to be a good person, *and also* by money, security, and status? Or is this an essentially unstable position? We have

---

[16] The reader may have by now made up his or her mind as to whether we have a 'skill *analogy*' or the conclusion that virtue is itself a kind of skill.

[17] 'Happiness studies' that give us *Consumer Reports* types of suggestions (see n. 5) on 'how to be happy' by being healthy, having good marriages, and so on, notice that these things are important constituents of many people's idea of happiness, but fail to notice that more is involved, namely the way we deal with these things.

seen that it is part of our everyday views about happiness that stuff alone doesn't make you happy. Could it be part of what living happily requires? If so, how important a part? Could money, status, and the like make you happy only if you are a good person, and not if you are evil? What about the mediocre—are they made happy by these things?

If virtue is necessary for happiness, then someone who fails to live virtuously is not happy, however much stuff she has and however many feelings of pleasure and satisfaction she has. This is a position we need to be persuaded of by philosophical argument; it does not just emerge from reflecting about virtue and happiness. We should note, though, that we need argument to reject it also; everyday reflection does not just rule it out, though philosophers surprisingly often think that it does and that argument is not necessary here. We can always, of course point to evil people having what they take to be enjoyable lives; but clearly by now this misses the mark if thought of as a counterexample to the present claim. Given the complexity of our conceptions of virtue and of happiness, this is not surprising. Bernard Williams makes a claim which has been frequently repeated, that we can see horrible people who do not seem to be unhappy at all, but by the 'standard of the bright eye and gleaming coat' are doing very well. Those who quote this, however, generally fail to continue the thought, which is that it is unclear whether there are such people. We imagine them, but this may just be a projection of our own thoughts. Williams suggests that a sign that this is indeed the case is that we can imagine examples that are attractive, rather than repellent, only by focusing on the partly imagined past, rather than contemporary examples.[18] It is extremely difficult to produce examples both of real, current wickedness which are also convincing examples of happiness.

We need yet further philosophical argument to convince us that living virtuously is actually sufficient for living happily, so that living happily resides entirely in the living of your life, with its circumstances having a different kind of value which, while important to your life, does not itself contribute to living happily. To get to this position we have to become convinced that there is a latent incoherence in thinking of happiness as

---

[18] Williams (1985: 46). The bright eye and gleaming coat are in any case signs of animal flourishing rather than the kind of flourishing appropriate to humans, who live in a world of mortgages, marriages, and other mundane but essentially *human* conventions.

made up both of living virtuously and of items such as money and status, which belong with life's circumstances rather than with the living of it.[19]

These are philosophical positions with thousands of years of tradition of debate behind them, and contemporary debate is beginning to catch up with the ways that they arise in eudaimonist accounts.[20] Happiness is again becoming the site where ordinary reflection and philosophical argument intersect. The traffic is two-way: lived situations give rise to problems that require philosophical treatment, and philosophical conclusions require us to rethink the ways we live our lives.

[19] I myself tend to the sufficiency position, on the basis of arguments (such as the above), not just on the basis of our conceptions of virtue and happiness (although the position is not in fact as hopelessly unintuitive as it is sometimes claimed to be).

[20] Russell (forthcoming) discusses the appeal of the sufficiency thesis and its connection to different conceptions of agency.

10

Conclusion

The account developed in the previous chapters has been on a high level of generality as concerns happiness, and the ways that virtue involves a commitment to goodness. I have not argued for a particular version of the way virtue is committed to goodness. Nor have I tried to adjudicate among the claims that virtue is a part of happiness, that it is necessary for it and that it is sufficient for it. Rather, I have tried to set up the frameworks within which these adjudications take place.

The account has been definite, however, on virtue, its composition, and its structure. Central to it has been the idea that the kind of practical reasoning found in the development and exercise of virtue is like the kind of reasoning we find in the development and exercise of practical expertise. The skill analogy has been central. It is because of this that we can see that the fact that virtue is habituated, built up over time and from experience by a process of learning, is not in conflict with the fact that it is *intelligent*. The virtuous person acts by way of immediate response to situations, but in a way that exhibits the practical intelligence of the skilled craftsperson or athlete. It is at the opposite extreme from an automatic or routine response, one which bounces back mindlessly from whatever calls it forth.

Obviously there is more that can be said about virtue. I have suggested that we can do justice to the social embeddedness of virtue while not being pushed into relativism. The same considerations apply to accounts of virtue themselves. The present account is, unsurprisingly, embedded in the social and cultural contexts in which this book, and books like it, are written. We will achieve a strong and universal account of virtue only when we have several accounts like this one but from different societies and different perspectives, and can come to an informed view as to the extent to which they converge. Accounts and descriptions of virtues differ in different societies and different languages; we may eventually be in a position to say something more definite than we can at the moment as to the level at which differences matter, and the level at which what we find are different embodiments of the same virtues. Meanwhile the account I have put forward is clearly not intended to be the last word, or the definitive word about virtue and its roles in the different kinds of virtue ethics. Nor is it, obviously, intended as the kind of theory acceptance of which is intended to force the reader to reject, or to detach herself from, her previous ethical beliefs. Acceptance of the account may well tend to make a reader more critical about alternative forms of structure for ethical thought, but that is a distinct matter.

As I have stressed throughout, the account has been built from the ground up, rather than relying on theoretical accounts of what a virtue is or has to be. Accounts which define virtue in terms of a larger theory, such as consequentialism, can claim for themselves the independent status that the theory has, relying in part on formal properties of the theory. I do not think that this is the way to illuminate virtue, and have througout talked in terms of an account of virtue and happiness, rather than a theory, because of this point. I shall now return to the question I mentioned earlier, namely, what is the status of this account? I have throughout appealed to our everyday views about virtue and expertise, and about pleasure and happiness. Who are 'we' here? And why should we rely on our everyday views about virtue to enable us to build up a philosophical account of virtue?

Who *are* 'we' here? If you are still reading this book, you are part of the audience who are 'we'; the audience for this book is an audience of, I hope, open-minded readers who care enough about understanding virtue to read and think about this and similar books. The 'we' here is meant, as already indicated, to be an inclusive invitation, not parochially exclusive. If you have found yourself disagreeing with claims about 'our' everyday views, this is relevant evidence, and best put to use by showing how it does or doesn't suggest modifications to the account. (I am taking it, as I have throughout, that disagreement here is straightforward disagreement, not simply based on prior theoretical assumptions which the present account does not make.) Simple disagreement is, we have now seen, not in itself an adequate ground to reject the entire account (of course you might do so for other reasons), since we do not have here the pattern of a theory vulnerable to overturn by single counterexample. We have a holistic account whose force comes in part from the grounding in experience of virtue and happiness that we find, and in part from the way it holds together overall. Because the account is holistic, we also do not have the pattern of a theory which can be attacked by attacking its foundational parts.

Are our everyday views about virtue and happiness, however, good enough even to provide the starting-points for such an account? Could our views about ourselves and our psychological make-up be inaccurate or even mistaken? Philosophers have come to be professionally suspicious of accounts which rely on our everyday 'intuitions'. I have avoided talk of 'intuitions', since this has itself become a theoretical term through its use in debates.[1] Moreover, the present account does not fit debates about moral intuitions, since the skill analogy takes it further afield; whatever moral intuitions are, we don't have them about skating or translating. Moreover, in a holistic account we do not find *intuitions* opposed to *theory,* as though there were only these two options and we had to pick one of them. As often, this is a forced choice which obscures the need to find a different alternative by extending the resources we bring to bear. The present account has simply appealed to our views about virtue and happiness, along with plumbing and piano playing, as the starting-points for the account as a whole, which is supported, as holistic theories are, partly by the way it holds together and partly by the rooting of virtue and happiness in views that come from our lived experience.

The problem remains, though: are our views about virtue and happiness a reasonable source on which to draw to produce an account of virtue and happiness such as the present one? Here it is relevant that this account has emphasized the *aspirational* element in virtue. The question is not, then, whether the account will be endorsed by any and every view about virtue, but whether it presents itself as an *ideal* that we can endorse.[2] Responses that few people exhibit virtue, on this account, are not decisive. It would be important, however, if the account met with overwhelming rejection as an ideal—if most readers, for example, felt that their characters were incapable of improvement, or straightforwardly dismissed Socrates and Gandhi as losers, or thought that happiness can't mean anything but having fun. This leaves open the question of whether the ideal presented

---

[1] There is a perfectly good ordinary sense of 'intuition' in which what is meant is judgements for which we may not be able to produce explicit backing or justification. In this sense I have been appealing to intuitions. I think that it is clearer to avoid the term, however, given contemporary philosophical debates in which this idea has hardened into a technical term partly defined by its use in the philosophical debates.

[2] Cf. the pertinent comments in Tiberius and Swartwood (forthcoming).

is too ideal to be 'practical', as Aristotle puts it, or is an ideal that we can put to work in our lives as we live them. The account is meant to be a realistic one for us to live by, but a developmental account may well provoke a variety of responses as to its practicability.

The views on which this account draws are thus, though not foundational, philosophically ground-floor. This does not mean that they don't have, or need, other support. Perhaps they can get another kind of support from study of our lived experience, especially from psychology. This thought has acquired greater force recently since the emergence in contemporary ethics of the demand that ethical theories be shown to be compatible with an acceptable account of our 'moral psychology'—one whose acceptability tends to be equated with answering to recent experiments by psychologists. The present account is indeed more open than some to the demand to answer to such an account of our psychology, since it, like that of the psychologists (though for different reasons), does not think in terms of a special area of our 'moral' psychology, but simply in terms of our 'practical psychology', those aspects of ourselves which are relevant to action and to practical reasoning, as opposed to theoretical abilities to do chess, mathematics, and so on.

Here we find a challenge waiting from some contemporary philosophers who, inspired by 'situationist' social psychology[3] have put forward a 'situationist' challenge to theories and accounts of virtue. The upshot of the challenge is that virtue does not in fact answer to our practical psychology: we do not have the kinds of disposition that virtue is, and so thinking and guiding our lives in terms of virtue involves a naive mistake. This would obviously disable it as a central term in ethical theory. It is important, therefore, to meet this challenge. I think that we can also show how virtue might in fact be fruitfully studied by psychologists.

One challenge, the most radical, is that we do not have any character traits of the kind that include virtue, since we do not have character traits that are robustly reliably either over time or, more importantly, across different kinds of situation.[4] This is held to be established by experiments by psychologists which showed that a majority of the people in the experiments did not act in the way that either they or others predicted when faced by new situations that put them at a loss. Another position

---

[3] Ross and Nisbett (1991) is the standard text.
[4] Harman (1999), (2000), (2001), (2003).

draws from the same range of experiments the conclusion that we do have character traits, but that they lack the cross-situational consistency that we assume. Because we are motivated more than we assume by situational factors which we may reflectively reject, or sometimes not even be aware of, we develop traits only within the contexts of types of similar situations, and these traits are not robust enough to carry us over to acting in corresponding ways in different situations.[5] Even the weaker view contains a threat to making virtue central to an ethical theory that claims to guide our actions, for if most people's actions do not reveal such dispositions, the claims of virtue seem to have no traction. In all these experiments some people did do the right thing or behaved admirably, so we seem to find virtue in a few, and some have thought that this is all we need for theories of virtue, since they put forward ideals, and it is not news that these ideals are demanding and so that virtue is rare.[6] And in fact the results are not as deplorable as some discussions might suggest.[7] Still, part of the attraction of an ethics of virtue has always been the point that virtue is familiar and recognizable by all, so it would still be a damaging result if virtue is hopelessly unattainable by all but a few.

Are the psychologists' experiments, though, really studying the kind of dispositions that virtues are? By now it is clear from several discussions that the traits studied by the situationist psychologists are ones where results are got from noting what people do or don't do, and that this is entirely inadequate to make claims about virtue, on any understanding of virtue on which that is a disposition not just to act, but also to reason, respond, and feel in certain ways. The claims by the situationists are compatible with consequentialist and pluralist accounts of virtue, but not with any account which makes virtue a matter of learning and habituation in a way building up practical reasoning as an essential part of virtue. For such accounts of virtue are not about character traits which are acquired or expressed merely in acting in certain ways. By now claims that these experiments show that virtue ethics rely on a mistaken account of our psychology are generally seen to have been refuted.[8]

---

[5] Doris (1998, 2002).   [6] See DePaul (1999).   [7] See Badhwar (2009).

[8] See Athanassoulis (2000), Badhwar (1996) and (2009), Kamtekar (2004), Miller (2003), Sabini and Silver (2005), Sreenivasan (2002). See Russell (2009: pt. III) for a thorough philosophical investigation of the psychologists' results. Russell argues for a more sympathetic and helpful interpretation of these results than philosophers have generally made, one that supports an ethics of virtue rather than undermining it. Russell's work is complemented by

This does not make the issue go away, however, since once the point about virtue and practical reasoning is clear, situationist objections shift to the relevant notion of practical reasoning. There are psychologists' experiments which show that we in fact reason in strikingly bad ways; we are readily led to make inferences we know to be bad, to follow the reasonings of others when we have far better reason to disagree, and to act on reasons that we know to be completely irrelevant.[9] Does this show that an ethics of virtue is discredited if it relies on our building up virtues by way of our practical reasoning? The answer is not clearly yes. The results of the experiments show how easily our reasoning is tripped up, but this might well show that there are more ways than we suspected for reasoning, including practical reasoning, to go wrong, and thus greater care is needed in its development.[10]

One point outstanding here is that in all this discussion nobody has pointed to psychological work done on virtue which has taken the skill analogy seriously. If our practical model for virtue should be that of a practical skill, we have a fairly specific model of practical reasoning and its development, one which is determinate enough to be tested and examined in empirical ways by properly designed experiments.

This claim might seem mistaken, since virtue has been likened to practical skills in some discussions.[11] However, in these it has been understood as a kind of undifferentiated 'know-how' which does not distinguish between the learner and the expert, or as a kind of sensitivity which emphasizes the immediacy of response. There has been no sustained contemporary investigation[12] of virtue in the light of the skill analogy either in ethics or in the empirical or social sciences. In fact, some influential studies of automatic behaviour have tended to have a negative

Snow (2010), which also discusses the psychologists' results in a sophisticated way, and shows that, far from undermining virtue, they support an attractive version of virtue development.

[9] Among the more alarming results: if most people in a group draw a mistaken conclusion, subjects are easily led to follow them, though they can actually see that it is wrong; people are less ready to help if others are present, even when they are doing nothing relevant.

[10] See Badhwar (2009), Kamtekar (forthcoming).

[11] See Churchland (2000), Clark (2000*a* and *b*), Dreyfus and Dreyfus (1990).

[12] At least, none that I know of. The skill analogy is so central in ancient ethics that there are frequent discussions of it there, and, because of the ubiquity of practical skill in the economic life of the ancient world, references of all kinds to skills are found deeply and widely in ancient culture; but of course there is nothing corresponding to contemporary experimental study.

impact, leading to a premature assumption that habituated behaviour must be automatic and routine.[13] There have, however, been some interesting studies of the differences between being motivated to achieve a goal for its own sake, and being motivated to achieve it for the sake of a further end.[14] And the work of social psychologists such as Turiel and Smetana suggests interesting paths for research, although it will be important to free study of early ethical development from the uncritical assumption that it has to be a matter only of rules.[15]

If we are concerned about the empirical applicability of virtue, the way ahead would seem to be to promote empirical study of practical skills and the ways in which virtue can be taken to be similar. Such study would require close cooperation of philosophers and psychologists, since it is crucial that virtue be understood properly, and not in terms of routine or automaticity. We would learn a lot from study of the kind of habituation in a practical expertise which produces intelligent exercise rather than automatic reaction. Empirical study of this would put us in a better position to study the acquisition and exercise of virtue. With both practical skills and virtues it is the acquisition stage which will probably be easier to study than their exercise in adults, where there are so many complicating and potentially confounding features. It would also be fruitful to follow up in the case of virtue the kind of result studied by Csikszentmihalyi for engaged activity. Many empirical indications have been found that people tend to be healthier and to feel better when doing good than when engaged in more selfish activities,[16] and it would be fruitful to have closer

[13] Bargh and Chartrand (1999) has been influential, and has led some to think of all our actions as either consciously worked out or automatic. The studies actually deal with only a few types of action, provding no basis for considering habituation (still less ethical habituation) to be nothing but automatic response. See Snow (2010).

[14] See Ryan and Deci (2000) and Deci and Ryan (2000).

[15] See Smetana (1993) and Turiel (1983, 2002). Turiel and Smetana's work shows that children can distinguish from a surprisingly early age between merely conventional and ethical rules. The studies, however, use the notion of *moral rule* somewhat uncritically, and do not distinguish between virtue rules (such as 'don't be dishonest') and deontically stated rules (such as 'it's wrong to lie').

[16] Empirical work on this is beginning to mount up, done from several distinct perspectives. In social psychology Haidt (2006: 174) cites studies longitudinal studies showing a causal increase of happiness from volunteering (Thoits and Hewitt 2001). McCullough (2008) investigates forgiveness from the viewpoint of evolutionary biology. See also Post (2007), especially Witvliet and McCullough, for empirical studies on the relation of altruism to health. Empirical studies are mounting up in this area, and will increase in usefulness as investigators become aware of work in several different areas.

empirical study of the enjoyable side of virtuous activity, in so far as this is feasible.

The more virtue is studied in its own right, rather than in the nexus of independently developed theories, the more we will need to study the actual empirical contexts in which it is taught and exercised. While I think that empirical studies of the kind just mentioned are valuable, not least because of the general tendency in contemporary ethics to study our 'practical psychology', I think that we can also find further rich material for studying virtue in some branches of literature and history. Kinds of literature that give us extended studies of the psychology of individuals give us valuable case histories, and so too do some kinds of historical biography. In studying virtue we are not limited to the present as psychology is. Plenty of people have taken an interest in the virtues and vices of their own and others' lives, and given us masses of evidence to study. This kind of material should complement a more scientific approach, since both are empirical, though with different methodologies.

At the same time this development in studying virtue might open up more fruitful ways of studying happiness. In the case of happiness there are huge amounts of data, but it is unclear how it can be used in the absence of any methodological agreement as to what happiness is or how to study it. While this situation is probably going to continue, since our conception of happiness is hybrid, it would further clarity in the study of happiness if studies could separate different strands in our confused conception, so that research could be done on them separately. We will get more usable results about virtue and happiness if we are clearly talking about virtue and *eudaimonia*, rather than virtue and pleasant feelings or desire-satisfaction.

All this is speculative, but I think not wildly so. The study of virtue ethics has exploded in the last twenty years, and is now an essential part of any ethical programme. 'Virtue ethics' has continued to expand, with different kinds of ethics of virtue being studied, and Aristotelian virtue ethics being joined by Kantian, Humean, Platonic, Nietzschean, and more kinds of virtue ethics. Within the field debates about virtue and 'right action', virtue and action guidance, and virtue and happiness are continually developing. I have tried to contribute to these debates by developing an account of virtue which I think is strong and defensible, together with a sketch of the many ways it can relate to happiness. I hope this study can supply resources for these and other debates.

Bibliography

Adams, Robert M. (2006), *A Theory of Virtue*, Oxford: Oxford University Press.

Annas, Julia (1992), 'Ancient Ethics and Modern Morality,' in J. E. Tomberlin (ed.), *Philosophical Perspectives* 6, Atascadero, Calif., 199–36.

——(1993), *The Morality of Happiness*, Oxford: Oxford University Press.

——(1999), *Platonic Ethics Old and New*, Ithaca, NY: Cornell University Press.

——(2001), 'Moral Knowledge as Practical Knowledge', in E. F. Paul, F. D. Miller, and J. Paul (eds.), *Moral Knowledge*, Cambridge: Cambridge University Press, 236–56.

——(2002), 'My Station and its Duties: Ideals and the Social Embeddedness of Virtue', *Proceedings of the Aristotelian Society*, 109–23.

——(2003), 'Should Virtue Make You Happy?' in L. Jost. (ed.), *Eudaimonia and Happiness*, *Apeiron*, special issue, 1–19.

——(2004), 'Happiness', *Daedalus* (spring issue on Happiness), 44–51.

——(2005), 'Virtue Ethics: What Kind of Naturalism?' in Gardiner (2005: 11–29).

——(2006a), 'Virtue Ethics', in D. Copp (ed.), *The Oxford Companion to Ethical Theory*, Oxford: Oxford University Press, 515–36.

——(2006b), 'The Phenomenology of Virtue', in U. Kriegel (ed.), *Phenomenology and the Cognitive Sciences*, special issue, 21–34.

——(2007), 'Virtue Ethics and the Charge of Egoism', in Paul Bloomfield (ed., *Morality and Self-Interest*, Oxford: Oxford University Press, 205–21.

——(forthcoming) 'Nietzsche, Ethics and Virtue'.

Anscombe, G.E. M. (1958), 'Modern Moral Philosophy', *Philosophy* 33.

Aristotle (1995), *Politics*, trans. Ernest Barker, rev. R. F. Stalley, Oxford World's Classics, Oxford: Oxford University Press.

——(2000), *Nicomachean Ethics*, trans. Roger Crisp, Cambridge: Cambridge University Press.

Athanassoulis, Nafsika (2000), 'A Response to Harman: Virtue Ethics and Character Traits', *Proceedings of the Aristotelian Society* ns 100, 215–21.

Badhwar, Neera (1996), 'The Limited Unity of Virtue', *Nous* 30/3, 306–29.

——(2009), 'The Milgram Experiments, Learned Helplessness and CharacterTraits', *Journal of Ethics* 13, 257–89.

Baier, Annette (1997), 'What Do Women Want in a Moral Theory?', in Crisp (1996: 263–77).

Bargh, J. A., and Chartrand, T. L. (1999), 'The Unbearable Automaticity of Being', *American Psychologist* 54, 462–79.

Barnes, Julian (1989), *A History of the World in Ten and a Half Chapters*, New York: Random House.

Baron, Marcia, Pettit, Philip, and Slote, Michael (1997), *Three Methods of Ethics*, Oxford: Blackwell.

Bentham, Jeremy (1983), *Deontology, together with A Table of the Springs of Action and the Article on Utilitarianism*, ed. A. Goldworth, Oxford: Oxford University Press.

Bradley, F. H. (1962), *Ethical Studies*, 2nd edn., introd. Richard Wollheim, Oxford: Oxford University Press.

Brannmark, Johan (2006), 'From Virtue to Decency', *Metaphilosophy* 37, 589–604.

Brobjer, Thomas H. (1995), *Nietzsche's Ethics of Character*, Uppsala: Uppsala University.

Brunt, P. A. (1998), 'Marcus Aurelius and Slavery', *Modus Operandi: Essays in Honour of Geoffrey Rickman*, BICS Suppl. 71, London: University of London, 139–50.

Campbell, John (1999), 'Can Philosophical Accounts of Altruism Accommodate Experimental Data on Helping Behavior?', *Australasian Journal of Philosophy* 77, 26–45.

Carr, David, and Steutel, Jan (eds.) (1999*a*), *Virtue Ethics and Moral Education*, London: Routledge.

————(1999*b*), 'Introduction: Virtue Ethics and the Virtue Approach to Moral Education', in Carr and Steutel (1999*a*: 1-18).

Chappell, T. (ed.) (2006), *Virtues and Values*, Oxford: Oxford University Press.

Churchland, Paul (2000), 'Rules, Know-How and the Future of Moral Cognition', in R. Thomason and B. Hunter (eds.), *Moral Epistemology Naturalized, Canadian Journal of Philosophy* suppl. vol. 26, 291–306.

Cicero (2001), *On Moral Ends*, trans. Raphael Woolf, introd. and notes Julia Annas, Cambridge Texts in the History of Philosophy, Cambridge: Cambridge University Press.

Clark, Andy (2000*a*), 'Word and Action: Reconciling Rules and Know-How in Moral Cognition', in R. Thomason and B. Hunter (eds.), *Moral Epistemology Naturalized, Canadian Journal of Philosophy* suppl. vol. 26, 267–89.

————(2000b), 'Making Moral Space: A Reply to Churchland', ibid. 307–12.

Copp, David, and Sobel, David (2004), 'Morality and Virtue: An Assessment of Some Recent Work in Virtue Ethics', *Ethics* 114/3, 514–54.

Crisp, R. (ed.) (1996), *How Should One Live? Essays on the Virtues*, Oxford: Oxford University Press.

————(2010), 'Virtue Ethics and Virtue Epistemology'. *Metaphilosophy* 41, 22–40.

————(forthcoming), 'Virtue Ethics: What Is It? And Why Should Anyone Believe It?'.

————and Slote, M. (eds.) (1997), *Virtue Ethics*, Oxford: Oxford University Press.

Csikszentmihalyi, M. (1991), *Flow: The Psychology of Optimal Experience*, New York: Harper.

Damasio, A. (1994), *Descartes' Error: Emotion, Reason and the Human Brain*. New York: HarperCollins.

Das, Ramon (2003), 'Virtue Ethics and Right Action', *Australasian Journal of Philosophy* 81, 324–39.

Deci, E., and Ryan, R. (2000), 'The "What" and "Why" of Goal Pursuits: Human Needs and the Self-Determination of Behavior', *Psychological Inquiry* 11, 141–66.

DePaul, Michael (1999), 'Character Traits, Virtues and Vices: Are There None?', *Proceedings of the World Congress of Philosophy* 1, Philosophy Documentation Center, 141–57.

——and Zagzebski, Linda (2003), *Intellectual Virtue: Perspectives from Ethics and Epistemology*, Oxford: Oxford University Press.

Doris, John M. (1998), 'Persons, Situations and Virtue Ethics', *Nous* 32/4, 504–30.

——(2002), *Lack of Character*, Cambridge: Cambridge University Press.

Dreyfus, H. L., and Dreyfus, S. E. (1990), 'What is Morality? A Phenomenological Account of the Development of Ethical Expertise', in D. Rasmussen (ed.), *Universalism vs Communitarianism*, Cambridge, Mass.: MIT, 237–64.

Driver, Julia (2001), *Uneasy Virtue*, Cambridge: Cambridge University Press.

——(2006), 'Virtue Theory', in J. Dreier (ed.), *Contemporary Debates in Moral Theory*, Oxford: Blackwell, 113–23.

Elster, J. (2009), *Alchemies of the Mind: Rationality and the Emotions*, Cambridge: Cambridge University Press.

Epictetus (1995), *The Discourses, The Handbook*, trans. Robin Hard, introd. and notes C. Gill, London: Everyman.

Foot, Philippa (2001), *Natural Goodness*, Oxford: Oxford University Press.

——(2002), *Moral Dilemmas*, Oxford: Oxford University Press.

Gardiner, S. (ed.) (2005), *Virtue Ethics Old and New*, Ithaca, NY: Cornell University Press.

Gill, Christopher (2004), 'The Stoic Theory of Ethical Development: In What Sense is Nature a Norm?', in Jan Szaif and Matthias Lutz-Bachmann (eds.), *Was ist das für den Menschen Gute/What Is Good for a Human Being?*, Berlin: de Gruyter, 101–25.

——(forthcoming), 'The Impact of Greek Philosophy on Contemporary Ethical Philosophy'.

Greene, Joshua, and Haidt, J. (2002), 'How (and Where) Does Moral Judgement Work?', *Trends in Cognitive Sciences* 6/12, 517–23.

——Sommerville, R. B., Nystrom, L. E., Darley, J. M., and Cohen, J. D. (2001), 'An fMRI Investigation of Emotional Engagement in Moral Judgement', *Science* 293 (14 Sept.), 2105–8.

Griffiths, Paul E. (1997), *What Emotions Really Are*, Chicago: University of Chicago Press.

Haidt, Jonathan (2001), 'The Emotional Dog and its Rational Tail: A Social Intuitionist Approach to Moral Judgement,' *Psychological Review* 108/4, 814–34.

——(2006), *The Happiness Hypothesis*, New York: Basic Books.

——with Joseph, Craig (2004), 'Intuitive Ethics', *Daedalus* (autumn), 55–66.

Harman, G. (1999), 'Moral Philosophy Meets Social Psychology: Virtue Ethics and the Fundamental Attribution Error', *Proceedings of the Aristotelian Society* ns 99, 315–31.

——(2000), 'The Nonexistence of Character Traits', *Proceedings of the Aristotelian Society* ns 100/1, 223–6.

——(2001), 'Virtue Ethics Without Character Traits', in A. Byrne, R. Stalnaker, and R. Wedgwood (eds.), *Fact and Value: Essays on Ethics and Metaphysics for Judith Jarvis Thomson*, Cambridge, Mass.: MIT, 117–27.

——(2003), 'No Character or Personality, a Reply to Robert Solomon', *Business Ethics Quarterly* 13/1, 87–94.

Haybron, Daniel (2001), 'Happiness and Pleasure', *Philosophy and Phenomenological Research* 62.

——(2002), 'Consistency of Character and the Character of Evil', in D. Haybron (ed.), *Earth's Abominations: Philosophical Studies of Evil*, Amsterdam: Rodopi, 63–78.

——(2008), *The Pursuit of Unhappiness*, Oxford: Oxford University Press.

Hochschild, Adam (2005), *Bury the Chains: Prophets and Rebels in the Fight to Free an Empire's Slaves*, Boston: Houghton Mifflin.

Hooker, Brad (1996), 'Is Moral Virtue a Benefit to the Agent?', in Crisp (1996: 141–55).

——(2002), 'The Collapse of Virtue Ethics', *Utilitas* 14/1, 22–40.

——and Little, M. (eds.) (2000), *Moral Particularism*, Oxford: Oxford University Press.

Hornby, Nick (2001), *How to be Good*, London: Viking.

Hume, David (2006), *Moral Philosophy*, ed. Geoffrey Sayre-McCord, Indianapolis: Hackett.

Hurka, Thomas (2001), *Virtue, Vice, and Value*, Oxford: Oxford University Press.

——(2006), 'Virtuous Act, Virtuous Dispositions', *Analysis* 66/1, 69–76.

——(2010), 'Right Act, Virtuous Motive', *Metaphilosophy* 41, 58–72.

Hursthouse, Rosalind (1995), 'The Virtuous Agent's Reasons: A Response to Williams', in R. Heinaman (ed.), *Aristotle and Moral Realism*, London: University College Press, 24–33.

——(1999*a*), *On Virtue Ethics*, Oxford: Oxford University Press.

——(1999*b*), 'Virtue Ethics and Human Nature', *Hume Studies* 25/1–2, 67–82.

——(2000), *Ethics, Humans and Other Animals: An Introduction with Readings*, London: Routledge.

——(2002), 'Virtue Ethics vs Rule-Consequentialism: A Reply to Brad Hooker', *Utilitas* 14/1, 41–53.

——(2004), 'On the Grounding of the Virtues in Human Nature,' in J. Szaif and M. Lutz-Bachmann (eds.), *Was is das für den Menschen Gute/What is Good for a Human Being?* Berlin: de Gruyter, 263–75.

——(2006), 'Are the Virtues the Proper Starting Point for Morality?', in J. Dreier (ed.), *Contemporary Debates in Moral Theory*, Oxford: Blackwell, 99–112.

——(2007), 'Environmental Virtue Ethics', in R. L. Walker and P. J. Ivanhoe (eds.), *Working Virtue*, Oxford: Oxford University Press, 155–71.

——(2008), 'Two Ways of Doing the Right Thing', in C. Farelly and L. Solum (eds.), *Virtue Jurisprudence*, New York: Palgrave Macmillan, 236–55.

Irwin, Terence (1988), 'Disunity in the Aristotelian Virtues', *Oxford Studies in Ancient Philosophy*, suppl., 61–78.

——(1996), 'Kant's Criticisms of Eudaemonism,' in S. Engstrom and J. Whiting (eds.), *Aristotle, Kant and the Stoics*, Cambridge: Cambridge University Press, 63–101.

Jacobson, D. (2005), 'Seeing by Feeling: Virtues, Skills and Moral Perception', *Ethical Theory and Moral Practice* 8, 387–409.

Johnson, Robert (2003), 'Virtue and Right', *Ethics* 113/4, 810–34.

Kamtekar, Rachana (2004), 'Situationism and Virtue Ethics on the Content of Our Character', *Ethics* 114, 458–91.

——(forthcoming), 'Updating Practical Wisdom', in C. Upton (ed.), *Virtue Ethics, Character and Moral Psychology*, Oxford: Oxford University Press.

Kant, Immanuel (1996), *Practical Philosophy*, trans. and ed. Mary J. Gregor, in *The Cambridge Edition of the Works of Immanuel Kant*, Cambridge: Cambridge University Press,

Kent, Bonnie (1999), 'Moral Growth and the Unity of the Virtues', in Carr and Steutel (1999a: 109–24).

Keyes, C. (2007), 'Protecting and Promoting Mental Health as Flourishing: A Complementary Strategy for Improving National Mental Health', *American Psychologist* 62, 95–108.

——and Annas, J. (2009), 'Feeling Good and Functioning Well: Distinctive Concepts in Ancient Philosophy and Contemporary Science', *Journal of Positive Psychology* 4/3, 197–201.

——and Haidt, J. (eds.) (2003), *Flourishing: Positive Psychology and the Life Well-Lived*, Washington, DC: American Psychological Association.

Kraut, Richard (1979), 'Two Conceptions of Happiness', *Philosophical Review* 88, 167–97.

——(1988), 'Comments on "Disunity in the Aristotelian Virtues"', *Oxford Studies in Ancient Philosophy*, suppl., 79–86.

Layard, R. (2005), *Happiness: Lessons from a New Science*, New York: Penguin.

LeBar, Mark (2004), 'Good For You', *Pacific Philosophical Quarterly* 85, 195–217.

——and Russell, Daniel (forthcoming), 'Well-Being and Eudaimonia: A Reply to Haybron'.

Lovibond, S. (2005), 'Virtue, Nature and Providence,' in C. Gill (ed.), *Virtue, Norms, and Objectivity*, Oxford: Oxford University Press, 99–112.

McCullough, M. (2008), *Beyond Revenge: The Evolution of the Forgiveness Instinct*. San Francisco: Jossey-Bass.

McDowell, J. (1979), 'Virtue and Reason', *The Monist* 62, 331–50.

MacIntyre, Alasdair (1985), *After Virtue: A Study in Moral Theory*, 2nd edn., London: Duckworth.

——(1999), *Dependent Rational Animals: Why Humans Need the Virtues*, New York: Open Court.

Manning, C. E. (1989), 'Stoicism and Slavery in the Roman Empire', *Aufstieg und Niedergang Der Romischen Welt*, 2nd ser., 36/3, 1518–43.

Marcus Aurelius (1997), *Meditations*, trans. Robin Hard, introd. and notes Christopher Gill, Ware: Wordsworth Editions.

Merritt, Maria (2000), 'Virtue Ethics and Situationist Personality Psychology', *Ethical Theory and Moral Practice* 3: 365–83.

——(2009), 'Aristotelean Virtue and the Interpersonal Aspect of Ethical Character', *Journal of Moral Philosophy* 6, 23–49.

Milgram, Stanley (1974), *Obedience to Authority*, New York: Harper & Row.

Mill, J. S. (1972), *Utilitarianism, On Liberty, Essay on Bentham*, ed. M. Warnock, London: Collins/Fontana.

Miller, Christian (2003), 'Social Psychology and Virtue Ethics', *Journal of Ethics* 7, 365–92.

Murdoch, Iris (1970), *The Sovereignty of Good*, London: Routledge.

Myers, David G. (1992), *The Pursuit of Happiness: Who is Happy and Why*, New York: Morrow.

Nichols, Shaun (2004), *Sentimental Rules: On the Natural Foundations of Moral Judgment*, Oxford: Oxford University Press.

Nietzsche, Friedrich (1997), *Daybreak*, ed. Maudmarie Clark and Brian Leiter, Cambridge: Cambridge University Press.

Nucci, L., and Turiel, E. (2000), 'The Moral and the Personal: Sources of Social Conflicts', in L. Nucci, G. Saxe, and E. Turiel (eds.), *Culture, Thought and Development*, Jean Piaget Symposium Series, Mahwah, NJ: Lawrence Erlbaum, 115–37.

Nussbaum, Martha (1999), 'Virtue Ethics: A Misleading Category?', *The Journal of Ethics* 3/3, 163–201.

——(2001), *Upheavals of Thought: The Intelligence of Emotions*. Cambridge: Cambridge University Press.

Oakley, Justin (1992), *Morality and the Emotions*, London: Routledge.

——and Cocking, D. (eds.) (2001), *Virtue Ethics and Professional Roles*, Cambridge: Cambridge University Press.

Österberg, Jan (1999), 'The Virtues of Virtue Ethics', in R. Sliwinski (ed.), *Philosophical Crumbs: Essays Dedicated to Ann-Mari Henschen-Dahlquist*, Uppsala Philosophical Studies 49, 277–89.

Parker, Ian (2004), 'The Gift', *The New Yorker*, 2 August, 54–63.

Peacock, Thomas Love (1948), *Melincourt*, in David Garnett (ed.), *The Novels of Thomas Love Peacock*, 2 vols., London: Rupert Hart-Davis, i. 91–343.

Peterson, Christopher, and Seligman, Martin (eds.) (2004), *Character, Strength, and Virtues: A Handbook and Classification*, Oxford: Oxford University Press.

Plato (1997), *Complete Works*, ed. J. Cooper and D. Hutchinson, Indianapolis: Hackett.

Pollard, Bill (2003), 'Can Virtuous Actions Be Both Habitual and Rational?', *Ethical Theory and Moral Practice* 6, 411–25.

Post, S. (ed.) (2007), *Altruism and Health: Perspectives from Empirical Research*. Oxford: Oxford University Press.

Ross, Lee, and Nisbett, Richard E. (1991), *The Person and the Situation: Perspectives of Social Psychology*. Philadelphia: Temple University Press.

Russell, Daniel (2009), *Practical Intelligence and the Virtues*, Oxford: Oxford University Press.

——(forthcoming), *Happiness, Virtue, and the Self*, Oxford: Oxford University Press.

Ryan, R., and Deci, E. (2000), 'Self-Determination Theory and the Facilitation of Intrinsic Motivation, Social Development and Well-Being', *American Psychologist* 55/1: 68–78.

Sabini, John, and Silver, Maury (2005), 'Lack of Character? Situationism Critiqued', *Ethics* 115, 535–62.

Seligman, M. (2002), *Authentic Happiness*, New York: Free Press.

Seneca (1989), *Epistulae Morales: Volume I*, trans. R.M. Gummere, Loeb Classical Library 214, Cambridge, Mass.: Harvard University Press.

——(1995), *Moral and Political Essays*, trans. John Cooper and John Procope, Cambridge Texts in the History of Political Thought, Cambridge: Cambridge University Press,

Shaw, Joseph (2001), 'Ancient Virtue Ethics and the Morality of Aspiration', in D. Baltzly, D. Blyth, and H. Tarrant (eds.) (2001), *Power and Pleasure, Virtues and Vices*, *Prudentia* Suppl., 339–65.

Sherman, Nancy (1989), *The Fabric of Character: Aristotle's Theory of Virtue*, Oxford: Oxford University Press.

——(1997), *Making a Necessity of Virtue: Aristotle and Kant on Virtue*, Cambridge: Cambridge University Press.

——(2005), *Stoic Warriors*, Cambridge: Cambridge University Press.

Sidgwick, Henry (1967), *The Methods of Ethics*, 7th edn., London: Macmillan.

Slote, Michael (2001), *Morals from Motives*, Oxford: Oxford University Press.

Smetana, Judith (1993), 'Understanding of Social Rules', in M. Bennett (ed.), *The Development of Social Cognition*, New York: Guilford, 111–41.

Snow, Nancy E. (2006), 'Habitual Virtuous Actions and Automaticity', *Ethical Theory and Moral Practice* 9/5, 545–61.

——(2010), *Virtue as Social Intelligence: An Empirically Grounded Theory*, New York: Routledge.

Solomon, David (1988), 'Internal Objections to Virtue Ethics', *Midwest Studies in Philosophy* XIII, 428–41.

Solomon, Robert (2003), 'Victims of Circumstances? A Defense of Virtue Ethics in Business', *Business Ethics Quarterly* 13/1, 43–62.

Spark, Muriel (1985), *The Stories of Muriel Spark*, London: The Bodley Head.

Sreenivasan, Gopal (2002), 'Errors about Errors: Virtue Theory and Trait Attribution', *Mind* 111, 47–68.

Sumner, L. W. (1996), *Welfare, Happiness, and Ethics*, Oxford: Oxford University Press.

——(2003), 'Happiness Then and Now', in L. Jost (ed.), *Eudaimonia and Happiness, Apeiron* special issue.

Svensson, Frans (2006), 'Some Basic Issues in Neo-Aristotelian Virtue Ethics', diss., University of Uppsala.

——(2007), '*Does* Non-cognitivism Rest on a Mistake?', *Utilitas* 19/2, 184–200.

Swanton, Christine (2003), *Virtue Ethics: A Pluralistic View*, Oxford: Oxford University Press.

——(2005), 'Nietzschean Virtue Ethics,' in Gardiner (2005: 179–92).

——(2006), 'Virtue Ethics, Role Ethics and Right Action', in Kim-Chong Chong and Yuli Li (eds.), *Conceptions of Virtue East and West*, Singapore: Marshall Cavendish.

Tännsjö Torbjörn (1995), 'Blameless Wrongdoing', *Ethics* 106, 120–7.

——(2001), 'Virtue Ethics', in Dan Egonsson, Jonas Josefsson, Bjorn Petersson, and Toni Rönnow-Rasmussen (eds.), *Exploring Practical Philosophy: From Action to Values*, Aldershot: Ashgate, 167–85.

Tessman, Lisa (2005), *Burdened Virtues*, Oxford: Oxford University Press.

Thoits, P. A., and Hewitt, L. N. (2001), 'Volunteer Work and Well-Being', *Journal of Personality and Social Behavior* 42, 115–31.

Thomson, J. J. (1997), 'The Right and the Good', *Journal of Philosophy* 94, 273–98.

Tiberius, Valerie (2008), *The Reflective Life*, Oxford: Oxford University Press.

——and Swartwood, Jason (forthcoming), 'Wisdom Revisited: A Case Study in Normative Theorizing', *Philosophical Explorations*, special edn.

Timmons, Mark (ed.) (2002*a*), *Kant's Metaphysics of Morals: Intepretative Essays*, Oxford: Oxford University Press.

——(2002*b*), *Moral Theory*, Lanham, Md.: Rowman & Littlefield.

Toner, Christopher (2006), 'The Self-Centeredness Objection to Virtue Ethics', *Philosophy* 81, 595–617.

Turiel, Elliot (1983), *The Development of Social Knowledge: Morality and Convention*, Cambridge: Cambridge University Press.

——(2002), *The Culture of Morality*, Cambridge: Cambridge University Press.

Upton, Candace (2009), *Situational Traits of Character*, Lanham, Md.: Rowman & Littlefield.

Walker, Rebecca and Ivanhoe, Philip (eds.), *Working Virtue: Virtue Ethics and Contemporary Moral Problems*, Oxford: Oxford University Press.

Watson, Gary (1984), 'Virtues in Excess', *Philosophical Studies* 46, 57–74.

——(1990), 'The Primacy of Character', in O. Flanagan and A. Rorty (eds.), *Identity, Character and Morality*, Cambridge, Mass.: MIT, 449–83.

White, Nicholas (2006), *A Brief History of Happiness*, Oxford: Blackwell.

Williams, Bernard (1973), 'The Makropoulos Case: Reflections on the Tedium of Immortality', *Problems of the Self*, Cambridge: Cambridge University Press, 82–100.

——(1985), *Ethics and the Limits of Philosophy*, London: Collins/Fontana.

——(1994), 'Pagan Justice and Christian Love', in M. Nussbaum and T. Irwin (eds.), *Virtue, Love and Form: Essays in Memory of Gregory Vlastos*, *Apeiron* special issue, 195–203.

——(1995*a*), *Making Sense of Humanity*, Cambridge: Cambridge University Press.

——(1995*b*), 'Making Sense of Humanity', in Williams (1995*a*: 79–89).

——(1995*c*), 'Ethics, Evolution and the Representation Problem', in Williams (1995*a*: 100–10).

——(1995*d*), 'Acting as the Virtuous Person Acts', in R. Heinaman (ed.), *Aristotle and Moral Realism*, London: University College Press, 24–33.

——(1996), '*The Women of Trachis*: Fictions, Pessimism, Ethics', in R. B. Louden and P. Schollmeir (eds.), *The Greeks and Us*, Chicago: Chicago University Press, 43–53.

Witvliet, Charlotte V.O., and McCullough, M. (2007), 'Forgiveness and Health: A Review and Theoretical Explanation of Emotion Pathways', in Post (2007: 259–76).

Wolf, Susan (2007), 'Moral Psychology and the Unity of the Virtues', *Ratio* 20/2, 145–67.

Zagzebski, Linda T. (2004), *Divine Motivation Theory*, Cambridge: Cambridge University Press.

——(2006), 'The Admirable Life and the Desirable Life', in Chappell (2006: 53–66).

Zyl, Liezl van (forthcoming), 'Virtue and Right: The Plight of the Non-virtuous', in D. Russell, *Cambridge Companion to Virtue Ethics*, Cambridge: Cambridge University Press.

Index